ROMAN ANNIVERSARY ISSUES

T0371310

ROMAN ANNIVERSARY ISSUES

AN EXPLORATORY STUDY OF THE
NUMISMATIC AND MEDALLIC COMMEMORATION
OF ANNIVERSARY YEARS
49 B.C.–A.D. 375

BY

MICHAEL GRANT

Professor of Humanity, University of Edinburgh

CAMBRIDGE
AT THE UNIVERSITY PRESS
1950

CAMBRIDGE
UNIVERSITY PRESS

University Printing House, Cambridge CB2 8BS, United Kingdom

Cambridge University Press is part of the University of Cambridge.

It furthers the University's mission by disseminating knowledge in the pursuit of education, learning and research at the highest international levels of excellence.

www.cambridge.org
Information on this title: www.cambridge.org/9781316603697

© Cambridge University Press 1950

First published 1950
First paperback edition 2015

A catalogue record for this publication is available from the British Library

ISBN 978-1-316-60369-7 Paperback

TO
MY MOTHER
WITH LOVE AND GRATITUDE

CONTENTS

KEY TO PLATES[1]

PLATE I

Augustus and Tiberius: Rare and Conjectural Pieces
facing page 20

Number	Collection	Reference in text
1	Paris	p. 20 and n. 3
2	London[2]	p. 25 and n. 5
3 (obv.)	London	p. 35 and n. 7
4 (rev.)	Paris	,, ,, ,,
5 (obv.)	Berlin	p. 42 and n. 5
6	London	p. 42 and n. 3
7	Paris	p. 42 and n. 4
8	London	p. 42 and n. 8
9	Paris	p. 57 and n. 7
10	Copenhagen	p. 62 and n. 2

PLATE II

Tiberius, Caligula and Claudius: Rare and Conjectural Pieces
facing page 62

1	Berlin	p. 62 and n. 3
2	Athens	p. 65 and n. 4
3 (obv.)	Paris	p. 68 and n. 3
4 (rev.)	Berlin	,, ,, ,,
5	Berlin	p. 68 and n. 4
6	London	p. 47 and n. 9
7 (obv.)	Budapest	p. 70 and n. 1
8 (obv.)	Budapest	,, ,, ,,
9 (obv.)	London	p. 69 n. 3
10	Berlin	,, ,,
11	Berlin	p. 77 and n. 2

1 As is explained in the Introduction, the coins shown here are not intended as representative illustrations of the anniversary theme, for which the time has not yet come. They are selected rather as pieces of special rarity, most of which do not occur in the principal catalogues or descriptive works; and they are therefore chosen from the one period in which I have had to consider pieces omitted from those works, namely that of the Julio-Claudians. See also Appendix IV.

2 I.e. British Museum.

INTRODUCTION

This study was foreshadowed in my Inaugural Lecture at Edinburgh University in October 1948.[1] Its purpose is to show that a large number of Roman imperial coins and medallions owe their types, wholly or in part, to coincidences in date with important 'anniversary years'.[2] These coincidences are either deliberately arranged, or are accidental coincidences of which advantage is taken for purposes of propaganda.

The 'anniversary' years which are thus signalised are the centenaries, or multiples or subdivisions of centenaries (or occasionally of 110-year *saecula*), of important happenings in the history of the State. These happenings include, *inter alia*, the births and deaths of Augustus and other leading persons; the various events that contributed to the inauguration of the imperial régime (Actium, the 'restoration of the Republic', etc.); and the foundation or dedication of temples and altars. Moreover, the sanctity of the mint and of its products (pp. 9 f.) enabled the process to be extended to the commemoration of the centenaries and half-centenaries of actual coinage: the numerous 'restoration' issues reveal a high degree of numismatic self-consciousness which was readily expressed by the selection of anniversaries for these repetitions.

The contention that coincidences with anniversary years so greatly influenced the coinage is one which may well provoke certain queries even from those who are, in principle, inclined to accept it. I propose in this Introduction to anticipate a few of these queries, and to endeavour to answer them.

First, is it not strange that these anniversaries should have been so carefully and so long remembered? It is strange in one sense, in that it reveals habits of thought alien from our own. It is not strange in another and less anachronistic sense, for it is entirely in harmony with the picture that modern research has given us of the mentality and customs of the ancient Romans. For example, we have abundant evidence of the meticulous observation, generally according to mathematical or political calculations based on 100- or 110-year

1 *PR*.; cf. also *AC*. (see Abbreviations).
2 For the use of this inexact but convenient phrase, and the distinction between the commemoration of 'anniversary *years*' and that of annually recurrent *days*, see p. 1.

intervals, of successive *saecula* from the supposed date of the foundation of the city (p. 2).[1] It would, however, be most unreasonable to
suppose that this must needs be the only such occasion commemorated in this way: the history and legend of Rome contained many
highly venerated events besides its foundation, and antiquarian references to them are persistent and emphatic.[2] Again, we know that
the *decennia* and *vicennia* of imperial accessions were punctiliously
celebrated: it was only to be expected, therefore, that the first and
greatest of all 'accessions', that of Augustus—his assumption of
imperium, Actium, the 'restoration' of the Republic, the *aureum
saeculum*—should be granted a recollection overlapping into the
reigns of the devoted Augustans which his successors almost invari-
ably professed themselves. Accessions, births and deaths were all
long and scrupulously commemorated; the recently edited *Feriale*
of Dura[3] has further revealed how extensive this process was,
even in the remotest areas and even when the Principate was far
advanced.

If I may repeat from the text (p. 171) a quotation from my lecture
introducing this subject, "the Romans are seen to be a people with
an abnormally developed sense, not only of the past, but of its single
ritualistic landmarks. These are the people, we recall, who cherished
dates in *Fasti*, who attributed divinity to single momentary happenings,
to a voice that spoke once and saved them, or to the Fortune of an
individual day; so it is not surprising that they outdo anything in
our own experience in their elaborate and almost morbid attention
to religious anniversaries. The institutions...were thought of...
as linked with the remote past by an unbroken chain of continuity."[4]
Altheim sees this peculiar stress on chronological landmarks as a
characteristically Roman "emphasis on the temporal element....
The individual moment...was raised to an importance hitherto
unknown.... Everything is concentrated on single decisive acts;
the special quality of the different moments of history is persistently
felt."[5]

1 Precisely centenary were the Secular
Games of Claudius (A.D. 47) and Philip
(A.D. 248); cf. a commemoration in 348, p. 153.
For the divergent methods of calculation on
other occasions see below, p. 12.
2 E.g. Toynbee, *An Imperial Institute of
Archaeology as revealed by Roman Medallions*,
Archaeological Journal, 1943, pp. 34 ff.

3 Fink, Hoey and Snyder, *YCS.* 1940. See
below, Indices II and IV, *ss.vv.* 'Dura'
and '*Ferialia*' respectively.
4 *PR.* pp. 239 ff.
5 *History of Roman Religion*, pp. 190 f.

Altheim goes on to show how this attitude applies to temple-foundations. "For all Roman temples the year and day, not only of dedication, but also of vowing, lives on in memory." Now anniversaries of the various stages of these temple-foundations seem to account for a considerable number of the coins and medallions that I am going to cite (see Indices III and IV, *s.v.* 'temples'). It may at first appearance seem curious that the authorities retained so careful a memory of these dates. But that they did, in fact, retain this memory happens to be confirmed independently. For, as a result of the attitude to which Altheim refers, there has survived to this day— just as there survived throughout the Roman Principate—a record of the alleged dates at which very many temples were vowed, dedicated and consecrated.[1] This record was handed down from the early *pontifices*, and, at least among the upper classes from which the priestly colleges were drawn, it was clearly well known in historical times. And if it was well known to these people, it requires no stretch of the imagination—especially in thinking of a nation with the Romans' attitude to past happenings—to suppose that they arranged for the important anniversaries of these dates to be duly celebrated. This being so, it is far from improbable that such anniversaries and celebrations were known of in advance to a circle at least wide enough to include the mint-authorities; so that the latter were able to signalise these occasions, either by issuing special coins and medallions or by adapting the types of those which were in any case due to be issued.

A modern reader, even if and when he has accepted the foregoing remarks, is likely to pause at this point and wonder about the general public. How could the general public be sufficiently well informed about this sort of thing for numismatic commemoration of such occasions to prove worth the government's while? Here again, I submit that doubts would be anachronistic. Rome was a city which had *acta diurna*[2] and other means of communicating current events to its people; and inhabitants of the capital at least, as well as a number of Roman citizens in colonies and *municipia*,[3] could very easily have such anniversaries—and the ceremonies which are likely

1 Ibid. pp. 249 f.
2 For references see Balsdon, *OCD*. p. 6. Here is one reason why external evidence for this type of commemoration is lacking: one could hardly expect such *acta* to have survived.

3 The *Feriale Cumanum* gives a selection of Imperial anniversary days celebrated at a Roman colony: Snyder, *YCS*. 1940, pp. 305 f., n. 150. Cf. a Theveste inscription, ibid. pp. 297 ff.

often to have accompanied them—brought to their attention by public announcement. Besides, one of the greatest gains in the study of Roman religion during the last decades has been the demonstration that the traditional cults were very far from forgotten during the Principate. There is nothing strange or forced about an assumption that the centenaries of great temples are likely to have been known to a wide enough circle to justify their commemoration on the coinage.[1]

Some readers, especially those familiar only with the literary tradition, might concede this point as regards the earlier part of the Principate, but find it less easy to envisage the same situation in the third and fourth centuries when religious tendencies of so very different a kind had taken root. But for those epochs, too, recent research has provided abundant evidence of the extreme tenacity of the traditional worship. In the third century "what our witnesses, one and all contemporary, reveal, is a vigorous emphasizing of Roman religion":[2] the *Feriale Duranum*, and intensified numismatic study, have brought this home in impressive and decisive detail. Indeed, as the Chronographer of A.D. 354 ('Philocalus') bears witness, "it is clear that down to the fourth century A.D. it was widely held that the prosperity and even the safety of Rome depended on the accurate performance of traditional ceremonies".[3] For these reasons it is no more surprising that official recollections of the early anniversaries occur in the fourth century, and abound in the third century, than that they are characteristic of the first and second centuries.

I have suggested that this celebration corresponded with, and was accompanied by, a considerable amount of justificatory public appreciation. But I would not, of course, suggest that anything like all the adult inhabitants of the empire, or even all those who understood Latin, possessed so high a degree of awareness. Many did, and many did not. Now it is this latter division of the population which provides the answer to a further question which sceptical or enquiring

---

1 The *accuracy* of the alleged foundation-dates is, of course, quite another matter. If the dates are wrong, then coinage commemorating their centenaries may be described as 'pseudo-anniversary'; see below, p. 128 n. 2. But Altheim, loc. cit., is optimistic about the reliability of these traditions. When they vary, this may sometimes be because one date refers to the foundation and one to the dedication; see pp. 12 f. and n. 7.

2 Altheim, loc. cit. p. 463.

3 Nock, *CAH.*, x, p. 465.

readers are likely to ask: if these coins and medallions owe their types, wholly or partly, to coincidences with anniversary years, why is it that, with the exception of Secular and *vota* coinages, this connection is practically never specified?[1]

This is only part of a wider, and demonstrable, circumstance, namely that any date whatever on a Roman imperial issue (other than that of a Regnal Year) is excessively rare.[2] One reason for this rarity, and for the corresponding absence of references to anniversaries, is that the authorities were intensely alive to the 'propagandist' importance of the coinage—which was very great owing to the ancients' habit of *looking at* their money[3]—and wanted its types to appeal to the widest possible public.[4] If, in (say) making an issue on the half-millenary of the temple of *Salus*, they had specified the occasion, the allusion would have been lost on the thousands who had not heard of the anniversary and were not interested in it. But, by referring to *Salus* in general terms without any special allusion to the half-millenary, the government was aiming to secure the comprehension both of those who knew about the anniversary and those who did not.[5] The former would read into the general type a connection with the current anniversary occasion; and be it noted that since they mostly lived in or near Rome many of them would see the coinage at an early date, while the occasion in question was still topical.[6] On the other hand these coins would not reach many of the outlying subjects of the emperor until a long time afterwards, when

---

1 A partial analogy is provided by inscriptions celebrating anniversary *days*, for these likewise often (though not so often) omit to specify their occasions, cf. Snyder, *YCS*. 1940, p. 225; cf. below, p. 3 and n. 2.

2 Apart from Secular pieces (including one for a 1001st year, p. 11 n. 7) it appears that the *only* coin of such a character is Hadrian's ANN. DCCCLXXIIII. NAT. VRB. P. CIR. CON., *BMC*. *Imp.* III, p. cxxxii, cf. W. Schmidt, *Geburtstag im Altertum*, p. 81 n. 1.

3 This can be safely concluded from the considerations indicated on p. 8. It would be interesting to collect external evidence pointing to the same conclusion (just as it would be to assess public interest in the series of commemorative postage-stamps issued by some governments to-day). Certain passages of ancient literature could be mobilised; but this is peculiarly ill-suited as evidence for

'mass observation', cf. Farrington, *Science and Politics in the Ancient World*, pp. 179 ff. However, the internal evidence is here adequate without the need for supplementation: it shows us three hundred years of unremitting changes and elaborations of coin-types made by a government hardly likely to do this just for fun.

4 This part of the Introduction has benefited from suggestions by Dr Toynbee.

5 Sutherland, *NC*. 1945, p. 67, makes a similar distinction: some points, "however much appreciated in the keen and suspicious political atmosphere of Rome, would probably be lost on the average provincial".

6 But not topical enough for the coinage to be a very appropriate vehicle for the commemoration of annually recurrent *days* (p. 2): anniversary *years* suited this medium better.

the anniversary had passed and was obsolete; but this did not matter, for in any case a large proportion of such people would not have understood, or been interested by, a reference to it. It is therefore for the benefit of this less educated and less Romanised section of the population that anniversary issues are made to omit any direct allusion to the occasions on which they were struck.

The result was a strong tendency to *generalise* coin-types. Plain PIETAS, for example, with a non-committal head, is preferred to any more explicit description. The word by itself conjured up from its rich store of semantic properties a whole host of different associations. One or more of these associations would occur to this person, one or more to that person, and thus the type would exercise the maximum effect (pp. 36–7; cf. pp. 54, 73, 168).[1] Such a procedure was more economical, and exercised a wider influence, than would have any explicit specification of occasions which possessed a less than universal significance; it is therefore easy to see why the Roman authorities preferred not to specify on their coins the anniversary occasions which contributed to their appearance and issue.[2]

But other critics of my theory may be less worried by this absence of specification than by a further lacuna, the deficiency of explicit references to the signalisation of anniversary years (other than Secular celebrations and *decennia* of emperors) in the literary authorities. I submit, however, that the whole trend of current investigations is against regarding this as a valid objection. It is only necessary to look at the Notes on Sources in the *Cambridge Ancient History*, Volumes x, xi and xii, and see how they stress, with ever sharply increasing emphasis, the extent of our dependence on non-literary records. The verdict of Baynes in the last volume is this: "for a period of history where our sources are so meagre the student must seek to base his chronology on all the available evidence, whether of inscriptions, papyri, coins or the dating of imperial 'constitutions'."[3]

---

1 The same motives were responsible for the alternative custom of depicting not a simple, generalised type but a highly complex and composite one (see Index IV, *s.v.* 'composite types'). For example, a goddess can be represented syncretistically with several adjuncts and attributes of quite other divinities (pp. 70 ff.): by this method, as by that of the generalised type, a correspondingly varied range of thought-associations was evoked in the minds of the general, or at least the educated, public. On these complex types see *CSNM*.

2 Cf. below, p. 3 and n. 1.

3 *CAH*. xii, p. 713. In *CAH*. xi, see pp. vi, 855, 857.

And Mattingly has no difficulty in justifying a special claim on behalf of his own branch: "in the coins lies a treasure... which, failing new discoveries of inscriptions or manuscripts, offers almost our only chance of penetrating the thick darkness that still envelops so much of the history of the third century."[1]

In selecting these quotations which stress the non-literary sources I would wish my attitude to be quite clear. I do not want to imply the slightest opposition or competition between the literary and non-literary branches of Latin studies. Nor is it my intention, or that of the distinguished authorities whom I have quoted, to aggrandise epigraphic, numismatic or papyrological research at the expense of attention to the literature.[2] Such an attempt would be entirely futile, for two reasons. First, because the vital task to-day is to consider all the various kinds of evidence *in conjunction*, or, where certain kinds fail, in mutual supplementation; and this aim would be ill served by any attempt to exalt one at the expense of the other.[3] Secondly, because the heart of Latin studies is manifestly Latin literature,[4] and historical fashions will never stray so far that serious students will try to displace it from that central position.

But a body contains other parts besides its heart; and it is unmistakably the student not of epigraphy or numismatics, but of the literature, who has right up to the present time been the worst offender in minimising the importance of the historical record derivable from sources other than his own. It is true that no one

---

1 *CAH.* xii, p. 720. Cf. Sutherland, *Royal Numismatic Society, Presidential Address,* 1948–9, p. 6: "surely, and clearly, numismatics have climbed into the rank of primary historical material, which a historian can neglect only at his own risk."

2 Cf. the salutary words of A. E. Housman, *Introductory Lecture, University College, London,* 1892: "everyone has his favourite study, and he is therefore disposed to lay down, as the aim of learning in general, the aim which his favourite study seems specially fitted to achieve, and the recognition of which as the aim of learning in general would increase the popularity of that study and the importance of those who profess it."

3 Numismatics especially suffers from being treated as a self-contained subject. This has long been deprecated (e.g. von Luschin, *NZ.* i, 1869, cf. Loehr, *Numismatik und Geldge-*

schichte), but the tendency dies hard, and the recent warning of Sutherland is very timely: "the numismatist who ploughs his furrow independently of the historian is asking for disastrous trouble... the ideal before us is the return, in some degree, to the tradition of an earlier age, in which there was no arbitrary distinction between related branches of study" (loc. cit., pp. 7 f.). It is very true that the special techniques of a subject must be throughly applied before it is fit to associate with other branches (cf. Instinsky, *Hamburger Beiträge zur Numismatik,* i, 1947, p. 81, on coins; and *AC.* on constitutional history): but the process of inter-relation must not be postponed too long. However, the numismatist need not feel exceptionally guilty in this matter, for many students of literature and *MSS.* are much worse offenders; see next paragraph of the text.

4 Cf. *PR.* p. 230.

would now deny categorically that the ancient historian must derive many of his conclusions from non-literary sources. But this injunction is still much better known in theory than in practice, and still receives much more lip-service than active discipleship. Even some of the very latest historical writers operate at variance with it; for they quote a great deal of ancient literature—much of it more valuable as literature than as history—and exceedingly few of the inscriptions, coins or papyri which likewise require consideration.

These are the people who would be most worried by the sparseness of the literary tradition about anniversary years. But their worry would be no less illogical in quality than a claim by the numismatist that only the coins are worth studying. All sources are seriously inadequate, and no category is sufficient by itself; moreover, our surviving literary record, like other forms of record, only represents a very small proportion of what originally existed.[1] Just as the coins and inscriptions completely fail to tell us many things which we learn from literature, so too there are whole categories of investigation—such as the present study of anniversary years—for which we have to apply exclusively to non-literary records.

The facts which we thus know, but which the literature has *not* told us, include such necessary pieces of information as the very names of *Augusti* set up outside Rome,[2] not to speak of the dates and titles even of those in the capital.[3] But what is particularly important to our present purpose is the existence among the weakest points of the literary record of precisely the three main topics most relevant to our present study—coinage, imperial publicity and religion. Coinage of almost inconceivable bulk, and with corresponding variety of type, lasted for century after century; yet the surviving literary commentary on it is ludicrously sparse, fragmentary and obscure,[4] exemplifying thereby the singular indifference

---

1   The historian need only think of Cato's *Origines* (7 books), almost all speeches other than Cicero's, the *Histories* of Sallust and Pollio, Q. Mucius Scaevola's 18 books *De Iure Civili*, Varro's 45 books of *Antiquitates*, Livy, XLVI–CXLII, Claudius' *Histories of Carthage and Etruria* (of 8 and 20 books respectively), and the autobiographies and memoirs of many imperial personages and politicians.

2   E.g. L. Julius Aurelius Sulpicius Uranius

Antoninus in Syria (Delbrueck, *NC.* 1948, pp. 11 ff.), Domitianus in Gaul (Webb, M. & S. v, 2, p. 590), Carausius II and 'Censeris' in Britain (Sutherland, *NC*, 1945, pp. 125 ff., Hill, ibid. 1948, pp. 91 ff.), Salbannacus (M. & S. IV, 3, p. 105); cf. Dryantilla *Augusta* in Pannonia (Webb, loc. cit. p. 588).

3   Mattingly, *CAH.* XII, p. 717.

4   It is time that it was collected.

of ancient writers to economics and public finance.[1]. Equally striking is the failure of our surviving literary tradition, over a very large part of the period, to tell us the imperial point of view. We should not have at all a clear idea of how Augustus or Tiberius presented their policy if we had to depend on Suetonius, Dio and Tacitus.[2] For Claudius, "inscriptions and papyri now become of great importance and have helped to correct and ameliorate the traditional literary portrait."[3] The coins entirely outstrip the literary record in informing us of the publicity of Domitian, Commodus, Pescennius Niger or Gallienus.[4]

It has long been notorious that the same discrepancy in value between the literary and non-literary sources exists in regard to Roman religion, and particularly to the early religion[5]—and to the ritual and routine of religious practice at all periods, which provides many of the occasions for anniversary celebration. Wissowa said of a non-literary record (the calendar): "hoc paene unum superest sincerum documentum."[6] He was speaking of the early period; but for the religion of the empire, too, the best sources are, to an over-whelming extent, non-literary. "We learn it in the main from temple-foundations, from coin-types, from dedications by the *princeps* or the Arval Brothers, and from the actions of the *quindecimviri sacris faciundis.*"[7]

Thus for information neither about the coinage itself, nor about the imperial publicity and religion which are its chief concerns, can we rely primarily on the surviving literary sources. It was hardly, therefore, to be expected that a theme which partakes of all these subjects, the numismatic celebration of anniversary years, would be confirmed by the literary record. At all events, it is in no way surprising that this is not so. The most that we might expect would be that writers (like inscriptions) should fortuitously divulge facts which illustrate the importance attached by the Romans to

1 Cf. A. H. M. Jones, *Ancient Economic History* (*University College, London, Inaugural Lecture,* 1948), p. 3.

2 For Augustus it is only necessary to think of the *Res Gestae.* For Tiberius see Pippidi, *Autour de Tibère,* pp. 67 ff., 188; cf. *APT.,* Preface.

3 Charlesworth, *CAH.* x, p. 653 n.

4 Cf. the weakness of the literary sources in telling us of ancient political eras: Kubitschek, *PW.* I, 610.

5 See now Rose, *Ancient Roman Religion,* pp. 11 ff.

6 *De Feriis,* p. 1; cf. Warde Fowler, *The Religious Experience of the Roman People,* pp. 14 ff., id. *Roman Festivals,* pp. 17 ff.

7 Nock, *CAH.* XII, p. 412. Snyder, *YCS.* 1940, p. 225, mentions the predominance of inscriptions over literary records as evidence for the celebration of anniversary days.

anniversary years; and this proves to be the case (pp. 3–5). It would be wrong to feel surprised that they do not say more.

I have tried here very briefly to answer possible objections to my general contention that many coins and medallions owe all, or something, of their type or timing to anniversary years. But this has been a negative process, and it remains to carry out a positive demonstration of my thesis. This will be attempted in the main part of the book. Here it may be desirable to point to certain analogies from other parts of the empire. I have suggested in *From Imperium to Auctoritas* that this practice of numismatic commemoration of anniversary years is identifiable on a considerable scale in the coinages of provincial cities. Especially significant is the custom of Roman colonies and *municipia*. Let us take, for example, the Julio-Claudian period, not because it is peculiar in this respect but because a large proportion of the coinages of these cities is concentrated in it. On examination of these issues it becomes clear that many of them—at some cities most of them—were intended to celebrate important local anniversaries—the fifth, tenth, twenty-fifth, fiftieth or hundredth jubilees of their privileged status.[1] The only reviewers of my book who have commented on this theory, Mattingly[2] and Tourneur,[3] have quoted it as representing a fact. This evidence from Roman cities is worth bearing in mind from our present point of view, since we should not expect to find such a custom prevalent in them unless it was also known at the Roman city *par excellence*, the capital itself.

Indeed, the latter supposition is by no means a new one, for the existence of this custom in certain forms is a well-known fact. I have already referred to the commemorations of *saecula* of Rome, and of the *decennia* of emperors. The monetary and medallic issues made in connection with these celebrations have been widely recognised. But these are the only anniversary occasions which have received anything approaching systematic attention from numismatists. However, certain scholars have also, cursorily and in isolated contexts, hinted at the much more extensive range of such occasions to which I believe the types of coins and medallions to refer (cf. p. 9). For at least six writers have each identified a single coinage celebrating an anniversary year of some occasion. These writers include

1 *FITA.* p. 295 (summary).
2 *NC.* 1946, p. 129.

3 *Revue Belge de Numismatique,* 1947, p. 144.

Laffranchi (p. 88), Strack (p. 101), Wruck (p. 65) and—less categorically—Gagé (p. 127) and Dobiaš (p. 73); Mattingly, too, adopts
Laffranchi's interpretation and ascribes to two comparable occasions
further mintages also (p. 74, Appendix III).

These writers have identified isolated numismatic commemorations of anniversaries of Actium, the "restoration of the Republic",
an emperor's birth, a prince's death, a great temple, and a coinage.
Yet these are only six happenings, and no attempt has been made to
bring even these into relation with each other; when this is done, the
coins concerned add up to no more than a few dozen. But it is my
aim to show that the anniversary years of some seventy-two different
events and occasions were celebrated on the imperial coinage—often
repeatedly on successive anniversaries—and that this commemoration was performed by means of many hundreds, or indeed perhaps
thousands, of different coins, not to speak of a considerable number
of medallions.

That is what I hope to show. The arrangement that I shall adopt is
largely chronological.[1] That is to say, after a preliminary chapter,
I shall proceed according to the chronological order of emperors.
This has obvious advantages as regards orderliness; but it also has
one disadvantage. Chronological order is clearly not identical with
the order of arguments that would be most persuasive. So this book,
as it is arranged, does not respond satisfactorily to any who still may
doubt the plausibility of my thesis, or who consider that its probable
scope is likely to be smaller than I have suggested. I would recom-
mend these readers, and any others who may wish to obtain a general
view of the subject without reading the book right through, to adopt
a procedure which puts before them a selection of the material
in a more cogent order. This procedure might take the following
form:

(1) Read Chapter I (pp. 1–13), showing the non-numismatic
evidence for the celebration of anniversary years, and indicating
special features applying to the coinage.

(2) Read Chapter VIII, section i (pp. 160–8), summarising the
extent of the numismatic evidence that I am putting forward.

(3)–(6). Next I would suggest attention to a few selected portions
of the subject, classified under four different headings—individual

---

1 Though not necessarily in chronological order *within* each principate.

emperors, categories of coins and medallions, occasions chosen for anniversary commemoration, and types:

(3) Emperors. Among those whose issues illustrate my thesis (though some readers may find other periods more illuminating) are Claudius (pp. 70–8), Vespasian (pp. 88–91 and Appendix III), Antoninus Pius (pp. 104–6) and Septimius Severus (pp. 114–22).

(4) Categories of coins and medallions. Series in which an extremely high proportion of known issues coincide with anniversary years include (*inter alia*) the following:

    (*a*) gold medallions (pp. 23–4, 59–60, 68, 95, 110, 124–6, 135 n., 140);

    (*b*) silver medallions (pp. 94–5, 100–1, 117–18, 123–4, 126, 132, 151–2);

    (*c*) gold and silver *quinarii* (Appendix I);

    (*d*) Eastern tetradrachms (pp. 20 n., 61, 76–7, 83–5, 88, 92, 98, 101–2, 121 n., 125).[1]

(5) As examples of occasions chosen for anniversary celebration, it is perhaps possible to single out Actium and the capture of Egypt, and the death and deification of Augustus.[2]

(6) Instances of types habitually bearing this significance are those of legions (pp. 86, 107, 137) and *Tutela* (pp. 88ff., 138f.).

I hope that this selection of the evidence will demonstrate that the numismatic commemoration of anniversaries attained a considerable scale. I must stress, however, the exploratory character of this book. I am very far from regarding every argument that I have put forward here as infallible. It is possible, indeed probable, that this or that example cited by me may prove susceptible to refutation. These examples necessarily depend to some extent on *argumenta a silentio*, that is to say on apparent peculiarities of issues due to significant chronological gaps, e.g. gaps of exactly fifty or a hundred years, between them and their predecessors or successors. Arguments of this kind always contain an element of risk. For rare and little-known series like those of the colonies, this is particularly true; though even in such cases it does not invalidate a sufficiently powerful array of anniversary coincidences.[3] With regard to the great metropolitan series, the prodigious feats of listing that have been performed by

---

1   For summaries of (*a*), (*b*) and (*d*), see pp. 165–6, 169.

2   For summaries see pp. 163–5.
3   Cf. *CMG*.

Mattingly and others have authorised us to feel nowadays that a very large percentage of the total major variants of this series have duly been included in our records.

The percentage may well be slightly lower in the case of some of the rarer categories, even of metropolitan mintage.[1] But I do not believe that future discoveries of major variants will invalidate my general interpretation or method. They will not be very many; only a small proportion of them will relate to my present material; and even if one of these effectively disposes of this or that significant gap between known issues, it will only have modified or destroyed one of a large number of cumulative pieces of evidence, without infringing the validity of any of the others. Even in the unlikely event of this happening thirty times, it is doubtful whether my general thesis would be adversely affected. In view of these considerations, based on the comparatively advanced state of our knowledge of the major variants,[2] I have not been afraid to make use—albeit tentatively and with the necessary mental reservations—of *argumenta a silentio*; and I hope that any that are demonstrably erroneous will be shown to possess this character as soon as possible (cf. Appendix IV).

This tentative, exploratory character of the book has another aspect also. For, just as I may have included certain evidence that may eventually be disproved, so I suspect that the examples of anniversary issues that I have quoted are very far from exhaustive. I hope that these processes of addition and subtraction will be attempted. In more general terms, I hope that some importance will be attached to this subject, in view of its repercussions on our understanding of coinage and of imperial publicity, and so of Roman history and religion.

Since, therefore, criticism and further information are needed before any degree of definitiveness can be claimed, I have not thought it desirable to try to assemble in my Plates a representative collection of illustrations; it seems better to wait until so unfrequented a subject has taken on a more definitive appearance. Instead I have merely chosen for reproduction here a few of the rarest coins of the Julio-Claudian period that are cited in the text (not necessarily those

1 For the distinction in kind between the commoner and rarer categories, a distinction stressed by Pink, Strack and Elmer, see below, p. 60. One of the rarer categories is that of the *quinarii*; see Appendix I.

2 That is to say, our knowledge of their existence and external appearance: I do not believe that our understanding of the significance of their types is nearly so advanced.

which best illustrate the theme of the book), this being the one period for which I have needed to discuss coins absent from the leading catalogues and works of reference. For the rest, illustrations are rarely needed for my argument, and those who require them will need to use the book in conjunction with those fundamental works.[1] References to them and to other works are given in connection with each coin—indeed, my debt to published writings can be seen on every page; but the subject has received too fragmentary treatment hitherto for any bibliography to be possible. I hope, however, that the general and other Indices will facilitate reference to the bibliographical information that is included in the footnotes.

It remains for me to acknowledge the help, besides that of published works, which I have received in preparing this book. I owe gratitude to Dr J. M. C. Toynbee for a letter which has greatly assisted me to formulate the present Introduction; to Professor R. Syme and Dr C. H. V. Sutherland for reading the proofs and offering valuable suggestions, and to the latter for showing me an important forthcoming work in draft; and to Mr C. M. Kraay for information about Flavian coinage. I want to express my thanks to the British Museum and to the national collections at Athens, Berlin, Budapest, Copenhagen and Paris, for the casts which the Chiswick Press has reproduced here. I am indebted to the Turkish Director-General of Museums and Antiquities, Bay Hâmit Zubeir Koşay, for enabling me to see unpublished coins in provincial collections; to the *University of Edinburgh Journal* for allowing me to reproduce from it passages from my Inaugural Lecture; and to Vienna University and Professor A. Betz, and also Professor P. W. Duff, for various kinds of assistance. I am, too, very grateful to the Cambridge University Press for undertaking the publication of the book, and to the Master and Fellows of Trinity College for defraying the costs of its preparation and thereby adding another to their many acts of generosity towards me.

MICHAEL GRANT

EDINBURGH, 1949

1 See Abbreviations: Cohen, Gnecchi, Mattingly, Mattingly-Sydenham-Sutherland-Webb, Strack, Toynbee; also Alföldi, *Die Kontorniaten*, Budapest, 1942/3.

CHAPTER I

THE CELEBRATION OF 'ANNIVERSARY YEARS'

(i) *Roman attention to 'Anniversary years'*

The celebration of past events played an extensive and vital part in the public religion and daily life of Romans of all periods.[1] The present study is intended to indicate certain evidence of this preoccupation, provided by the coins and medallions and relating in particular to anniversaries. But a distinction must be drawn between two quite different senses of the word 'anniversary', that is to say between two different categories of anniversary for which these coins and medallions might be, and were, issued:

(*a*) the annually recurrent noteworthy *day* of the month[2] or more usually of the year; e.g. the New Year Day,[3] the reigning emperor's 'Regnal New Year Day'[4] and birthday,[5] and probably other days also, hitherto uninvestigated from this point of view.[6]

(*b*) the *year*[7] in which was celebrated the centenary, or multiple or subdivision of a centenary—or other such 'round' anniversary—of an important event:[8] here loosely described as the 'anniversary year'.

1 Cf. Altheim, *History of Roman Religion*, pp. 190 f. (temples; cf. G. Rohde, *Die Bedeutung der Tempelgründung im Staatsleben der Römer*, pp. 1 ff., 8, 12 ff.), 386 (deaths; cf. K. Sauer, *Untersuchungen zur Darstellung des Todes*, Frankfurt Diss. 1930, W. Schultze, *Kleine Schriften*, pp. 138 ff.); cf. *PR.* (*Fortuna huius diei*, Aius Locutius).

2 Lambrechts, *L'Antiquité Classique*, 1944, p. 48; id. *Latomus* (*Mélanges Heuten*), 1946, p. 327.

3 For commemorative issues (some of the instances questionable) see the following writings: coins (*BMC. Imp.* III, pp. 448, 476; ibid. IV, pp. lxxvii, 282; M. & S. IV, 1, p. 76; Toynbee, p. 76; id. *JRS.* 1945, pp. 117 f.; ibid. 1946, p. 236; Alföldi, ibid. 1940, p. 9), medallions and semi-medallions (Toynbee, pp. 33 ff., 73 ff., 89; cf. *BMC. Imp.* IV, pp. xciv, clxxxii; Alföldi, *Die Kontorniaten*, Pl. I. 1, 3) and contorniates (Toynbee, *JRS.* 1945, pp. 117 ff.; ibid. 1946, p. 236, accepts a proportion of the attributions of Alföldi, loc. cit. pp. 37 ff.).

4 Cf. Nock, *CAH.* x, p. 489; Toynbee, pp. 74 ff.; Snyder, *YCS.* 1940, p. 266.

5 Cf. Pippidi, *Recherches sur le Culte Impérial*, pp. 44 f., 116 f. n. 3; Nock, *CAH.* x, loc. cit.; Kornemann, *Gestalten und Reiche*, p. 100; Ensslin, *SB. München*, 1943. Censorinus wrote a work *De Die Natali*; cf. below, p. 2, nn. 6, 7.

6 Cf. Toynbee, p. 73 n. 1.

7 For this distinction cf. Altheim, loc. cit. p. 191: 'the year and day...live on in memory.'

8 Here, too, the commemoration centres on the *day* in so far as it is on this, in all probability, that its climactic point is reached: but this is so, not only or not even principally because this annually recurrent day of the year has again been reached, but because the *year* (of which for this purpose the day in question is the central point) is of peculiar importance as the 100th (or similarly 'round' anniversary; for the importance of 50 see Roscher, *Abh. Leipzig*, 1917, Rose, *OCD*. p. 614) of the event which is commemorated.

As regards (*a*), there is abundant evidence of keen attention by Romans of all periods to anniversary days and to coincidences connected with them,[1] and this interest is reflected in coins and medallions. But this book is about (*b*), for which, indeed, the coinage is rather more appropriate; for it took some time to pass from hand to hand, and was therefore better suited for the celebration of a year than for that of a day. Up to the present, we have known much more about (*a*) than about (*b*), since it is naturally the former, rather than the latter, type of occasion with which *Fasti* and *Ferialia* are concerned. But there are two exceptions to our ignorance about (*b*). First, an interest has long been taken (it was stimulated by Laffranchi)[2] in the *decennalia, vicennalia*, etc. of emperors, and in the celebrations which accompanied, preceded and followed those occasions.[3] Secondly, great progress has been made, especially by Gagé[4] and Piganiol,[5] with regard to the *ludi saeculares*, which on a number of occasions commemorated intervals of 100[6] or 110 years,[7] or artificial intervals fixed for political reasons, in the history of Rome.[8] In the

1 E.g. Augustus (Gagé, *RGDA*. pp. 159 n. 1, 167 f., 175, 182 f.; Snyder, *YCS*. 1940, pp. 233 f. [especially p. 234 n. 21], 236; Weber, *Princeps*, I, pp. 99*, 101*; Taylor, *The Divinity of the Roman Emperor*, p. 206); Tiberius (Weber, loc. cit. pp. 94*, 99*; cf. Rogers, *Studies in the Reign of Tiberius*, p. 57); Caligula (Pippidi, *Recherches sur le Culte Impérial*, p. 109); Claudius (Weber, loc. cit. p. 101*); Nero (Laffranchi, *Atti e Memorie dell' Istituto Italiano di Numismatica*, 1921, p. 58; cf. *BMC. Imp.* II, pp. lxxvii, xcv); Severus (Fink, *YCS*. 1940, pp. 77 ff., 81; cf. Weinstock, *JRS*. 1942, p. 128); Macrinus (Fink, loc. cit. p. 81, cf. n. 256); Diocletian (Alföldi, *Röm. Mitt.* 1935, pp. 98 f.); Maxentius (Besnier, *Histoire Romaine*, IV, 1, p. 354). One of many Republican instances is provided by Cicero (cf. Gagé, *RGDA*. p. 156 n. 1).
2 E.g. *Atti e Memorie dell' Istituto Italiano di Numismatica*, 1921, pp. 54 ff.
3 There is some reason for thinking that certain developments in the official Alexandrian coinage occurred not every five, but every seven years after accessions (cf. Milne, loc. cit. p. xxxix: for the religious significance of the number, see Nock, *CAH*. XII, p. 421 n. 1, and references). Asia on the other hand was particularly attentive to Σεβαστά occurring at intervals of four years (cf. *FITA.* p.

362: on Greek quadrennial and octennial festivals see Thomson, *JHS*. 1943, pp. 59 ff.; on Roman quadriennial intervals, Ginzel, II, pp. 250 f.; Bolton, *CQ*. 1948, pp. 82 ff.). Fourth and seventh centenaries are correspondingly stressed. Cf. Rose, *OCD.* p. 614.
4 *Recherches sur les Jeux Séculaires, Saeculum Novum (Transactions of the International Numismatic Congress of* 1936); *Mélanges d'Archéologie et d'Histoire*, 1934, pp. 1 ff., etc.
5 *Revue des études anciennes*, 1936, pp. 219 ff.; *Histoire de Rome*, pp. 43, 60, 67, 71, 229, 239, 251, 412, etc. See also now Pighi, *Pubblicazioni dell' Università Cattolica del Sacro Cuore*, (ser. v, sc.-fil.), XXXV, 1941.
6 Censorinus, *De Die Natali*, XVII, 13; cf. Ginzel, II, p. 201 and n. 2; *CAH.* X, p. 150 n. 1.
7 Censorinus, loc. cit. XVII, 9; cf. Ginzel, loc. cit. This interpretation leads (as coins will show) to emphasis on multiples of that figure (and especially on 550) in connection with events other than the foundation of Rome. It is recorded by Horace, *Carmen Saeculare*, 21.
8 For the persistence of the *saeculum* motif see Mattingly, *CAH.* XII, p. 719; id. *The Emperor and his Clients (Todd Memorial Lecture*, II, Sydney, 1948), pp. 16 f., 26; Manni, *Atene e Roma*, 1938; id. *Rendiconti R. Ac. Bologna*, 1939.

present volume no attempt will be made to discuss the secular celebrations or the well-known coinages in honour of them, though these will be used as evidence in an endeavour to pierce the obscurity surrounding other anniversary issues. The same will apply to our attitude to *decennalia*, etc., and their coinages; except that, in the early empire, some attempt will also have to be made to identify various neglected and unapparent issues of decennial character, since these will be found to throw light on the problems of anniversary coinages as a whole.

Unfortunately mint-masters often preferred to generalise their types, being aware of what was familiar to some contemporaries and careless of the worries of future historians: so that many pieces carry no specific allusion to the occasions of their issue.[1] This applies to anniversary issues as much as any others, and has caused students to ignore the possibility that such issues may celebrate *decennia*, centenaries, etc., of events quite other than the foundation of Rome or the accession of the reigning emperor. For, even viewed as a general hypothesis apart from specific evidence, this possibility must be admitted. A people which was so attentive to the centenaries of its city or to the *decennia* of its ruling *princeps* was not likely to neglect similar anniversaries of other great events in its history. Least of all could such neglectfulness be considered a likely trait in the traditionally minded Roman. Indeed, quite apart from the coins, there is—though ancient authors took such matters too much for granted to comment on them[2]—specific evidence to the contrary; though it has not, as far as the present writer knows, been collected. For example, under the Republic, the Romans being deeply attentive to the years of temple foundations,[3] it had surely not been fortuitous that the temple of *Concordia in arce* was vowed in the 150th year (218 B.C.)[4] of the traditional foundation-date of the first known temple of Concord in 367;[5] that the temple of *Fortuna Primigenia* was dedicated in the 100th year (194 B.C.)[6] of the temple of *Fors*

1 Cf. Sutherland, *Numismatic Review*, II, I (July 1944), pp. 7, 9. See also Introduction.
2 Snyder, *YCS*. 1940, p. 225, refers to scattered references by the literary authorities to anniversary *days*.
3 Cf. Rohde, *Die Bedeutung der Tempelgründung im Staatsleben der Römer*; Altheim, *History of Roman Religion*, p. 191.

4 Cf. Platner and Ashby, *Topographical Dictionary of Ancient Rome*, p. 137.
5 For references, see Altheim, *History of Roman Religion*, p. 282; Pippidi, *Recherches sur le Culte Impérial*, p. 64 n. 1.
6 Cf. Wissowa, *Religion und Kultus der Römer*², pp. 260, 596, Rose, *OCD*. p. 368.

Fortuna (293 B.C.);[1] that the second temple of Mars (138 B.C.) was dedicated just a quarter of a *millennium* after the traditional date of his first temple (388 B.C.);[2] and that C. Sosius is likely to have completed his restoration of the temple of Apollo in the quadringenary year (*c.* 32 B.C.) of the original date assigned to it (431 B.C.).[3] Similarly, the first attested *augurium salutis* (160 B.C.), a ceremony in honour of Peace, coincides with the centenary of a foundation with preeminently similar associations, the temple of Janus (260 B.C.).[4]

Another important type of religious occasion, the *deductio* of colonies, sometimes follows a similar pattern. Thus *colonia Copia* at Thurii (194–3 B.C.) is founded precisely a quarter of a *millennium* after the Greek colonisation of the same city (444–3 B.C.); and the very next colony to be called *Copia*, at Lugdunum (43 B.C.), is established just four centuries and a century and a half respectively after the two foundations of Thurii, whose coin-types it deliberately repeats.[5] Similarly, Caesar apparently planned the colonisation of Carthage just 100 years after its destruction (p. 120).[6]

If we turn to the Principate, Augustus timed his *ludi saeculares* to occur 10 years after the 'restoration of the Republic';[7] and he assumed the titles of *pontifex maximus* and *pater patriae*, with much ceremony, 15 and 25 years respectively after the same great event. His thirteenth consulate coincided with the same quarter-centenary occasion, just as his twelfth consulate had been timed to coincide with the quarter-centenary of *Aegyptus capta*. The second consulate of Tiberius was likewise arranged to fall on the *vicennium* of the *respublica restituta*.[8] Another *vicennium*, that of the first victories of Nero Drusus, was signalised by games in A.D. 6.[9] Attention should also be paid to the simultaneous dedication of altars to *Pax*, *Salus* and Janus (with *Concordia*). This took place in 10 B.C., the sesquicentenary

1 Wissowa, loc. cit. pp. 256, 595.

2 Cf. Platner and Ashby, loc. cit. p. 328.

3 Cf. Strong, *CAH*. x, p. 573. For the special importance of four (and its multiples), see p. 2 n. 3; for 'quadringenary', p. 53 n. 1.

4 *PR.*; see Liegle, *Hermes*, 1942, pp. 249 ff.

5 Bull; I hope to amplify elsewhere.

6 Mommsen, *Die römische Chronologie bis auf Cäsar*[2], p. 175, considers a different type of religious ceremony also to have a centenary character, namely the hammering of a nail into the wall of the Capitoline temple, of which he believed the first recorded example

(363–2 B.C.; Livy, VII, 3. 3 f.) to have related to a plague of 463–2 B.C. (ibid. III, 6); but this view is seriously contested; cf. Ginzel, II, pp. 204 f. (references).

7 Cf. Stuart Jones, *CAH*. x, p. 150. See also below, p. 84 and n. 9.

8 Cf. Sutherland, *NC*. 1943, p. 46. The *Carmen Saeculare* (29 f.) stresses *Tellus*, whose temple's quarter-millenary might have fallen in the previous year, Platner and Ashby, loc. cit. p. 511 against Weinstock, *PW*. VA. I.804.

9 Weber, *Princeps*, I, p. 231*; cf. Dio 55. 27.

year of the first recorded *augurium salutis* in honour of peace, and the quarter-millenary of the temple of a deity indissociably linked with peace, Janus:[1] so that the occasion, like *decennia* and *quinquennia* of 27, 17, 12 and 2 B.C., had a multiple anniversary significance. Moreover, the *vicennium* of this same event of 10 B.C. seems to have been signalised by the foundation, or dedication, of a further altar of *Concordia* in A.D. 10.[2]

Similar coincidences occur later. Tiberius's restoration of Venus' temple on Mt. Eryx (A.D. 20)[3] was undertaken 200 years after the dedication of the temple of Venus *Erycina* at Rome (181 B.C.).[4] Likewise his *Ara Pietatis Augustae* in A.D. 22 was dedicated just 50 years after the probable establishment of the *Arcus Pietatis* in 29 B.C.[5] Claudius deified Livia in the centenary year of her birth (p. 70). Nero's closure of the temple of Janus in A.D. 66 (which could, as far as the cessation of warfare was concerned, have taken place several years earlier) coincided with the tercentenary of the first closure that is historically attested (235 B.C.).[6] Vitellius used the appellative *Germanicus* in a very special sense—initially it even seemed to replace Augustus,[7] whose precedents he partly neglected[8]—and his principate coincided with the half-centenary of the much commemorated Germanicus's death.[9] Domitian's *ludi saeculares*, at a date otherwise inexplicable (A.D. 88), fell in the 100th year of the no less carefully remembered inauguration of the imperial high priesthood. Later, Severus, in A.D. 203, restored the *Circus Maximus*, on which Trajan had spent large sums in *c.* 103;[10] and of the only three years in which the Arval brothers are known to have carried out special celebrations for all *divi*[11] (the third was for an accession),[12] one (A.D. 183) was the bicentenary year of the *saeculum aureum* of

1 *PR.*; cf. p. 3 and n. 4.
2 For the date see Pippidi, *Recherches sur le Culte Impérial*, pp. 63 f. (references on p. 64 n. 1).
3 Cf. Colin, *Revue archéologique*, 1946, p. 42.
4 Cf. Schilling, *Rev. de phil.*, 1949, p. 314.
5 Rushworth, *JRS.* 1919, pp. 37 ff., 53 ff.; cf. Platner and Ashby, loc. cit. p. 42.
6 *PR.*; see Momigliano, *JRS.* 1942, p. 63.
7 *BMC. Imp.* I, p. ccxxviii, cf. p. ccxxii. Here he was accentuating a tendency of the later Julio-Claudians, Snyder, *YCS.* 1940, p. 137 n. 592. On coinage he often writes *Germanicus* in full even when all titles are abbreviated, *BMC. Imp.* I, p. 379. 62, etc.

8 *BMC. Imp.* I, p. ccxxviii. His apparent employment of the title *consul perpetuus* (cf. Hammond, *The Augustan Principate*, p. 283 n. 42; Stevenson, *CAH.* x, p. 826) shows an attitude to the constitution very different from that of Augustus from 23 B.C.
9 For the persistence of this commemoration cf. Snyder, loc. cit. pp. 136 ff., 277; Taylor, *American Journal of Archaeology*, 1942, p. 310.
10 Cf. Longden, *CAH.* XI, p. 205 n. 3.
11 Henzen, *Acta Fratrum Arvalium*, p. 148; cf. Hoey, *YCS.* 1940, p. 185.
12 Of Elagabalus (A.D. 218).

Augustus, and another (A.D. 224) was the quarter-millenary year of the equally celebrated *respublica restituta*.[1] Constantine began his Arch, with its Trajanic designs, in A.D. 312–13,[2] just two centuries after the dedication of the *Basilica Vlpia* and *Forum Trajanum* (p. 149; cf. also pp. 41–2 n. 5).

There are other instances in which *principes* seem to have made use, for publicity purposes, of the *accidental* coincidence of important events with the 'anniversary years' of other occasions. Thus it seems that the cult of Actian Apollo under Augustus owed something, not only to the temple on the Epirote promontory, but also to the coincidence of the battle of Actium with the quadringenary of Apollo's temple at Rome—an occasion apparently signalised in the previous year by a political opponent, Sosius (p. 4). Similarly, Claudius made much of the coincidence of his accession with the fiftieth year of his life and of the *Ara Romae et Augusti* at his birthplace Lugdunum (pp. 70, 74). Caligula, too, in his extensive and immediate commemoration of Augustus,[3] was surely not unaware that his own accession (A.D. 37) fell in the centenary year of the latter's birth (63 B.C.) (cf. p. 69); and the coincidence of the same event's bicentenary with the accession of a better Augustan, Antoninus Pius (A.D. 138), is unlikely to have escaped notice. One of his first and most emphasised coin-types is the Augustan *Pax*; and Gordian I, by stressing the same type, shows awareness that his own accession (A.D. 238) took place a century after that of his model and kinsman[4] (p. 129).[5] Likewise Carausius, whose emphasis on *Pax* was even greater, may have been conscious that he, too, came to the purple

---

1 Snyder, loc. cit., has collected a number of inscriptions which, though not explicit, seem to tell a similar story (*CIL*. xi, 3781: thirtieth anniversary of adoption of Tiberius), 241 (Preisigke and Bilabel, *Sammelbuch griechischer Urkunden aus Ägypten*, 4583: fifteenth of *dies imperii* of Trajan), 245 (*CIL*. xiv, 4553: beginning of sixtieth year of life of Antoninus Pius), 250 (*CIL*. xii, 5905: fortieth birthday of Marcus Aurelius), 253 f. (*CIL*. xiv, 168, *ILS*. 6172: beginning of fiftieth year of life of Severus), 257 (*CIL*. vi, 862: tenth year of *imperium* of Severus). Acclamations of later emperors often took the 'centenary' form *vivat centum annos*, cf. Alföldi, *Röm. Mitt.* 1934, p. 87. It may not be entirely fortuitous that the Theodosian *Codex* coin-

cided with the half-millenary of the birth of Augustus. For '50' see Rose, *OCD*. p. 614.
2 Toynbee, *JRS*. 1941, pp. 190, 193.
3 E.g. the dedication of his temple, Balsdon, *The Emperor Gaius*, p. 35, and coinage.
4 Constantius II and his colleagues may likewise have appreciated the quadringenary character of their accession year, A.D. 337.
5 The conqueror of Gordian I, Maximinus, may, by his assumption of the title *Germanicus* in A.D. 235–6 (M. & S. iv, 2, pp. 133 f.), show consciousness that his German victories (ibid. pp. 146 f.) occurred just a quarter of a millennium before the first German victories (15 B.C.) of the first imperial figure to be granted the same title, Nero Drusus—whose same victories, on an earlier anniversary, had

in an anniversary year (the 150th) of the accession of Antoninus, a year which was also the 350th after the birth of Augustus (p. 144). Again, Constantius II, by issuing medallions with the Augustan legends AVGVSTVS–CAESAR for his visit to Rome in 357, seems to indicate that he appreciated its coincidence with the quadringenary of a year in which contemporaries believed the Principate to have begun (43 B.C.) (p. 152).

(ii) *The numismatic record of 'Anniversary years'*

The coincidences, deliberate or accidental, to which the last section has called attention, are only the concern of this book in so far as they are recorded by coins and medallions; and its aim is to suggest the extent to which these, like other instruments of official policy, coincided with, and celebrated, years possessing an anniversary character. As monetary and medallic issues play a great part in commemorating *ludi saeculares* and *decennalia,* there is no reason why they should not equally have joined in the celebration of other anniversaries. Moreover, the strongly marked anniversary character of the coinage at Roman colonies and *municipia* and even at *civitates peregrinae*[1] would be strange if similar customs did not prevail at Rome. This would harmonise with the intensely traditional appearance of the Roman coinage, illustrated, for example, by the numerous 'restorations' and revivals of earlier emperors' portraits and types.[2] Indeed, *Fasti, Acta* and *Ferialia* show clearly that even at late periods the celebration of recurrent rites dating from Republic or early empire was by no means limited to *ludi saeculares* or *decennalia*; and it is on general grounds likely that the coinage was included among the media of propaganda utilised for such commemorations.

Finally, there is a special reason for believing this probable: namely, the peculiar attention devoted to their coins by the Roman

received special commemoration (see above, p. 4). Among recent writings on Maximinus are those of Bersanetti, *Studi sull' Imperatore Massimino il Trace*; Passerini, *Epigraphica,* III, 1941; id. *Athenaeum,* 1942, pp. 150 ff.; Hohl, *Klio,* 1941, pp. 264 ff.; ibid. 1942, pp. 287 f.; Altheim, *Rheinisches Museum,* 1941, pp. 192 ff.; d'Ors Perez Peix, *Emerita,* 1941, pp. 200 f.; Ensslin, *Philologische Wochenschrift,* 1943, pp. 253 ff.

Domitian had already perhaps, at an earlier date, especially honoured the centenary of Nero Drusus' death for a similar reason (p. 96).

1 *FITA.* pp. 295 ff., 338, etc.
2 E.g. Mattingly, *BMC. Imp.* II, pp. xxxvii f., lxxvii, xcvi; III, pp. 1, lxxxvi f., xc; id. *NC.* 1920, pp. 179 ff.; Mattingly and Salisbury, *NC.* 1924, pp. 235 ff.; Gagé, *Revue archéologique,* XXXIV, 1931, pp. 40 f., etc.

authorities and so by the people of the empire.[1] This is a topic on
which the present writer has enlarged elsewhere[2] as follows: 'Roman
coinage is a branch of archaeology which has two arresting features.
First, it is enormously varied, offering a kaleidoscopic variety of
types, usually numbering hundreds in every reign. And secondly—
the reason for such variety—it served a propagandist purpose far
greater than has any other national coinage before or since. This
was the means which the Roman government, lacking modern media
of publicity, used to insinuate into every home in the empire each
changing nuance of imperial achievement and policy. Their unremitting use of this means is evidence enough, if evidence is needed,
that in the course of their vast circulation these coins were studied
with an attentiveness that is quite alien to our own practice. Their
subtle and highly differentiated symbolism is often hard for us to
understand, but millions of contemporaries must have been immune
from this difficulty. For if this were not so, the hard-headed Roman
government would not have been so foolish as to continue, for centuries, this lavish outlay of energy and ingenuity. I do not mean that
everyone who saw a coin would necessarily understand each of the
often complex significances of its type; but I do mean that most
people, or most educated people, noted and understood at least some
of the several imperial themes imprinted thereon; and to us, as to
them, the fluctuations of these themes are of peculiar interest as
reflecting the principles which successive imperial governments
wished to have identified with the bases of their rule.'

A particular aspect of this attentiveness to coinage which is
relevant here is the religious character not only of the mint (which
was in the temple of Juno *Moneta* and was, from the second century
A.D., described as *sacra*),[3] but even of coin-types, and especially
portraits.[4] MONETA itself begins, before the death of Caesar, to
appear on the coinage (on an anniversary occasion) as a religious
concept (p. 15); and before the end of the next century it has become
MONETA AVGVSTI.[5] Indeed, not only were old and unusual pieces

1 Cf. Charlesworth, *The Virtues of a Roman Emperor*, p. 8; and *PR*.
2 *PR*.; cf. *CSNM*., and below, p. 171.
3 *ILS*. 1638 (Hadrian); cf. Hirschfeld, *Die kaiserlichen Verwaltungsbeamten*², p. 186 n. 3; Ensslin, *CAH*. xii, p. 362.
4 Cf. Clerc, *Les Théories rélatives au Culte des Images* (Diss. Paris, 1915), p. 57;

Rolland, *Courrier numismatique*, 1931, p. 11; Cahn, *RS*. 1944, p. 58.
5 *BMC. Imp.* iii, pp. xxxv ff. (cf. ii, pp. xii, lxxxiii, lxxxiv n. 1, xc); Strack, i, pp. 154 ff. (references on p. 161 n. 675); cf. Dieudonné, *Rn.* 1940; Mattingly, *NC.* 1943, p. 36. See also Grimal, *Lettres d' Humanité*, iv, 1945, pp. 29, 120.

selected by Augustus for his *Saturnalia* presents (p. 24), but coins,[1] as well as medallions and medallic objects,[2] were themselves objects of consecration. They were thus very easily utilisable for the commemoration of the great anniversaries of public religion. But the coins' own religious character leads to a further point also: we ought not to be surprised if we find coins commemorating the anniversaries, not only of earlier events, but of earlier coins—just as a number of emperors, of whom the most thoroughgoing is Trajan,[3] stress the significance of much earlier coinage by reviving or 'restoring' a large number of its types.[4]

These points will be illustrated during the identification and discussion of anniversary issues which will follow. These will be seen to be of considerable number. Modern writers have identified a minute proportion of them.[5] For example, Laffranchi and Mattingly appreciated that certain issues of Vespasian commemorated the centenary of Actium and of the *respublica restituta* of Augustus in 27 B.C. (p. 88); and Strack has rightly ascribed Hadrianic innovations to the 150th anniversary of the latter occasion (p. 101). Mattingly has also attributed a Lugdunese *quadrans* of Claudius to his fiftieth birthday (p. 74). Wruck assigned the Eastern S.C. *aes* of Tiberius to the half-centenary of the inauguration of that series by Augustus (p. 65).[6] Gagé, too, noted the lapse of 100 years between the consecration (?) of the Temple of Venus and Rome and a reminiscent medallion of Severus Alexander. He did not pursue this topic, but rightly added *cette coincidence nous paraît mériter réflexion* (p. 127). The same thought was probably also in the mind of Dobiaš, who observed (without comment) that the issues of Claudius in honour of Nero Drusus were made just half a century after the latter's death (p. 73). There may be similar references that have escaped the present writer's notice. But in any case such allusions are very few indeed, and only refer to an insignificant percentage of the issues

---

1 Cf. Mabbott, *Numismatic Review*, I, 3 (Dec. 1943), p. 29 n. 4; M. & S. II, p. 303; cf. later, Laurent, *Cronica Numism. si Arheol.* 1940, pp. 119 f. Laum, *Heiliges Geld*, p. 154, restricts this unduly to Greece.
2 E.g. Nemausus *patte de sanglier* pieces; cf. Babelon, *Rn.* 1943, p. 2.
3 *BMC. Imp.* III, pp. lxxxvi ff., 132 ff.—he was 'one of the first to recognise Numismatics as an aid to History' (M. & S. II, loc. cit.) (on an anniversary, p. 100).
4 Republican issues remained a very long while in circulation: cf. *BMC. Imp.* III, p. lxxxviii and n. 2.
5 Von Schrötter's *Wörterbuch der Münzkunde*, p. 297, s.v. *Jahrhundertmünzen*, mentions no ancient examples.
6 I would express it differently.

to which, in the present writer's view, an anniversary character is to be ascribed.

Before an attempt is made to review these issues, certain observations are necessary regarding the methods which we may expect the coinage to adopt in celebrating anniversaries. Nowadays we should often confine our attention to the actual day, or at any rate to the week or other brief period, in which the centenary (or its multiple or subdivision) falls. The Romans took a rather more elastic view, according to which celebrations might instead (or in addition) be held within the year immediately preceding, as well as the year immediately following, the anniversary day. To take the former of these two marginal years, Vespasian,[1] Septimius Severus[2] and Gallienus[3] are among the numerous emperors who celebrated their *decennalia* not on the tenth, but on the ninth, anniversary of their accession—that is to say at the beginning, not the end, of the tenth year of their reigns. Likewise, Augustus chose Livia's 49th birthday for the dedication of the *Ara Pacis Augustae*;[4] and Tiberius dedicated a statue of Divus Augustus on the 49th anniversary of his own assumption of the *toga virilis*.[5] The second Republican temple of Concord was vowed not much more than 149 years after the first, and 99 years separate two Republican temples of *Fortuna* (pp. 3 f.); while inscriptions possibly commemorate the 59th and 49th birthdays of Antoninus and Severus respectively, and the ninth anniversary of the latter's *dies imperii*.[6]

Our understanding of this emphasis on the year preceding an anniversary (which the coins and medallions may be expected to share) is assisted by entries in the *Acta Arvalia* such as the following: *vota quae superioris anni magister voverat persolvit et in proximum annum...nuncupavit.*[7] Thus anniversary celebrations came to have two parts, one of which was naturally felt to be concerned with the

1 Cf. *BMC. Imp.* II, p. liii.
2 Cf. Miller, *CAH.* XII, p. 19.
3 Cf. Piganiol, *Histoire de Rome*, p. 425; von Domaszewski, *Rheinisches Museum*, 1902, pp. 510 ff.; Alföldi, *Röm. Mitt.* 1935, pp. 90 f. n. 2.
4 Cf. Snyder, *YCS.* 1940, p. 234. For recent contributions to the voluminous literature on the *Ara*, see Strong, *Quaderni di Studi Romani*, II, 1939, pp. 23 f. (bibliography); Picard, *Revue des études Latines*, 1941, pp. 279 ff.

(bibliography); Momigliano, *Journal of the Warburg and Courtauld Institutes*, 1942, p. 228; id. *JRS.* 1944, p. 110; Poulsen, *Acta Archaeologica*, 1946, pp. 1 ff.
5 Weber, *Princeps*, I, pp. 94*, 99*.
6 *CIL.* XIV, 4553, 168, VI, 862: cf. above, p. 6 n. 1.
7 Thus restored by Henzen, *Acta Fratrum Arvalium*, pp. xxxiii, 95; cf. Gagé, *Revue archéologique*, 1931, pp. 24 f.; Pearce, *NC.* 1937, pp. 118 ff.

past and the other with the future.[1] The coin-types celebrating Philip's millenary games look both backwards and forwards;[2] indeed, some of them were probably struck well in advance of the actual anniversary. An obvious point ahead of an actual anniversary date was 1 January of the anniversary year. This was one of the commonest occasions for the issue of medallions (p. 1 n. 3). These are especially frequent in years of imperial consulships;[3] but the largest of all New Year issues occurs precisely on the occasion of Philip's *millennium*.[4] The same may well apply to Regnal New Years. Occasionally, moreover, the anniversary occasion was anticipated by more than a few months, or even by more than a year, as, for instance, when Antoninus Pius began to issue 'secular' types several years before his *ludi saeculares*.[5]

Sometimes, too, the commemoration of an anniversary continued for a year or so *after* the main occasion.[6] The clearest example is that of the usurper Pacatianus (A.D. 249–50), who inscribes his coins ROMAE AETER. AN. MILL. ET PRIMO[7] (*Romae aeternae anno millesimo et primo*). But, though the references are not customarily so explicit, it is equally certain that the numismatic publicity for the *ludi saeculares* of Augustus in 17 B.C. continued without diminution at least in the year 16.[8] Again, Strack[9] has noted that the *ludi* of Antoninus Pius continue to receive belated attention on the coinage of A.D. 148–9. These examples recall the demonstration attempted by the present writer elsewhere[10] that the foundation (and thus probably the anniversary) issues of Roman colonies and *municipia* were habitually followed by a second mintage—usually of the following year—before numismatic silence descended. The first year after a great occasion appears to have been thought of as a period in which celebration might justifiably continue.[11] Thus, too, it is possible that Antoninus Pius celebrated his restoration of the temple of

---

1 Cf. Piganiol, *JRS*. 1937, p. 153 n. 1.
2 Cf. Gagé, *RGDA*. p. 180; Toynbee, p. 103.
3 Toynbee, pp. 83 ff.
4 Ibid. p. 86.   5 Ibid. pp. 143, 194.
6 For long gaps between *vota suscepta* and *soluta*, see Pearce, *NC*. 1937, p. 119; cf. also, for the religious importance of round numbers +1, Rose, *OCD*. p. 614.
7 Cohen, v, p. 182, no. 7; cf. Kubitschek, *NZ*. 1908, p. 48; Elmer, ibid. 1935, p. 39; Ensslin, *CAH*. xii, p. 92. The same occasion perhaps produced the novel and exceptional

double *sestertii* of Trajanus Decius and Etruscilla (Mattingly, *Roman Coins*, p. 127; Pink, *NZ*. 1936, p. 13).
8 Cf. Sutherland, *NC*. 1943, pp. 43 ff.; Nock, *CAH*. x, p. 478.
9 III, p. 140.
10 *FITA*. pp. 290 f., 291 n. 1, summarising nineteen suggested examples.
11 Anazarbus (peregrine) even seems to coin specially for the conclusion of its first *quadriennium* after its 1000th year, Hill, *BMC. Lycaonia*, etc. p. cv.

Augustus and Livia in the 201st year after the conferment of *imperium* on Augustus (p. 106).[1] Or the delay might perhaps be longer: Momigliano[2] suggests that the foundation of the *Porta Argentariorum*, though of A.D. 204, may represent a belated echo of the *decennalia* of Severus which, due in 203, had been celebrated in 202.

Such considerations add to the difficulty of identifying anniversary issues; and so do others. One of them is the extremely uncertain dating of so many of the great Republican occasions which were appropriate for celebration. Nor, even if such dates are discoverable with some probability, does it by any means follow that the Roman moneyers employed accurate chronographical systems. The sources which they used, *Fasti, Annales*, Varro, Diodorus, etc., often differ very widely from each other;[3] and we cannot usually be quite sure which reckoning was 'official' at a given moment of Roman history. Furthermore, even if the Roman authorities knew, or believed that they knew, the date of a famous early occasion, there is always the danger that, for political reasons, they might have celebrated its anniversary on quite a different date. It is only necessary to quote here the extraordinary disparity of the intervals between the *ludi saeculares* of the Republic, Augustus, Claudius, Domitian, Antoninus Pius, Severus and Philip.[4] Similarly, the *dies imperii* celebrated for a *divus* did not necessarily correspond with the date celebrated during his lifetime.[5] A further difficulty lies in the fact that an important religious edifice was often not fully inaugurated until at least two ceremonies had taken place, its foundation and its dedication[6] (in addition to its preliminary vowing). These ceremonies are often separated by a number of years, and either of them, or both, may at a later epoch be selected for anniversary celebration.[7]

1 Is there a similar 'schematisation' in Pliny, *NH*. xxxiii. 42: 'gold coinage first issued 51 years after first silver'?
2 *JRS*. 1940, p. 214.
3 Cf. Beloch, *Römische Geschichte, passim*; Piganiol, *Histoire de Rome*, pp. 43 f., 55, 70; Cornelius, *Untersuchungen zur frühen römischen Geschichte*, pp. 7 ff.; Momigliano, *JRS*. 1945, pp. 128 f. etc.
4 Cf. Gagé, *RGDA*. p. 120; Mattingly, *BMC. Imp*. II, pp. lxxvii, xcv; Pighi, *Publicazioni dell' Università Cattolica del Sacro Cuore* (ser. V, sc.-fil.), 1941, vol. xxxv;

Bernini, *Athenaeum*, 1943, p. 148; Scramuzza, *The Emperor Claudius*, p. 237 n. 113; M. &. S. IV, p. 69, etc.
5 Fink, *YCS*. 1940, p. 79 n. 243.
6 For the various occasions cf. Rohde, *Die Bedeutung der Tempelgründung im Staatsleben der Römer*; Altheim, *History of Roman Religion*, p. 191; Paoli, *Revue historique du Droit français et étranger*, 1946–7, p.180; etc.
7 E.g. for the *Ara Pacis Augustae*, although the date of foundation remained the more celebrated (cf. Gagé, *RGDA*. pp. 167, 174; Welin, ΔΡΑΓΜΑ *Martino P. Nilsson dedi-*

With this and the other peculiarities of Roman anniversaries in mind, an endeavour will now be made to identify some at least of the issues commemorating such occasions.

catum, pp. 500 ff.), the dedication date also seems to have been remembered (cf. Hanell, *Det Kungliga Humanistiska Vetenskapssam-fundets i Lund, Årsberättelse*, 1935–6, pp. 131 ff.). This duality of occasion may also account for the variant dates given for so many of these altars, e.g. the *Arae Romae et Augusti* at Lugdunum (12, 10 B.C.; cf. *FITA*. p. 115, cf. n. 9), *Fortunae Reducis, Iustitiae Augustae, Gentis Iuliae, Concordiae Augustae, Clementiae*, and especially the *Ara Numinis Augusti* (A.D. 9: Piganiol, *Histoire de Rome*, p. 229; A.D. 10: Pippidi, *Recherches sur le Culte Impérial*, p. 65; A.D. 13: Pettazzoni, *Augustus*, p. 226; A.D. 15: Weber, *Princeps*, I, p. 99* n. 436); cf. also, among later foundations, the temple of Venus and Rome (p. 127). Dates of vowing also add complications.

CHAPTER II
CAESAR AND AUGUSTUS

(i) *Caesar and Octavian*

Before the time of Caesar there is no certain example of a coinage issued on an anniversary or jubilee occasion. This uncertainty would not by any means justify the assumption that no such coinages were issued. Indeed, the later history of the anniversary issues will unavoidably raise the question whether this institution, like others clearly attested for the Principate, was not based on Republican precedents: the history of the Secular Games shows that the Republic was interested in anniversaries from an early date.[1] (If we consider another and not wholly dissimilar category of coinage—namely issues celebrating contemporary foundations of Roman colonies and *municipia*—we find that, though these, too, cannot be identified on a considerable scale until the last half-century B.C.,[2] there are signs that earlier mintages had performed a similar function.[3])

A search for anniversary issues of the Republic is hampered by various obscurities. Some of these are identical to the difficulties which hinder the identification of foundation issues. For example, it is still very uncertain at what dates many, or most, of the Republican *denarii* were struck.[4] Secondly, the significance of their types is often scarcely less uncertain. But we also encounter, in a particularly acute form, the various problems peculiar to anniversary issues. These obscurities make an examination of Republican issues necessarily unproductive as far as the identification of anniversary coinages is concerned. At best one can tentatively single out a few issues, with the conjecture that future research may enable an anniversary character to be assigned to some of them.[5]

1 These were first celebrated in 249 B.C. according to Nock, *CAH.* x, p. 477; Pighi, loc. cit. p. 4; cf. Bernini, *Athenaeum*, 1943, p. 148. Other theories have preferred *c.* 348 B.C. (Taylor, *American Journal of Philology*, 1934, p. 101; Piganiol, *Revue des études anciennes*, 1936, p. 219) or *c.* 456 B.C. (Altheim, *History of Roman Religion*, p. 459 n. 13, etc.).
2 *FITA.* p. 290 (summary).
3 Cf. Mattingly, *Roman Coins*, pp. 32, 78 f., 95, 98.

4 Cf. Pink, *NZ.* 1946, p. 114: 'es müssten alle Beobachtungen, die Willers, Bahrfeldt, Mattingly, Häberlin und Giesecke gemacht haben, mit den alten Resultaten zusammen verwertet werden.' The publication of the late Rev. E. A. Sydenham on this subject is eagerly awaited.
5 For a very tentative conjecture regarding the coins of M. Plaetorius Cestianus, see p. 52 n. 2. Cesano, *Studi di Num.* I, 2, 1942, collects significant evidence.

At last, half-way through the first century B.C., we come upon a group of issues which supplies more definite evidence. Admittedly, the first of these, signed by Dec. Postumius Bruti f. Albinus,[1] is again of somewhat uncertain date: but Grueber's ascription to 49 B.C.[2] is preferable to the former attribution to 43.[3] Albinus shows his adoptive father A. Postumius Albinus,[4] who had been consul in 99 B.C.—exactly 50 years before the probable date of this issue. Granted that a consular father would in any case constitute a normal type for coinage by a Republican moneyer, it may well be that the coincidence of the half-centenary with the moneyership of Dec. Albinus provided additional inducement for the type; and that this jubilee occasion was intended to come to the minds of those who saw these coins. This conjecture seems particularly justifiable in view of the still unusual expedient of the actual depiction of the honoured relative's portrait.

This possible analogy encourages us to ask whether M. Cordius Rufus, who portrayed Castor and Pollux in c. 46 B.C.,[5] did not intend the public to relate this type to the 450th year of the vowing of the temple of the Dioscuri, which, according to one reckoning, fell in precisely that year:[6] the Dioscuri were by now a far from usual type for coinage, and celebration of temple anniversaries was typically Roman (pp. 3 n. 3, 160). Evidence again seems to be provided by the issues of T. Carisius (c. 45 B.C.)[7] and L. Flaminius Chilo (probably 44 B.C.).[8] Carisius attributes to Juno the explicit designation of MONETA, showing a new self-consciousness of moneyers regarding the religious character of coinage (p. 8); and Chilo's type appears to be the same. Here is the numismatic début of this important word, an occasion recognised by the 'restoration' of this *denarius* by Trajan.[9] It does not seem fortuitous that the temple of Juno *Moneta* traditionally passed through its 300th year in precisely 45–4 B.C.[10] This theme is given added prominence by the still

---

1 *BMC. Rep.* I, p. 509.3966.
2 Ibid., cf. Mattingly, loc. cit. p. 277; id. (tentatively), *NC.* 1933, p. 245.
3 As Ulrich, *Pius-Pietas als politischer Begriff im römischen Staate* (*Historische Untersuchungen*, VI, 1930), p. 13, etc.
4 For the portrait see Vessberg, *Skrifter utgivna av Svenska Institutet i Rom*, VIII, 1941, Pl. IV, 8–10, V, 1–2, pp. 133 f.
5 *BMC. Rep.* I, p. 523. 4037.
6 Beloch, *Römische Geschichte*, p. 193; cf. Dionys. Hal. VI, 2; Livy, II, 21.3 (B.C. 496).

The other date is B.C. 499: Livy, II, 20; Altheim, loc. cit. p. 242.
7 *BMC. Rep.* I, p. 527. 4056; cf. *Roman Coins*, p. 274.
8 *BMC. Rep.* I, p. 565. 4198; cf. *Roman Coins*, loc. cit.
9 *BMC. Imp.* III, p. 136. 688.
10 Beloch, loc. cit. p. 3; Warde-Fowler, *The Religious Experience of the Roman People*, p. 135; cf. Livy, VII, 28. 4 f.; Ovid, *Fasti*, VI, 183 f. Vowed 345 B.C., dedicated 344, cf. Rose, *OCD*. p. 578.

unusual appearance of Juno *Sospita* on coins of M. Mettius, a moneyer of *c.* 44 B.C.:[1] it was just 150 years since the temple of this deity also had been erected, in 194 B.C.[2]

With these issues it may perhaps be felt that anniversary coinages have emerged from the thickest of the mists which had enshrouded their beginnings; and it is desirable to glance at the contemporary historical scene. The *denarii* of L. Flaminius Chilo and M. Mettius may have been issued after Caesar's death,[3] but those of M. Cordius Rufus and T. Carisius are attributable to his last years.[4] The traditional character of their types is fully in keeping with the picture of Caesar's régime which has been given us by Adcock and Syme. Caesar, as *Pontifex Maximus*, cared for the historic features of Roman religion and, like his contemporaries, regarded it as the symbol of the *respublica* and of its greatness.[5] Patricians of his time were well informed regarding ritual; and not only were the Julii an ancient priestly family, but Caesar himself showed on various occasions his *expertise* in sacerdotal matters.[6] It is, therefore, fitting that he should have paid careful attention to anniversary coinages; though, in spite of the vagueness of precedents, we need not necessarily suppose that he created the custom, which was in any case well suited to the atmosphere of the last years of the Republic.[7] We shall find that Tiberius and Claudius, as antiquarian as Caesar, revert to the numismatic theme of temple anniversaries; and this was to be vigorously revived by the Antonines and Severi.

The precedent of Caesar has prepared us for numismatic references to anniversary occasions by Octavian also. To begin with, we find possible or probable allusions of this kind on no less than three *denarii* of the important CAESAR DIVI F. class. The coins in question bear types of Venus,[8] Neptune[9] and Mercury.[10] The present writer

1 *BMC. Rep.* I, p. 542. 4135. Grueber, ibid. n. 2, conjectures Lanuvian origin.
2 Cf. Warde-Fowler, loc. cit. p. 354 n. 7; Wissowa, *Religion und Kultus der Römer*[2], p. 188.
3 Cf. *FITA.* p. 16 n. 4.
4 For a recent note on the iconography of coins of this period, see Mamroth, *Deutsche Münzblätter*, 1942, pp. 545 ff.
5 Cf. Adcock, *CAH.* IX, p. 722.
6 Cf. Syme, *JRS.* 1944, pp. 94, 97; *The Roman Revolution*, p. 68, cf. n. 4.
7 Cf. Piganiol, *Histoire de Rome*, p. 188: an

epoch *marquée...par un effort pour trouver les sources primitives et mystiques de la réligion.* A recent work, not seen by the present writer, is Giovanetti's *La Religione di Cesare*; cf. Seel, *Gnomon*, 1940, pp. 421 ff.
8 *BMC. Imp.* I, p. 100. 609; cf. p. cxxiii, correcting Grueber; *BMC. Rep.* II, p. 9; Babelon, loc. cit. II, p. 409. 105.
9 *BMC. Imp.* I, p. 100. 615; cf. p. cxxiii and n. 2.
10 Ibid. p. 98. 596; cf. p. cxxiii and n. 2, and Chittenden, *NC.* 1945, p. 41, who accepts Mattingly's date.

has already endeavoured to show that this series was inaugurated as early as 36 B.C. or even a year or two earlier.[1] The Venus coin strikes the eye as the earliest since, unlike the remainder of this class, the composition of its type relates it very closely to the preceding group of moneyers' *aurei* and *denarii*, which terminated in *c.* 38–7.[2] The portrait of Octavian harmonises with this view, being clearly one of the earliest in the CAESAR DIVI F. group. Neptune is no less suitable to the Sicilian war which ended in 36 B.C. than to Actium; and Mercury is appropriate to the restoration of commerce and prosperity which was intended to follow the close of the Sicilian hostilities.

Let us now look at the coinage just 50 years before. The first half of the 80's B.C. was a period when deities and personifications were beginning to multiply on the Roman *denarii*; and among those apparently making their first appearance on such coinage just at this very period are Venus under L. and C. Memies (Memmii) in *c.* 87,[3] and both Neptune[4] and Mercury[5] on the coins of L. Rubrius Dossennus in *c.* 89–6 B.C.[6] It is unlikely to be accidental—especially as similar echoes of Republican coinages occur later (pp. 26, 51)—that Octavian portrays the same trio precisely half a century after their first introduction to the silver issues. This curious, carefully timed echo of apparently insignificant mintages (rather than of actual events) is characteristic of the religious importance of the coinage and its types (cf. pp. 8 f.); for the same reasons, many more Republican *denarii* were to be 'restored'—again apparently on an anniversary occasion—by Trajan (p. 100).

The 30's B.C. were a time when Rome was in the grip of new religious feelings. Certain aspects of them had very recently and vividly been expressed by the fourth *Eclogue*. Venus was a deity who had acquired a novel significance in the previous decade, though

1 *FITA*. pp. 49 f. n. 14, corrected by Errata, ibid. p. vii. But the elimination of C. Clodius Vestalis from the Roman series is now felt to be premature. His issues appear to be Roman, and datable to *c.* 42–1 B.C. (his later career is recorded in a Cyrenian inscription, Oliverio, *Bericht über den VI. Internationalen Kongress für Archäologie*, 1939, p. 457). There are, however, still a lot of secrets to be extracted from the gold, silver and *aes* issues of the period. But at all events Bahrfeldt, *Die Römische Goldmünzenprägung*, pp. 106 ff., is justified in considering a group

of the CAESAR DIVI F. issues to be pre-Actian.
2 *BMC. Rep.* I, pp. 591 ff. gives the latest pieces in this category.
3 *BMC. Rep.* I, p. 307. 2421; cf. Mattingly, *Roman Coins*, p. 35.
4 *BMC. Rep.* I, p. 312. 2459.
5 Ibid. p. 313 (exceptionally a jugate head, with Hercules, on an *as*).
6 *BMC. Imp.* III, p. 133, prefers *c.* 89 to Grueber's *c.* 86 B.C. Other coins of Dossennus were 'restored' by Trajan, ibid. nos. 676 f., perhaps only for the intrinsic interest of their types, ibid. p. xc; cf. p. 139.

possibly the Venus of Julius Caesar was not so very different from the Venus of Sulla.[1] One of the most curious aspects of Augustan religion was to be the identification of the *princeps*, at least in private and provincial cult, with Mercury.[2] As for the third deity on this group of coins, Neptune, he too gained a new significance at this time by virtue of his special association with Agrippa, who was to dedicate a temple to him in 25 B.C.[3]

Thus Venus, Mercury and Neptune alike gained new life in these years. But the anniversary character of these coinages illustrates the fact that this new life had old roots. The religious revival in all its manifestations, like other Augustan institutions, was firmly based on the Republic. This idea is compendiously expressed by the CAESAR DIVI F. *aurei* and *denarii*. This series, while portraying deities who were taking on new aspects, selects for their portrayal the half-centenaries of their Republican débuts on the silver coinage. It would probably be misguided to detect any particular political relevance to Octavian in the careers of the Memmii or Dossennus. The triumvir was rather alluding to the Republic in general terms, and thus stressing the traditional Roman character of his public policy.[4] A good way of doing so was to call attention to the anniversary of the numismatic inauguration of this or that religious type. Against this background Octavian's commemorative gesture gains point, and enriches the significance of his coinage by combining a topical allusion with a traditional motif.

(ii) *Augustus*

We now come to the period when Octavian became Augustus and, having 'restored the Republic', ruled it as *princeps*. There is considerable inherent probability that a traditional custom like that of the anniversary issues should have flourished in this antiquarian period. Augustus was not only superstitious,[5] but also interested in anniversaries. Indeed, his attention to them has already been illustrated by the frequency with which he 'timed' important ones to coincide with his doings (pp. 4f.). But the most striking examples

1 Cf. Piganiol, *Histoire de Rome*, p. 163; Leopold, *Mededeelingen van het Nederlandsch Historisch Instituut te Rome*, vi, 1936, pp. 1 ff.
2 Cf. Altheim, loc. cit. pp. 365, 531 n. 49; Chittenden, *NC.* 1945, pp. 41 ff.

3 Weinstock, *PW.* xvi, 2528; cf. Dio 53. 27. 1.
4 Cf. *BMC. Imp.* iii, pp. lxxxvii, lxxxix f., on the 'restorations' of Trajan.
5 Cf. Gagé, *RGDA.* p. 159.

of his interest in anniversaries are provided by the issues celebrating the recurrent *decennia* of the *respublica restituta*. These would have been known, under later emperors, as *vota* coinages,[1] and as such would not come within the general theme of this book. But certain special reasons justify us in briefly considering the decennial, vicennial, etc., issues of Augustus and Tiberius. First, these issues celebrate not only the *vota* of an individual *princeps* but also the more permanently significant event of the 'restoration of the Republic'. This event was of a universal significance, and was still to provide the occasion for anniversary coinages at a much later date (p. 163). Secondly, the decennial and vicennial issues of Augustus and Tiberius have been only imperfectly recognised and appreciated. An attempt must be made to remedy this deficiency since they play their part in the history of anniversary issues as a whole. Tiberius will be considered in the next chapter, but here let us briefly review the issues of Augustus commemorating the *decennia* (and the quarter-centenary) of the restored Republic.

The first *decennium* (17 B.C.) coincided with the Secular Games, a tremendous occasion which in a sense constituted the foundation-date of the Principate in Roman public religion.[2] The new *saeculum* was likewise celebrated on official coinage,[3] and also perhaps by a 'medallic' issue bearing the portrait of Numa,[4] for which there is no sort of precedent at this period. The Secular Games of 17 B.C. were also remembered on the anniversary coinages of later emperors (pp. 44, 109). It was characteristic of Augustus to 'time' this celebration to coincide with the first *decennium* of the new order. The assumption of the responsibilities of *pontifex maximus* coincided with the fifteenth anniversary of the same event (p. 4):[5] and this combined occasion is possibly the *raison d'être* of an unusual *aes* mintage by Scato, proconsul of Cyrene and Crete.[6] Important anniversaries of the same great event of 12 B.C. were to be commemorated under at least two considerably later *principes* (pp. 5, 110).

---

1 The actual *vota* themselves may have started later than A.D. 10: Fink, *YCS.* 1940, p. 52 n. 115, *pace* Marquardt, *Die Römische Staatsverwaltung*, III², p. 266 and n. 9; Nock, *CAH.* x, pp. 482 f.

2 Cf. Stuart Jones, *CAH.* x, p. 150; Sutherland, *NC.* 1943, p. 42; ibid. 1945, pp. 65 f.; Mattingly, *Roman Coins*, p. 171, etc.

3 *BMC. Imp.* I, pp. 13, 74; Sutherland, *CR.* 1944, pp. 46 ff., etc.

4 See *SMACA.*

5 It was perhaps at this date that the *princeps* was first associated with the cult of the Lares: cf. Nock, *CAH.* x, p. 485. Pettazzoni, *Augustus*, p. 224, prefers c. 10 B.C.

6 *FITA.* pp. 138 f.

It appears highly probable that a number of official issues likewise celebrate the second *decennalia* of the new régime, which fell in 7 B.C.[1] —an occasion which has not, in modern times, received the notice that has been accorded to 17 B.C.[2] Two of these issues are the rare and medallic-looking *sestertii* probably issued by proconsuls of Africa[3] and Asia.[4] They are dedicated to Augustus with the words O.C.S. and OB CIVIS SERVATOS respectively. This was the dedication— made by the senate and Roman people (S.P.Q.R.)—which had accompanied the presentation to him in 27 B.C. of the *clipeus virtutis*, which likewise figures on these pieces.[5] The African issue (Plate I, 1) is specifically dated to 7–6 B.C. (TR. POT. XVII), the proconsul apparently being L. Volusius Saturninus.[6] The Asian specimen resembles it closely in type, module, isolation and general character. Possibly the proconsul who issued it was P. Cornelius Scipio, who, like L. Volusius Saturninus,[7] was an *amicus principis* whom a city honoured by coin-portraiture.[8] These rare issues are the forerunners of that large group of *sestertii* of many reigns which lack S.C. but instead bear a dedicatory formula with S.P.Q.R.[9] Dr Toynbee accounts for the variant formula by 'specially personal connections with the emperor'. But it is also possible to hold that S.P.Q.R., including as it does a mention of the senate, almost implies S.C.[10] In either event,

1 The *quinquennia* actually fell in 17, 12, 7 and 2 B.C. (though celebrations may well have begun in the earlier years); cf. *FITA.* p. 434.
2 The *vicennium* was apparently signalised by local coinages also: (i) it is perhaps for this occasion (starting in either 9–8 or 8–7 or 7–6 B.C.) that African colonies (Hadrumetum, Achulla, Hippo Diarrhytus) and Asian cities (Pitane, Temnus, Hierapolis) began honouring their proconsuls with coin-portraiture (*FITA.* pp. 224, 228, 230, 387, and Errata [ibid. p. vii] to pp. 229, 458); cf. a further group of honorary mentions under Tiberius, perhaps again (in Africa) starting on an anniversary occasion (*APT.* Ch. II, sect. ii). The governors chosen are in both cases *amici principis*, and political reasons for the innovation are suggested. (ii) P. Quinctilius Varus, perhaps arriving in Syria in *c.* 7 B.C. (*FITA.* p. 228 n. 8; for him see also Bernhart, *Blätter für Münzfreunde*, 1941, p. 204), started there the new so-called 'pseudo-autonomous' *aes* of Antioch, on which the ethnic was accompanied by ΕΠΙ ΟΥΑΡΟΥ (*FITA.* pp. 396 ff.), ΕΠΙ denoting at this time a pro-

cess of collaboration (ibid. pp. 398 ff.). (iii) Another unprecedented series began at Antioch in 7–6 B.C., namely *dupondii* and *asses* with ΑΡΧΙΕΡΑΤΙΚΟΝ ΑΝΤΙΟΧΕΙΣ in wreath (ibid. p. 376)—possibly also celebrating the *quinquennium* of the Roman high priesthood, perhaps together with an allusion to its Antiochene counterpart. (The next year, 6–5 B.C., occasioned a revival of the Antiochene silver tetradrachms [*FITA.* pp. 376, 398 and Errata to both pages], which may constitute a belated reference to the same occasions.)
3 Ibid. p. 139.   4 Ibid. p. 145.
5 Weber, *Princeps*, I, p. 257*, rightly points to the vast emphasis on this theme.
6 *FITA.* p. 228 n. 7. But de Laet, *Samenstelling*, p. 245, attributes P. Quinctilius Varus to this year.
7 *FITA.* p. 229, cf. n. 4.
8 Ibid. p. 387, cf. n. 2; *APT.* Ch. II, sect. ii (*a*).
9 Toynbee, p. 28.
10 Sutherland, *CR.* 1945, p. 74, Mattingly, *NC.* 1944, p. 124.

PLATE I

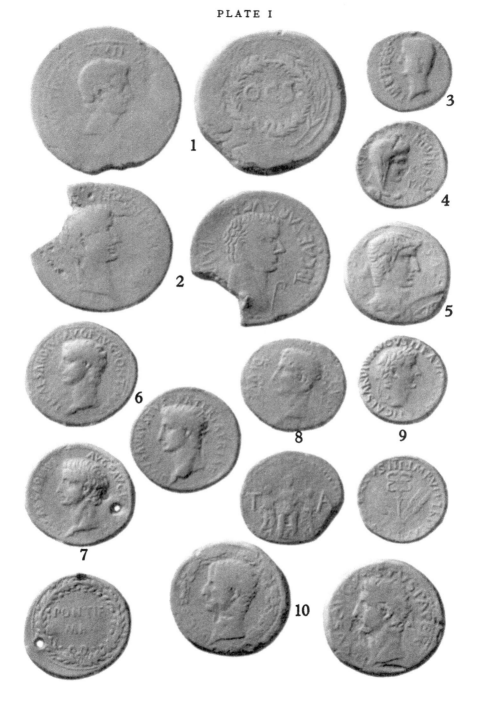

AUGUSTUS AND TIBERIUS:
RARE AND CONJECTURAL PIECES

the present *sestertii* were presumably issued under the same adminis trative arrangements as governed the remaining official *aes* of east and west alike, namely *senatusconsulto Caesaris auctoritate* (p. 28). Dr Toynbee rightly points out that the s.p.q.r. *aes* issues of later prin cipates are not medallions but coins. But it is doubtful whether this can apply to the present pieces, with their rarity and peculiar character.

Equally rare is a Roman series which appears to have been influenced by the same vicennial occasion. This consists of the so-called ' Triumphal' *aes*—large pieces (whether of bronze, *orichalcum* or copper is still unknown) bearing laureate (?) heads of Augustus to left, with globe at point of bust,[1] and, behind, Victory draped,[2] holding *cornucopiae*.[3] These rare specimens display the signatures of the *tresviri a.a.a.f.f.* P. Lurius Agrippa,[4] M. Maecilius Tullus [5] and M. Salvius Otho.[6] Their immediate occasion is very likely to have been the triumph of 7 b.c.[7] The 'Victory' type is closely associated with *vota*,[8] and will occur again in this connection under Tiberius (p. 34) and Nero (p. 81): and, just as 12 b.c. witnessed the fif teenth anniversary of the régime as well as the high priesthood, so 7 b.c. was no less noteworthy for the *vicennium* of Augustus than for the triumph. This issue appears to carry a combined reference to the topical and the anniversary occasions.

Now the pieces in question bear the letters s.c., but—exactly as is the case with the 'Numa' issue of perhaps 18–17 b.c. (p. 19)—their rarity and exceptional character sharply differentiate them in purpose from the common and orthodox coinage of the three moneyers who signed them. This distinction, and their apparent failure to fit into the metrological system, strongly suggest that these 'Triumphal' pieces were issued for private distribution.[9] In this character they are, in a sense, the successors of the framed 'pseudo-medallions' that

---

1 Sydenham, *The Coinage of Nero*, p. 32, notes this as precedent for the usage of Nero.
2 Cf. on an official African coin of 25 b.c., *FITA*. p. 81.
3 This leads Pink, *NZ*. 1946, p. 116—pro bably with justice—to call her *Fortuna-Victoria* (cf. the Seleucid *Tyche-Nike*).
4 *BMC. Imp.* I, p. 41 (Levis coll.).
5 Ibid. p. 42. 217.
6 Ibid. p. 43. 224. See also *SMACA*.
7 *BMC. Imp.* I, pp. xcviii, c; cf. Willers, *Gesch. der römischen Kupferprägung*, p. 152; Weber, *Princeps*, I, p. 80*. Laffranchi, *Bollet-*

tino del Circolo Numismatico Napoletano, 1940, *Estratto*, p. 12 n. 17, doubts the allusion to the triumph, partly on the dubious grounds that Augustus is wearing an oak- and not a laurel-wreath. The present writer, for reasons that cannot be given here, does not accept Pink's attribution (*NZ*. 1946, p. 125) to 12 b.c.
8 Cf. Gagé, *Revue historique*, 1933, pp. 27 f.; Alfoldi, *Röm. Mitt*. 1935, p. 98 n. 3; Fink, *YCS*. 1940, p. 59.
9 Cf. Pink, loc. cit. pp. 117 f. (who attri butes the occasion tentatively to Augustus' assumption of the high priesthood).

had already occurred under earlier moneyers, and were also to recur later. This interpretation of the 'Triumphal' *aes* as medallic is supported by analogies drawn from the Julio-Claudian emperors. For under them, too, we shall find similar examples of rare and peculiar pieces with s.c. forming part, or issued alongside, of large and common contemporaneous issues (pp. 60, 78).

It is reasonable to conclude that, in these years before the production of medallions was standardised, such rarities were issued with the explicit, varying to implicit, authority of the *senatusconsultum Caesaris auctoritate* which permitted the simultaneous main issue. Dr Toynbee has referred to various issues which, although they display the letters s.c., are to be classified as medallions[1] or as examples of 'border-line' categories including 'pseudo-medallions'[2] and 'medallic coins'.[3] The 'Triumphal' *aes* might almost be considered to fit within the definition of 'medallic coins'. But the contemporary official issues of Asia and Africa, like later issues of Tiberius and Claudius, form a new category, since they are indistinguishable by structure or style from ordinary issues. They are, however, differentiated from those by their rarity and by the probability that, on the commemorative occasion of 7 B.C., their purpose was distributive rather than monetary.[4] Pink and Elmer have pointed out the importance of segregating exceptional issues from the main lines of development, and these pieces constitute cases in point (cf. p. 60).

Our next landmark is the quarter-centenary of the Augustan régime. Until the second century A.D., it was only on the occasion of such quarter-centenaries that *quinquennia*, as opposed to *decennia*, receive much notice. The quarter-centenary of the *respublica restituta* fell in 2 B.C. So, too, according to the chronology of the *Fasti Capitolini*, did the 750th anniversary of the foundation of Rome.[5] The *princeps* selected this composite anniversary year for his assumption of the title *pater patriae*[6] and for his thirteenth consulate—only

---

1   Toynbee, pp. 21, 25 n. 28.
2   Pp. 25 ff.
3   P. 32.
4   It was apparently in this year that the reorganisation of the city-wards (closely connected with the worship of the *genius Augusti*) was completed; cf. Nock, *CAH.* x, pp. 479 f., etc.

5   Cf. Ginzel, II, p. 198; Piganiol, *Histoire de Rome*, p. 55. According to Taylor, *Classical Philology*, 1946, the Capitoline *Fasti* had originated in *c.* 21–17 B.C. For other reckonings of the foundation of Rome see p. 160 n. 2.
6   For bibliography, see *FITA*. p. 444 n. 6.

the second since 23 B.C. Such an occasion was particularly apposite for numismatic celebration, and it is tempting to relate to it the inauguration of the great C. L. CAESARES series of *aurei* and *denarii*.[1] These are considered, on independent grounds, to have been first struck in *c.* 2 B.C., and they could not have begun much later.[2]

The probability that this important mintage coincided with a special occasion, such as the year 2 B.C. provided, is reinforced by consideration of the great gold medallions of Augustus.[3] For it was now that one of his mints produced the first gold medallions (as far as we know) that any Roman had ever issued. These were apparently two in number, and no others are known for nearly a century afterwards (p. 95). The first of these two Augustan medallions, the famous Este piece—if genuine, as it is likely to be[4]—shows a minor variant of the usual C. L. CAESARES types. It is well suited by its clearly commemorative character to the circumstances of 2 B.C., and was possibly issued by the Lugdunum mint which produced the *aurei* and *denarii* of the same type. It is not unlikely that such a piece was intended for distribution to Gallic notables, like much later medallions of the same metal.[5] But, if so, the donor cannot have been any local Roman official, for there was not even a *legatus pro praetore* at Lugdunum: for some years past, the highest resident official had been a *procurator*,[6] and surely such pieces can have been issued by no Augustan *procurator*. It is perhaps just possible that the *legatus pro praetore* of the province, apparently L. Domitius Ahenobarbus,[7] had a hand in the issue from his distant headquarters on the frontier. But it is more probable that the initiative for such a striking innovation, and for such valuable gifts, lay with the *princeps*.

1 *BMC. Imp.* I, pp. 88 ff., 513 ff. There is a sharp distinction between this and the earlier period of activity of the 'Lugdunum' mint for gold and silver; *FITA.* p. 467 n. 6. On the earlier issues see *CSNM.*

2 *BMC. Imp.* I, p. cxiv.

3 Milne, *JRS.* 1945, p. 135, objects to Dr Toynbee's phrase 'money medallions'.

4 Cesano, *Atti e Memorie dell' Istituto Italiano di Numismatica*, 1934, pp. 107 ff.; *Quaderni Augustei*, III, 1937, pp. 32 ff.; Rizzoli, *Atti e Memorie della Reale Accademia di Padova*, 1926; Bahrfeldt, *Blätter für Münz-*freunde, 1931, pp. 243 f.; *pace* Laffranchi, *Historia*, 1933, pp. 600 ff.; *Bollettino del Circolo Numismatico Napoletano*, 1940, *Estratto*, pp. 3 ff. See also *Archäologischer Anzeiger*, 1928, p. 122; Toynbee, pp. 45 n. 2, 114 n. 10, 127, 231 n. 2; id. *JRS.* 1946, p. 236. For a false medallion with type of hippopotamus, see Cesano, Rizzoli, Laffranchi, loc. cit., C. P., *Bullettino del Museo dell' Impero Romano*, 1941, pp. 116 f.

5 Toynbee, pp. 117 f.

6 Cf. *FITA.* p. 118.

7 Cf. de Laet, *Samenstelling*, p. 233.

We may conjecture, then, that this medallion was a gift distributed by Augustus to celebrate the varied significance of 2 B.C. In this event, even if Lugdunum was the mint, it is unlikely that distribution was limited to Gaul. Indeed, the provenance of both the known gold medallions of Augustus is Italian,[1] and the rarity of such Italian finds of gold medallions may possibly suggest Roman origin. Augustus was accustomed to giving old or unusual coins as presents for the *Saturnalia*.[2] From such a custom, it was an easy stage to issue special pieces for an occasion like 2 B.C., or any other important anniversary; and later emperors will provide examples of the same practice.

The second of the gold medallions of Augustus, represented by the piece from Pompeii at Naples museum,[3] repeats a type of Diana which had been introduced to the gold and silver coinage of the mint at Lugdunum (?) in *c.* 14 B.C.[4] The medallion, however, is inscribed IMP. XV. SICIL., and must therefore be attributed to *c.* A.D. 1–4.[5] On the analogy of the foregoing conjecture regarding the C. L. CAESARES medallion, the Diana medallion too can be plausibly ascribed to an anniversary of the *respublica restituta*—in this case to its thirtieth year in A.D. 3–4. C. Sentius Saturninus was *legatus* at this time,[6] but the medallion may have something to do with the arrival of Tiberius in Gaul to take command in A.D. 4.[7]

The twentieth anniversary of the *respublica restituta* had been celebrated numismatically by an African proconsul (p. 20). Another equally isolated and rare 'sestertius' bears the signature of the pro-consul L. Passienus Rufus, who. is best attributed to *c.* A.D. 3–4.[8] Probably his coinage, like the IMP. XV. SICIL. medallion, com-memorates the end of the third, and beginning of the fourth, decade of the restored Republic. Incidentally the prolific colonial mint of Corinth produced an extraordinarily large and manifestly 'pro-gramme' issue in *c.* A.D. 4–5.[9] This, too, may have referred to the Roman celebrations of A.D. 4, though it might equally have been

1   Toynbee, p. 63.
2   Suetonius, *Aug.* 75; cf. Toynbee, p. 73 n. 1.
3   Gnecchi, I, pl. I, 1; Toynbee, pp. 45 n. 2, 127, 140, 206; Gabrici, *Augustus*, p. 400, pl. IV, 1.
4   For the date, see *CSNM*.
5   For the *terminus post quem*, see Kolbe, *Germania*, 1939, p. 104; Momigliano, *JRS.*

1944, p. 114. Siber, *Abh. Leipzig*, 1940, ascribes *Imp.* XVI. to *c.* A.D. 2/3–6; but see Syme, *JRS.* 1946, p. 156.
6   Cf. de Laet, *Samenstelling*, p. 233.
7   Ibid. p. 232.
8   *FITA.* p. 139.
9   West, *Corinth*, VI, p. 7; for the Augustan coinage of Corinth in general, see *FITA.* pp. 268 f.

intended to commemorate the half-century (or beginning of the fiftieth year) of the colony.[1] It may even have been designed to celebrate conjointly both the Roman and the Corinthian occasion, as one of the 'double occasions' which were so much in favour.[2]

It was also to be expected that numismatic notice would be taken of A.D. 13–14. This year combined the fortieth anniversary of the restored Republic, the quarter-centenary of the imperial high priesthood, and the fifteenth anniversary of the title *pater patriae*. It is natural to attribute to this occasion the exceptional *aes* of M. Granius Marcellus, proconsul of Bithynia in *c*. A.D. 14–15.[3] Probably this is also true of the scarcely less unusual pieces issued by Q. Caecilius Metellus Creticus Silanus, *legatus* of Syria at the same time,[4] and by a contemporary proconsul of Africa (Plate I, 2),[5] possibly L. Caninius Gallus or L. Nonius Asprenas.[6]

This, the last year of the life of Augustus, is also, on iconographical grounds, the most likely date for the issue, not only of much Lugdunese *aes* honouring Tiberius as IMP. VII.,[7] but of *aurei* and *denarii* honouring both men,[8] and of others bearing (for the first time) the sole reverse inscription PONTIF. MAXIM.[9] If, as appears probable, these coins allude to the important jubilee occasion of A.D. 14, they provide a further example of the custom by which types were sometimes designed to combine an anniversary occasion with a topical allusion. For the long sceptre held by the seated figure on the reverse of this series is likely to be that of *Iustitia*,[10] to whom an altar appears to have been dedicated in A.D. 13.[11] There is a certain interest in the apparent selection of *Iustitia* as the deity for special attention by the *Pontifex Maximus* on this anniversary. *Iustitia* had

---

1 For the foundation of the colony, see *FITA*. p. 266.

2 Cf. *CMG.*, for colonial coinages of Nemausus and Patrae jointly celebrating their own half-centenaries and the accession of Caligula.

3 *FITA.* p. 145 (Augustus and Livia).

4 Ibid. p. 128.

5 Ibid. p. 139. The fiftieth year after Naulochus, a much celebrated occasion (cf. Snyder, *YCS*. 1940, p. 196), also began in A.D. 14.

6 Cf. de Laet, *Samenstelling*, pp. 36, 66, 246; *PIR.*² II, p. 93. 390, *PIR.* II, p. 409. 93.

7 *BMC. Imp.* I, pp. 95 f., 579 f. For the date of the salutation see Schwartz, *Revue de Philologie*, 1945, p. 36.

8 *BMC. Imp.* I, p. 87. 506 ff.

9 Ibid. p. 91. 544 ff., *APT*. Laffranchi attributes to *c*. A.D. 11–12 (*R. it.* 1913, p. 316), cf. Mattingly, loc. cit. p. cxiv).

10 Strack, I, p. 52 n.128. *BMC. Imp.* I, p. 91. 544, ascribed to this figure, as its other emblem, the corn-ears of Ceres instead of the olive-branch of *Pax* (which recurs constantly on the same type under Tiberius [pp. 39 f.]), cf. Grether, *American Journal of Philology*, 1946, p. 226 (references ibid. and p. 227 n. 24 are confusing). Liegle, *Hermes*, 1942, p. 304, unplausibly interprets as *Salus*.

11 Cf. Latte, *PW*. x, 2. 1339 (not a temple, pace Ovid, *Pont*. III, 6. 23); Schwartz, *Revue de Philologie*, 1945, p. 32.

been one of the four cardinal virtues specified on the *clipeus virtutis* presented to Augustus just 40 years earlier, in 27 B.C.[1] Since then there had been no numismatic mention of her;[2] but she was to be greatly emphasised under Tiberius (pp. 38f.). It looks, however, as though·the decisive step in this direction was taken just before the death of Augustus. Many Tiberian institutions are traceable to the somewhat obscure last years of Augustus in which the two men ruled together,[3] and probably those years represented a more decisive stage in the foundation of the imperial philosophy than has been believed.

Thus the jubilee occasions of the *respublica restituta* attained numismatic celebration in keeping with the importance that was attached to them, and thereby set a precedent for the *vota* coinages of successive centuries. But the first *princeps* and his moneyers paid attention to other anniversaries also. Issues of *c*. 37–29 B.C. had deliberately revived, with added significance, the types of precisely half a century before (p. 17). It seems that the moneyers of *c*. 19–18 B.C. did the same. In *c*. 70–68 B.C.[4] M. Plaetorius Cestianus appears to have introduced to *denarii* the deity *Fortuna*;[5] and his is the type which may have been in the mind of Q. Rustius when, probably in 19[6] or 18 B.C.[7]—some 50 years later[8]—he stressed *Fortuna* in no less than three of her aspects (*Redux*, *Victrix* and *Felix*).[9] Again, in 19–18 B.C., two further moneyers, M. Durmius and a contemporary P. Petronius Turpilianus, depict Hercules and a lyre respectively.[10] This combination of types may have been intended to recall the

1 Markowski, *Eos*, 1936, pp. 110 ff., etc.
2 There had, however, been literary mention of the *vir iustus*, Horace, *Odes*, III, 3. 1.
3 See now Schwartz, loc. cit., on this period.
4 Mattingly, *Roman Coins*, p. 275, prefers *c*. 70 to Grueber's 68 B.C.
5 *BMC. Rep.* I, p. 443. 3519; cf. n. 1.
6 So Mattingly, *BMC. Imp.* I, p. ci.
7 So Willers, *Geschichte der römischen Kupferprägung*, p. 186; Bahrfeldt, *Die römische Goldmünzenprägung*, p. 144. Cf. also Macrea-Berciu, *Apulum*, I, 1939–42, p. 183 n. 41.
8 Pink, *NZ*. 1946, pp. 119, 123, now attributes Rustius to *c*. 13 B.C.; but this is unlikely, cf. *SWC*. However, calculations of intervals by mint-masters might well be inaccurate; cf.

the ignorance of Trajan's, *BMC. Imp.* III, pp. xci, xcii n. 3.
9 *BMC. Imp.* I, p. I. 1 f.
10 *BMC. Imp.* I, p. 11. 59, p. 5. 22. Other coins of Turpilianus, showing the exceptional type of *Feronia* (ibid. p. 2. 6, p. 3. 8 f.), may conceivably illustrate another anniversary occasion: 18 B.C. was the 200th year after the presentation, in 217 B.C., of a gift to *Feronia* by the *libertinae* (Livy, XXII, 1; cf. Warde-Fowler, *Roman Festivals*[5], p. 253). A parallel type of Turpilianus is *Liber* (*BMC. Imp.* I, pp. 2 ff.) who was connected by Romans with *Libertas* (ibid. p. cii n. 1). Servius (*Aen.* VIII, 564, cf. Warde-Fowler, loc. cit.) tells us of the devotion of *libertini* to *Feronia*. For her see further Marconi, *Storia e Religioni* IV, 1939, pp. 302 ff.; Untersteiner, *Rivista di Filologia*, 1940, pp. 211 f.

introduction of Hercules *Musarum* to the coinage half a century before, in *c.* 67 B.C., by one Q. Pomponius.[1] The comparison of these coincidences with those provided by similar Republican reminiscences under Octavian and Tiberius (pp. 16, 51) suggests that the 50-year intervals were not fortuitous.

In each case there may well have been, indeed there is likely to have been, a topical or 'family' occasion as well; but either or both would combine comfortably enough with an anniversary, and such blends are highly characteristic of Roman coinage. For example, *Fortuna* received special attention, including the dedication of an altar in her capacity as *Redux*,[2] on Augustus' return from the East in 19 B.C.;[3] and Hercules too gained new and special associations at this time.[4] The commemoration of these deities here repeats the custom by which, when a god or personification is given a new 'topical' aspect, allusion is simultaneously intended to this new aspect and also (on a suitable anniversary of an earlier coinage) to his or her traditional aspects.

Many of these moneyers' coinages for Augustus carry family allusions alongside the national references;[5] and the Augustan recollections of M. Plaetorius and Q. Pomponius may convey some honorific implication concerning their families also—especially as the coinages of M. Plaetorius were, half a century later, again to be recalled by Tiberius (p. 51).[6] But the reasons for this twofold reminiscence may merely lie in the fact that his was a good 'senatorial' issue—it bears the letters s.c.—made during a fleeting period in which the senate reasserted its peaceful control.[7] Such recollections of not very important Republican issues, of which the most conspicuous example is Trajan's series of 'restorations', bear witness to the religious significance attached to earlier mintages and indeed to the coinage in general (pp. 8 f.).

1 *BMC. Rep.* I, p. 441. 3602.
2 Cf. Gagé, *RGDA.* pp. 182 f., 185.
3 For *Fortuna* see now Marconi, loc. cit. p. 231; Untersteiner, loc. cit. p. 212; Dejaeger, *Fortuna: de oude cultus*, etc. (Diss. Louvain, 1941); Lyngby, *Historische Studien*, 1939 (not seen), etc.
4 Cf. *CSNM.* (coinage of *c.* 14–13 B.C.); Pippidi, *Revista Clasica*, 1941–2; *Autour de Tibère*, p. 162 n. 1 (refs.).
5 For those of Durmius and Petronius see *BMC. Imp.* I, p. cii.

6 But there were no senatorial Plaetorii (as far as is known) in the early principate, and the Sulpicii Platorini were not very eminent: *PIR.* III, pp. 42 f.
7 Cf. Last, *CAH.* IX, p. 341. It is also not impossible that the coinage of Plaetorius was influenced by the end of the fourth *saeculum* (110 years) from the beginning of the Republic (four being a particularly stressed number, p. 2 n. 3).

Augustus ruled for so long that, in the end, the half-centuries that he celebrated were his own and no longer those of the Republic. A very important period from a numismatic point of view was c. A.D. 10–11. In one of these years, or at a date very close to them, at least two major developments of the coinage occurred. The Roman mint revived after at least a decade of quiescence, and made a vast issue of *asses* with portraits first of Tiberius and then of Augustus[1] (as well perhaps as beginning to issue *quadrantes*).[2] Another great output of *asses* occurred at the other chief official mint, Lugdunum (in the *legatio* of L. Aelius Lamia,[3] serving under Tiberius), with the addition of *sestertii, dupondii*, and *semisses*.[4] (It is not necessary to consider these two series as distinct in administrative character, i.e. the Roman as 'senatorial' and the Lugdunese as 'imperial' or 'provincial', on the grounds that one is inscribed s.c. and the other is not. The present writer has endeavoured to demonstrate[5]—and his attempt has met gratifying support[6]—that much of the principal official *aes* of the period emanated from a *senatus-consultum* moved by the *auctoritas principis*, intervening by virtue of his *tribunicia potestas*; though varying procedures occurred.)

Thus the period c. A.D. 10–11 witnessed the apparently simultaneous, and no doubt co-ordinated, revival of the Rome and

---

1 BMC. *Imp.* I, p. 50. 271 ff., cf. p. xciv.
2 On these see *BMC. Imp.* I, pp. xcviii ff.; Willers, *Geschichte der römischen Kupferprägung*, pp. 129 ff.; Elmer, *NZ.* 1934, pp. 21 f.; *SMACA.* Willers, loc. cit., and Borghesi, *Oeuvres*, II, p. 423, are alone in considering them *semisses*; cf. Fluss, *PW.* XVI, 1653. They are usually ascribed to the last decade B.C., e.g. by Mattingly, Elmer, loc. cit.; Pink, *NZ.* 1946, p. 123. The present suggestion of a later date (which cannot be defended in detail here) is based on clear stylistic differences from other *aes* of Augustus's moneyers —differences which were noted by Laffranchi, *R. it.* 1911, pp. 323 ff. But, as was seen by Mattingly, *NC.* 1914, pp. 261 ff., the *quadrantes* do not suit the late Tiberian date postulated by Laffranchi (and Nicodemi, *Catalogo delle Raccolte Numismatiche del Castello Sforzesco*, I, pp. 62 ff.). Yet Mattingly's arguments, while disposing of attribution to the 30's or later, do not (and do not attempt to) prove that the *quadrantes* were as early as the first decade B.C. In the present writer's view (admittedly a tentative one) their real

analogies of style and letter-formation are with the Roman *aes* of c. A.D. 10–14 and with Sicilian issues of the same period (*FITA.* pp. 197 n. 6, 199). The latter seem actually to have been imitated from the *quadrantes* just before and just after A.D. 14. Prosopographical considerations have been adduced in favour of attribution of the *quadrantes* to the last decade B.C., but from this point of view also—though the prosopographical argument can only be used with the utmost caution, cf. Mattingly, loc. cit. p. 262—they actually suit a later date as well or even better.
3 Cf. de Laet, *Samenstelling*, pp. 20, 233; *PIR.*[2] I, 34. 200, II, Add. 200.
4 BMC. *Imp.* I, pp. 94 f. 565 ff., cf. p. cxviii.
5 *FITA.* pp. 97 ff., 446; but see *SMACA.*
6 E.g. by Bellinger, *American Journal of Archaeology*, 1947, p. 339; Mattingly, *NC.* 1946, p. 132; Sutherland, *JRS.* 1947, p. 211; id. *CR.* 1947, p. 115; de Laet, *L'Antiquité Classique*, 1946, p. 374; Vallejo, *Emerita*, 1946, p. 407. Further evidence regarding the workings of *Auctoritas Principis* has now been collected in Magdelain's study of that name.

Lugdunum *aes* mints on a large scale. It has already been suggested that many of the major numismatic enterprises of Augustus, as of his successors, were related to important anniversaries. Now it is revealed by Augustan and Tiberian *Fasti* that particular importance —indeed, perhaps an unexpected degree of importance—was attached to anniversaries of the first *ovatio* of Octavian in 40 B.C.[1] The significance attributed to that occasion is apt to be lost sight of in the light of Roman imperial history as a whole. For Augustus celebrated anniversaries of his first *imperium*,[2] as well as those of his first *ovatio*; and most of his successors, with regard to their own persons, laid more emphasis on the date of their first *imperium*, or first imperial salutation,[3] than on their first triumph or ovation. But one of the most important occasions in the *Fasti* of the first *princeps* —and one which, demonstrably, was remembered until and beyond the end of his life—was his first *ovatio* in 40 B.C.[4] The fiftieth year after that event was A.D. 10–11, and that is precisely the period to which the vast revivals of the Rome and Lugdunum *aes* have been attributed.

It must, then, be considered likely that the issues beginning in *c.* A.D. 10–11, apart from their task of providing *aes* for the Roman world, were timed to commemorate the half-centenary of the first *ovatio* of Augustus. Furthermore, they included an enormous number of *asses*—the denomination primarily designed to pay the soldiers.[5] The Roman *asses* ascribe to Augustus the *praenomen imperatoris*, a title conspicuously omitted on the vast majority of *aes* issues of the age of his rule by *auctoritas* (27 B.C.–A.D. 14).[6] This title is, however, included here with reference not so much to the measure of *imperium* which survived, but to the *Victoria Augusti* and his great military past, in which an early distinction had been his first *ovatio*.[7]

1 Cf. Gagé, *RGDA*. p. 184.
2 Ibid.
3 For confusions between the two, cf. Hohl, *Klio*, 1941, p. 281 n. 7.
4 For imperial *ovationes* see now Rohde, *PW*. XVIII, 2. 1902 ff.
5 Cf. Mattingly, loc. cit. p. xlviii; Willers, *Geschichte der römischen Kupferprägung*, pp. 168 ff.
6 *FITA*. pp. 440 ff.
7 Ibid. p. 442, cf. p. 440 and nn. 1, 4. A conjecture may be added here regarding a possible

connection of the *ovatio* with the *quadrantes* here tentatively attributed to *c.* A.D. 10–11 (p. 28, cf. n. 2). Moneyers whose coins look early among the four groups of *quadrantes* display a type of clasped hands—a theme which incidentally is to recur, described as IVNCTIO, on a colonial issue of Ilici honouring Germanicus and Drusus junior only a very few years later (Vives y Escudero, *La Moneda Hispánica*, IV, p. 42. 10). Is it, or is it not, a coincidence that Octavian's first portrayal of the clasped-hands type had occurred on

The history of anniversary issues has, in spite of obscurities of chronology, become somewhat less dim under Augustus. Indeed, it appears at first sight as though coinages of this type multiplied considerably during the triumvirate and first principate; but this appearance may be exaggerated by the obscurity of the Republican origins of such issues. At all events, under Augustus anniversary coinages did not diminish. The occasions to which they refer show a cross-section of the traditional bases of the Augustan programme. The Republic is not neglected, nor perhaps is the foundation of the city; but great emphasis is also laid on the *respublica restituta* and its anniversaries. We have also detected a likely reference to the first *ovatio*, which symbolised Augustus's early military achievements. It has been argued elsewhere that cities also coined to celebrate their own half-centenaries and other jubilees.[1]

Yet even this list of occasions seems slender in comparison with the numerous Augustan anniversaries recorded in the *Fasti*.[2] The application of this technique to the coinage was apparently not yet sufficiently developed to do justice to all the great Augustan events —many of which, indeed, were not yet far enough removed in date for their centenaries or half-centenaries to have arrived. Subsequent chapters will endeavour to show that later *principes* did much to fill the gaps.

a gold *quinarius* referring to the Treaty of Brundusium (*BMC. Rep.* II, p. 498. 128), which had immediately preceded the first *ovatio*?

1   *FITA.* p. 295. The Roman cities are Dyrrhachium, Cnossus, Patrae (?), Uselis (*mun.*), Cirta (??), Carthage (?), Lugdunum (?), Lystra. Cf. Lepcis Minor, ibid. p. 338.

2   Possibly gold *quinarii* of 11–10 B.C. celebrate the *vicennium* of Actium or *Aegyptus Capta*: see Appendix I.

CHAPTER III

TIBERIUS

(i) *The half-centenary of the restored Republic*

In the principate of Tiberius anniversary issues, as well as remaining prominent on the local coinage,[1] seem to have formed a considerable proportion of the total official mintage of their period.[2] The identification of these issues will, it is hoped, enable the coinage of this principate, often criticised as dull and undescriptive, to gain somewhat in significance as a historical source.

Let us first consider the issues starting in *c.* A.D. 23. It does not cause surprise to learn that Tiberius scrupulously celebrated the termination of his tenth and twentieth years of sole rule (A.D. 23–4 and 33–4).[3] Dio's suggestion that this was not necessary since he had assumed the *imperium* once and for all in A.D. 14 is anachronistic and misguided. The celebration by Augustus of his *decennia* had had little or nothing to do with his *imperium*, and the same applies to Tiberius. It had been the *respublica restituta* of which Augustus had celebrated the *decennia*; and Tiberius is to be expected to do the same. He is also to be expected to commemorate the death of the first *princeps* and his own accession. (In the case of later *principes* we are accustomed to speak of celebrations, contemporary and anniversary, of their *accessions*. But the known attitude of Tiberius, as well as the character of his coinage and *Fasti*, leaves little doubt that, in such commemorations, at least as much stress was laid on the death and consecration of Augustus as on the accession of Tiberius himself [cf. p. 99 n. 1].)[4]

We have, then, two sets of possible anniversaries, those of the *respublica restituta* and those of the change of rulers in A.D. 14. But, in examining the coinage, there is no need for us to decide which of

---

1 For Roman cities, see *APT*. Appendix 6: Antioch in Pisidia, Dertosa (*mun.*), Parium (perhaps an official coinage), Pella (?), Hippo Diarrhytus and Thapsus (apparently for official rather than local anniversaries). Cf. peregrine communities, e.g. Damascus, which only (?) seems to coin for the accession, *decennium* and *vicennium* (*FITA*. p. 332).

2 The only other important occasion for issues was perhaps his accession.

3 Dio 57. 24, 58. 24; cf. Charlesworth, *CAH.* x, p. 612 n. 2; Strack, *Gnomon*, 1937, p. 678; Piganiol, *Journal des Savants*, 1937, p. 153.

4 For this as a general tendency see W. Schmidt, *Geburtstag im Altertum*, p. 76.

these alternatives Tiberius favoured. For the year of his accession coincided, within a few months, with the fortieth year after the *respublica restituta*: thus the later anniversaries of the two occasions fell in the same years. The existence of such a multiple occasion will prepare us sufficiently for the allotment of emphatic celebration to the years A.D. 23–4 and 33–4.

The former of these periods represents the *decennium* of Tiberius, and also the half-centenary of the new Republic; Vespasian was to celebrate its centenary with vigour (p. 91). The decennial year of Tiberius began in August A.D. 23 and ended in August 24. The half-centenary year of the *respublica restituta* lasted from January A.D. 23 until January 24. It is not fortuitous that a monetary revival of great significance occurred between June A.D. 22 and June 23.[1] The latter half of this period fell within the anniversary year of the *respublica restituta* and shortly preceded the decennial year of Tiberius; but we are already familiar with the Roman custom of commemorating anniversaries well in advance of the actual occasion (pp. 10f.), and the *decennium* forms part of the occasion of issue.[2]

But before we can proceed to discuss the issues of this date an endeavour must be made to define their extent and content. It has, until recently, been customary to attribute to A.D. 22–3 all *aes* coinages bearing the titulatures of Tiberius as TR. POT. XXIIII. and of Drusus junior as TR. POT. ITER. (or II). The Tiberian issues in question include the following: *sestertii* with CIVITATIBVS ASIAE RESTITVTIS (Tiberius seated),[3] DIVVS AVGVSTVS PATER (Augustus seated by altar),[4] and S.P.Q.R. IVLIAE AVGVST. (*carpentum*);[5] *dupondii* with the busts of IVSTITIA[6] and SALVS AVGVSTA;[7] and *asses* with the head of Tiberius.[8] The coins with the name of Drusus junior comprise *sestertii* with the heads of his twins, each on *cornucopiae*;[9] *dupondii* with a veiled bust of PIETAS;[10] and *asses* with the head of Drusus himself.[11] Two undated groups of *dupondii* of Divus Augustus

1   Not A.D. 21–2, as Willers, loc. cit. p. 210. For the tribunician month see now Giles, *Classical Review*, 1946, p. 44.
2   Cf. *BMC. Imp.* I, p. xviii n. 6.
3   Ibid. p. 129. 70.
4   Ibid. p. 130. 74. Lederer, *RS.* 1942, p. 12 n. 2, ascribes the altar to *Providentia*.
5   *BMC. Imp.* I, p. 130. 76.

6   Ibid. p. 131. 79.
7   Ibid. p. 131. 81.
8   Ibid. p. 133. 91. Some specimens look un-Roman; e.g. Vautier and Collignon (Naville) sale, 1922, no. 214.
9   *BMC. Imp.* I, p. 133. 95.
10 Ibid. p. 133. 98.
11 Ibid. p. 134. 99.

Pater, with round temple[1] and Victory (S.P.Q.R.S.C.)[2] respectively, are now attributed to the same period.[3]

With regard to those of the foregoing coins which bear the Tiberian date TR. POT. XXIIII., it is now considered exceedingly unlikely that the whole of the series so inscribed was issued as early as June A.D. 22–June 23,[4] and the present writer has suggested that the dating only bears witness to the fact that the *senatusconsultum* from which the whole series emanated was passed during that period.[5] This view has appeared to justify the attribution to a later date of the S.P.Q.R. IVLIAE AVGVST. and SALVS AVGVSTA issues, both of which seem to commemorate topical events rather than anniversaries.[6] It will be shown in another section that a later date is likewise more suitable for the *sestertii* with CIVITATIBVS ASIAE RESTITVTIS; and that there are reasons for asking whether the *asses* of Drusus junior may not be posthumous. A later date will also be preferred for the Tiberian *dupondii* inscribed CLEMENTIAE and MODERATIONI (pp. 47 f.).

However, this pruning operation leaves still undetached from A.D. 22–3 a group of issues fully worthy of the great combined occasion of the half-centenary and *decennium*. This group seems to consist of the DIVVS AVGVSTVS PATER *sestertii* (Augustus seated by altar) and *dupondii* (round temple and 'Victory'); the IVSTITIA and PIETAS *dupondii* of Tiberius and Drusus (and his *sestertii*); and possibly the *asses* of Tiberius. This dating of the *asses* admits of no definite corroboration; but a monetary reform and revival comprising a large output of *orichalcum* issues is very likely to have been accompanied by a copper series.[7] We have still to demonstrate, however, that this large output of *orichalcum* in fact occurred in A.D. 23 or thereabouts, and not later, like some of the components of the group dated TR. P. XXIIII. In this task we may bear in mind

---

1 Ibid. p. 140. 142.
2 Ibid. p. 140. 141.
3 Sutherland, *NC*. 1941, p. 106. Some of the 'Temple' coins may conceivably have been issued outside Rome: a possible example is illustrated, ibid. Pl. I, 12, Pl. II, 1; *SMACA*.
4 References in *FITA*. p. 447; cf. Sutherland, *JRS*. 1947, p. 211, 'this will now be generally admitted'; *BMC. Imp*. IV, p. xvii n. 2.
5 *FITA*. pp. 447 f. Sutherland, loc. cit., points out that this conclusion raises important political and administrative questions.

6 I.e. the death of Livia (cf. *APT*. Ch. III, sect. ivb) and the conspiracy of Sejanus respectively. But the latter attribution is not certain: there were *auguria salutis* in A.D. 23 and 29, Liegle, *Hermes*, 1942, pp. 304, 311.
7 But the *asses* may have continued to be struck over a number of years: e.g. a specimen in the Paris collection (no. 4762) has a portrait differing considerably from the usual one.

the general probability that the *senatusconsultum Caesaris auctoritate*, from which this important revival of the *aes* coinage no doubt originated, did not precede by a very long period the first issues emanating from it.

For the two sets of Divus Augustus Pater *dupondii*, moreover, Sutherland's convincing analysis of this and other consecrationary *aes* concludes by preferring the date *c.* A.D. 22–3 (p. 33 n. 3). The round temple, found on one of these sets of coins, seems to be one of the temples of Vesta, possibly Vesta *in Foro*,[1] but probably Vesta *in Palatio*,[2] which was so closely connected with the worship of Divus Augustus.[3] Later coinages were to reserve representations of the Vesta temples almost exclusively for centenaries and half-centenaries of the death of Augustus (pp. 80 f., 135). The only exception to this general statement tends to prove its significance. For Vespasian, who celebrated other anniversaries of famous early events and coins, was to portray just such a temple, inscribed VESTA, in A.D. 73 (p. 91). That year witnessed not only the centenary of the *respublica restituta* but also the half-centenary of the date which appears on the present issue of Tiberius. Vespasian's simultaneous revival of the IVSTITIA type of Tiberius suggests that he intended this and the temple of Vesta types alike to recall the Tiberian issues; and his timing of these reminiscences to coincide with the centenary of the *respublica restituta* suggests that he interpreted the coins of Tiberius as celebrating the half-centenary of the same Augustan occasion. Vespasian's interpretation seems to corroborate Sutherland's view that the *dupondii* with the type of Vesta's temple were issued at about the date of the half-centenary (*c.* A.D. 22–3).

If so, then the same is true of the 'Victory' *dupondii*, for these show die-identities with the Vesta coins.[4] This conclusion regarding the date of the 'Victory' coins receives external confirmation from two sources. First, there is a connection between 'Victory' and *vota* (p. 21), and the year A.D. 23 was an occasion *par excellence* for *vota*. Secondly, the shield inscribed S.P.Q.R., which 'Victory' is

1 As Bernhart, *Handbuch zur Münzkunde der römischen Kaiserzeit*, p. 129, etc.
2 Rizzo, *Bollettino della Commissione archeologica Comunale di Roma*, 1933, pp. 29 ff.; Brown, *Numismatic Notes and Monographs*, XC, 1940, p. 7; Sutherland, *NC.* 1941, p. 115 n. 25 (bibliography); see also the discussion of Weber, *Princeps*, I, p. 94* n. 428.

3 Cf. Sutherland, loc. cit. p. 116 n.; Gagé, *Revue archéologique*, xxxiv, 1931, p. 15 n. For connection of Vesta with *Aeternitas* of the dynasty, see Charlesworth, *Harvard Theological Review*, 1936, p. 124.
4 Sutherland, loc. cit. p. 105. But on this criterion see also *SMACA*.

carrying, is very likely (and is specifically indicated on pre-Tiberian coins of identical type[1]) to be the *clipeus virtutis* awarded to Augustus on the great occasion of 27 B.C.—of which the half-centenary year began in A.D. 23. Moreover, the twentieth anniversary of the same occasion had likewise been celebrated by a 'Victory' type (p. 21). A 'Victory' on a coin posthumously commemorating Augustus might well carry a *clipeus* relating to him rather than to the reigning *princeps*. But so, for that matter, might any 'Victory' of the principate of Tiberius, whose own victories had been won *auspiciis Augusti*.[2] The type was to be repeated by Nero and Domitian, in both cases to celebrate further Augustan anniversaries; and it was to be precisely imitated on the earliest of the 'imperial' contorniates, which seem to mark the 350th anniversary of the death of Augustus (p. 155).

To this evidence regarding the *dupondii* of Divus Augustus Pater, we cannot add much specifically bearing on the date of the *sestertii* in his honour. But the seated figure on the latter seems to represent his statue mentioned by the *Fasti Praenestini*.[3] This statue was apparently dedicated in *c.* A.D. 22; and the coins may well have commemorated that occurrence a year or so later, with special reference to a *pompa circensis* on the *decennalia* of his consecration.[4]

This conclusion is in line with the next series that we have to discuss, namely the PIETAS *dupondii*. *Pietas* is another type associated with *vota*.[5] It was, again, in *c.* A.D. 22 that an *Ara Pietatis Augustae* was vowed, on Livia's recovery from illness[6] (and on the half-centenary of an *Arcus Pietatis* [p. 5]). In the case of the PIETAS series, we have reason to believe that issue was not delayed long after A.D. 22–3. For the bust is imitated on two unpublished official issues of a *legatus Augusti pro praetore* of Galatia called Priscus (Plate I, 3, 4).[7] The present writer hopes to deal with the

1 Gagé, *Revue archéologique*, xxxiv, 1931, p. 32: cf. the Carthage Altar, Poinssot, *Notes et Documents, Direction des Antiquités de Tunisie*, 1929, pp. 14 f., discussed in *APT*. Ch. III, sect. i.

2 Cf. Gagé, loc. cit. pp. 31 ff.; id. *Revue des études Latines*, 1932, pp. 61 ff. He goes farther than this, but see Mattingly, *BMC. Imp.* III, p. xxxix.

3 Cf. Weber, loc. cit. I, p. 94* n. 428.

4 Cf. Beurlier, *Essai sur le Culte rendu aux Empereurs Romains*, p. 74, etc.

5 Cf. Mattingly, *Roman Coins*, p. 152.

6 Cf. Schweitzer, *Klio*, 1941, p. 347 n. 1; Koch, *PW*. xx, 1, 1228; Charlesworth, *CAH.* x, p. 634, etc. It was not dedicated until A.D. 43 (cf. Bloch, *Mélanges d'Archéologie et d'Histoire*, 1939, pp. 1 ff.; Piganiol, *Revue des études latines*, 1940, pp. 238 f.).

7 ΕΠΙ ΠΡΕΙΣΚΟΥ. The Paris specimen (a cast is in the possession of the present writer) shows this bust. Another specimen, in the present writer's collection, which has enabled the legend on the Paris piece to be

coins of Priscus in greater detail elsewhere, but here it must be mentioned that they bear the date '43' of the Galatian era—namely A.D. 23–4 (p. 92 n.). The PIETAS *dupondii* cannot, then, be later than A.D. 23–4. Moreover, as in the case of the 'Victory' pieces, there is a clear reference to the *clipeus virtutis* which had been presented to Augustus half a century before A.D. 23–4: for *Pietas* was one of its cardinal 'Virtues'.[1] It remains to discuss its particular implications.

A Republican, Q. Caecilius Metellus, who had used the same type (possibly just a century earlier),[2] had himself been called *pius* because of dutifulness to his father,[3] and this theme was highly relevant to the circumstances of the PIETAS coinage of *c*. A.D. 22–3. Drusus junior may or may not still have been alive when it appeared —he died in September A.D. 23,[4] and some at least of his coinage is posthumous (p. 67)—but, alive or dead, his piety to Tiberius and Livia was a subject very suitable for commemoration. So, indeed, was that of Tiberius to Augustus[5] (whose title PATER on the consecrationary coinage has at least some reference to his adoptive parenthood of the reigning *princeps*).[6] Tiberius might well also wish people to acknowledge his piety to his adoptive mother Livia, whatever his inward feelings on the subject: it was in her honour that the *Ara Pietatis Augustae* had been dedicated a year or so earlier. It was, moreover, she of whom people almost everywhere would think when they saw the bust of an idealised female described as PIETAS;[7] the government must have known this.

All these filial aspects of *Pietas* might well come, and be intended to come, to the minds of recipients of these coins. But it would be a mistake to consider that these, or any one of them, were the only aspects of *Pietas* of which those who saw this carefully generalised type were expected to think. The 'Virtues' or 'Blessings'[8] on coins are sometimes depicted in the most general manner possible, and

---

restored, has instead the 'seated priestess' type (*APT*. Ch. III, sect. iv *b*). Later emperors appear to celebrate Galatian anniversaries of 25 B.C., but this cannot be true of the present coins, for it would place the *Pietas* issues too early. The identity of Priscus is a difficult question which will not be discussed here.

1 Cf. Markowski, *Eos*, 1936, p. 124.

2 *BMC. Rep.* II, p. 357. 43, cf. n. 2. This (like the issues of Tiberius) is omitted by Dodd, *NC.* 1911, pp. 20 ff., in his survey of the *Pietas* type.

3 Cf. Liegle, *ZfN.* 1935, p. 77, etc.

4 *Fasti Verul.*; cf. Charlesworth, *CAH.* x, p. 625 n. 4.

5 Cf. especially Weber, loc. cit. I, p. 6* n. 33.

6 Cf. (recently) Bloesch, *Antike Kunst in der Schweiz*, p. 69.

7 Cf. M. & S. I, p. 99, about the PONTIF. MAXIM. issues.

8 'Virtues' is the term preferred by Mattingly, *Harvard Theological Review*, 1937, pp. 108 f.; *BMC. Imp.* IV, p. xxv and n. 2; *JRS.* 1943, p. 77, etc.; but see p. 71 n. 5.

their topical allusions, if any, are so vague that they escape us.[1] But this was not due to inefficiency, or to an inadequate appreciation of the possibilities of coin-propaganda. Indeed, the anniversary ramifications of the official coinages have already revealed, under Augustus, striking, if (to our minds) strangely 'traditionalist', aspects of such propaganda. With such a medium at its disposal the Roman government did not feel the need to be particularly explicit about the topical references of its types. It could, instead, be sure that various relevant points would come to the minds of large sections of its public in the light of the centenaries, half-centenaries and *decennia* celebrated by its issues. We have noted that great occasions were not infrequently 'timed' so that the anniversaries of more than one of them fell on the same day of the year, or so that their *decennia* or centenaries fell in the same year (pp. 3 ff.). The same sort of principle was extended to the 'Virtues' or 'Blessings' on the coinage. These were often treated in the most general way possible so that more than one (or all) of their various aspects might be considered to participate in the allusion;[2] the extent to which particular aspects were intended to play their part on each individual occasion was, of course, governed by topical events and situations as well as by the past occasions or coinages of which the anniversaries were occurring at the moment of issue. As Tacitus said of the other utterances of Tiberius, *suspensa semper et obscura verba*.[3]

To revert to the PIETAS coinage. We have seen that there were reasons for this type to be connected in people's minds with Livia, but it is misguided to consider the bust to be, *tout simple*, that of 'Livia as *Pietas*'.[4] There is not the slightest attempt to make the features resemble those of Livia; there is no addition of *Augusta* to *Pietas* which might point to a special reference to her and to her altar. There was ample Republican and even Augustan precedent for numismatic busts of 'Virtues' possessing no apparent connection with dead or living personages. Likewise, there is no point in detecting an official identification of the PIETAS bust with

1 Cf. O. Schulz, *Die Rechtstitel und Regierungsprogramme auf römischen Kaisermünzen*, p. 15. See also Introduction.

2 A comparison between these official usages and the deliberate 'ambiguities' of Virgil, etc., is suggested in *CSNM.*; cf. Jackson Knight, *Roman Vergil*, pp. 203 ff.

3 *Annals*, I, 11; cf. Pippidi, *Ephemeris Dacoromana*, 1938 = *Autour de Tibère*, p. 37.

4 This long-standing interpretation is recently repeated by Koch, loc. cit. 1227; Grether, *American Journal of Philology*, 1946, p. 236 n. 82.

Antonia.[1] Any identifications with her suggested by later provincial or local imitations are irrelevant in view of the inevitability that cities would use official prototypes in this way. Though, here again, Antonia's supporters were naturally at liberty to think of the *Pietas* bust in connection with her if they wished to.

Similarly, we have seen that the type suggested several obvious filial allusions. But there is nothing either in its character or in the general probabilities to indicate that it was intended to exclude the other and equally important aspects of *Pietas*. For this concept alluded also to the relationship of the *princeps* to his country and his subjects,[2] and to their relations (especially those of the army) with him;[3] also—perhaps to some extent enhanced by the cult of the divine Augustus[4]—the concept of *pietas erga deos* was now prominent.[5] *Pietas* is thus often found linked with priestly emblems.[6] This 'Virtue', like so many others, had strong Greek and especially Stoic associations.[7] These blended with, and were modified by, not only purely Roman ideas but in due course the actual Roman history of the 'Virtue' herself.[8]

All these were factors in the thought-image created by the word PIETAS, and one or more of these factors would be brought to the mind of every literate member of the public who saw these coins (p. 8). It would be wrong to suppose that any one of the various aspects of *Pietas* was intended to be represented to the exclusion of the others, and this view is borne out by the scrupulously general character of the reference.

Let us now turn to the second great 'Virtue' attributed to A.D. 22–3, *Iustitia* (pp. 32 f.). It was in A.D. 23 that two significant anniversaries concerning *Iustitia* occurred. The *decennium* of the *ara Iustitiae Augustae*, and of the gold and silver mintage commemorating it (p. 25), coincided in that year with the beginning of the half-centenary year of the *clipeus virtutis* of Augustus (27 B.C.). The

1 Von Sallet, *ZfN.* 1879, pp. 61 ff.; cf. Ulrich, *Pius-Pietas als politischer Begriff im römischen Staate* (*Historische Untersuchungen*, VI, 1930), p. 50 n. 4. For a recent note on the iconography of Antonia, see Györkösy, *Archivium Philologicum*, 1942, pp. 114 f.
2 Cf. Charlesworth, *Proceedings of the British Academy*, 1937, p. 113.
3 Id. *JRS.* 1943, p. 1; Mattingly, *NC.* 1933, p. 245; Liegle, *ZfN.* 1935, p. 90.
4 Liegle, ibid. p. 126.

5 Cf. Dodd, loc. cit. pp. 24 f.; Warde-Fowler, *The Religious Experience of the Roman People*, p. 431; Liegle, loc. cit.; Markowski, loc. cit. p. 124 n. 7.
6 Abaecherli Boyce, *Museum Notes of the American Numismatic Society*, I. 1945, p. 51; Cesano, *Studi di Numismatica*, I. 2, 1942, p. 236.
7 Markowski, loc. cit. pp. 111 ff.
8 For early Roman references, see Altheim, *History of Roman Religion*, p. 532 n. 8.

clipeus had celebrated the *Iustitia* of the first *princeps* as well as his *Pietas*, and this pair of imperial virtues is particularly closely linked.[1] The next numismatic appearance of the type is in A.D. 73—exactly 50 years after 23. The same is true of the type representing the temple of Vesta (p. 91), and in that case the coincidence has been held not to be fortuitous. It is likely to be equally deliberate in the case of *Iustitia*.

Now we have seen that the representation of *Pietas* under Tiberius carried not only earlier Roman (as well as Hellenic and Hellenistic) associations, but also associations peculiar to his own period. *Iustitia* must be considered from the same viewpoint. The type had not been introduced to the coinage by Augustus until *c*. A.D. 13–14, when its emblem appeared on gold and silver inscribed PONTIF. MAXIM. (p. 25). But the same reverse continued without any major variation throughout the principate of Tiberius, and indeed after *c*. A.D. 15 no other type whatever appeared on the Western *aurei* and *denarii* (with the exception of a single very rare revival of a Divus Augustus type,[2] probably for the *decennium*). This persistence of a single type is unprecedented during the whole early imperial period, and has attracted comment.[3] On these coins the figure carrying the sceptre of *Iustitia* also bears the olive-branch of *Pax*.[4] *Iustitia* is very closely allied to *Pax*,[5] which was thus in any case likely to be thought of, as well as *Iustitia*, by those who saw these long-lived *aurei* and *denarii*:[6] in the principate of Tiberius the *Pax Augusta* gained in recognition and significance.[7] The PONTIF. MAXIM. type obviously—and intentionally—avoids close definition or particularisation, and it seems legitimate to suppose that, from its introduction in *c*. A.D. 13, its intention was to call *Pax* to mind as well as *Iustitia*. If this is so, the same intention may be attributed to the IVSTITIA *dupondii*, which belong to its *decennium*. This emphasis

1 Cf. Markowski, loc. cit. p. 119; Wagenvoort, *Quaderni Augustei, Studi Stranieri*, x, 1938, p. 13.

2 *BMC. Imp.* I, p. cxxx; cf. Bahrfeldt, *Römische Goldmünzenprägung*, p. 171.

3 E.g. Sutherland, *Numismatic Review*, II. 1 (July 1944), p. 9.

4 For this symbol see now d'Hérouville, *Revue des études Latines*, 1941, pp. 142 ff.

5 Strack, I, p. 52, cf. n. 128; cf. Bosch, *Die Kleinasiatischen Münzen*, II, 1, p. 184; *BMC. Imp.* III, pp. xxxviii n. 5, xcii n. 1.

6 There seems no reason to see a reference to *Salus*, as Liegle, *Hermes*, 1942, p. 304.

7 Cf. Ciaceri, *Tiberio Successore di Augusto*, p. 225; von Premerstein, *Vom Werden und Wesen des Prinzipats*, pp. 125 f. There is a little-known large *aes* piece (? medallion) of Tiberius at an unknown Western colony (Carthage ?) reading PACE AVG. PERP. (Berlin; cast in writer's collection; *APT*. Ch. II, sect. iv). For *Pax* in the early Empire, see *PR*.

on *Iustitia* is not surprising, in view of her special place as partner of *Pietas* on the *clipeus virtutis*, of which the half-centenary was commemorated at the same time. Inscriptions show that, not Augustus (as far as we know), but Tiberius, was known in Italy as *iustus* and *iustissimus princeps*.[1] The fact that Tiberius gave so unprecedentedly long a life to the PONTIF. MAXIM. series with *Iustitia-Pax*, as well as devoting the type of a *dupondius* to *Iustitia* herself, confirms that these inscriptional compliments were not out of harmony with his official policy.

Yet, here again, it would be erroneous to suppose that the one aspect of the 'Virtue' of which possessors of the IVSTITIA *dupondii* were intended to think was its applicability to the *princeps*, relevant though this was owing to his scrupulous desire for a just government and personal attention to judicial matters. The coins are not inscribed IVSTITIA AVGVSTI (this type of formula did not appear on official coins until Claudius)[2] or even IVSTITIA AVGVSTA, any more than *Pietas* is yet called, on Roman coinage, PIETAS AVGVSTA. As in the case of *Pietas*, it was inevitable that many who saw the idealised womanly features of the obverse of the *Iustitia* coins should think of Livia in the first instance. Others would call to mind the association of *Iustitia* with Augustus, and those well versed in Greek culture would know of the Hellenic and Stoic background of this component of the four cardinal virtues.

The types, then, that were officially called to the notice of the Roman world in A.D. 23, or very soon after, comprised *Pietas* and *Iustitia* as well as 'Victory', the temple of Vesta and the statue of Augustus. There is also a non-commemorative topical type of the heads of Drusus junior's twin sons, each on *cornucopiae*.[3] But the greater part of the coinage of *c.* A.D. 23 is of an anniversary character. In its anniversary ramifications as well as in the variety and execution of its types, the Roman *aes*, as revived in about this year, shows marked improvement over previous efforts. It is tempting to attribute this improvement to Sejanus, whose special position in the state was now well established. It was, however, not Sejanus but the

1 *ILS.* 159, 3783; cf. Rogers, *Studies in the Reign of Tiberius*, p. 88.
2 *BMC. Imp.* I, p. clvi, cf. n. 1. For the origins of this formula, see especially Otto, *PW.* VIII, 36 f.; Strack, loc. cit. pp. 49 ff.; *BMC. Imp.* I, loc. cit.; Nock, *Harvard Theological Review*, 1930, p. 266, etc.
3 For this, cf. Mowat, *Rn.* 1911, pp. 347 ff.; Alföldi, *Röm. Mitt.* 1935, p. 100 n.; Rogers, loc. cit. p. 97; Kornemann, *Doppelprinzipat und Reichsteilung*, p. 44 n. 1, etc.

princeps whose *auctoritas* (through his *tribunicia potestas*) still moved the *senatusconsultum* on which these mintages were based; though it may be wondered whether Drusus junior, who likewise possessed *tribunicia potestas* from A.D. 22 until his death in 23,[1] did not himself move the senatorial endorsement of the issue of *sestertii* and *dupondii* bearing his name. We cannot pursue this speculative theme here;[2] but whether or not Drusus, instead of his father, was the exerciser of *auctoritas* in this case, there was every reason for either of them—however Drusus felt personally about Sejanus—to incorporate in his motion before the senate the views of the leading *amicus principis*. Equally, or alternatively, the views of Sejanus might at a later stage (i.e. after the *senatusconsultum* was passed) have been included by the senate in its instructions on the subject to the *tresviri a.a.a.f.f.*; or he may even have let the last-named have the benefit of his *auctoritas* direct. In any case, we cannot reject the possibility that the developments of the anniversary theme which occurred in *c.* A.D. 23 were due to Sejanus. In allowing this possibility, however, we must bear in mind the cautionary consideration that other allusions to him have been read into the coinage in vain.[3] At all events, the great series which started in *c.* A.D. 23 represented not merely a revival of the *aes* coinage but—in art, standard and metal alike—a reform.[4] The fact that this reform was timed to coincide with a combination of anniversaries is directly paralleled by the practice of many later emperors,[5] as well as by that of Tiberius

---

1 Cf. Rogers, loc. cit. p. 146 n. 1.

2 Buckland, *CAH.* xi, p. 814, attributes all *senatusconsulta* to the *auctoritas* of the *princeps* himself.

3 E.g. by Wruck, *Die Syrische Provinzialprägung*, pp. 43, 48; Trassagnac, *Courrier numismatique et archéologique*, 1934, pp. 35 ff.; Cohen, Laffranchi. *Mun.* Bilbilis provides the only authentic example (Vives y Escudero, *La Moneda Hispánica*, iv, p. 56. 17).

4 Sydenham, *NC.* 1917, p. 266. There was no 'double standard' henceforward, as has been suggested, but a uniformly higher average of weight. *Orichalcum*, too, had not been issued at Rome for at least 30, and perhaps 40, years.

5 This appears to be true of Nero, Hadrian, Caracalla, Trajanus Decius, Aurelian, and perhaps Carausius. As regards the official mint of Alexandria, the same applies not only to Tiberius himself, but also to Claudius,

Nero, Caracalla, and Gallienus. It may be conjectured that the reform of Diocletian and Maximian in A.D. 295–6 was timed to coincide with the *decennium* of their joint rule and of the new system which this heralded. It may seem fanciful to pursue the matter into the Byzantine epoch, but it must nevertheless be pointed out that the great reforms of the coinage by Anastasius I and Justinian I also both coincided with famous anniversary occasions. It was in A.D. 498 that Anastasius entirely reformed and revived the *aes* coinage (Wroth, *BMC. Byzantine Coins*, i, pp. xiii and n. 3, lxxiv; Blake, *Studies in the History of Culture dedicated to W. G. Leland*; for a recent study of his policy see Laffranchi, *Rivista storica italiana*, 1940, v, p. 2). This was the 400th anniversary of the accession of Trajan, an emperor whose honours demonstrably persisted until the last period of the empire (p. 158). The next great reform was that of

himself at Alexandria (p. 61); such reforms, described as MON (*eta*) RESTITVTA,[1] were later thought worthy of specific numismatic commemoration.[2]

Before leaving this date, mention should perhaps be made of two exceedingly rare *aes* coins with heads of Tiberius and, on reverse, radiate head of Augustus (Plate I, 6),[3] and PONTIF. MAX. in oak(?)-wreath (Plate I, 7),[4] respectively. Resemblances of the two Tiberius portraits, especially in the truncation, indicate identity of mint; the features appear to be imitated from Roman *asses* of *c.* A.D. 23. Possibly, then, these pieces were issued by a provincial governor for the *decennium*—the same might apply to a *dupondius* of the two *principes* issued in Cyprus (Plate I, 5);[5] their style (admittedly a questionable criterion)[6] is somewhat suggestive of the Balkan area.[7] If this could be proved, C. Poppaeus Sabinus, *legatus Augusti pro praetore* of the whole peninsula, would be the likeliest minting authority: under Claudius another Balkan *legatus* was to issue equally rare and exceptional pieces (pp. 77 f.).

It is conceivable that a mysterious *as* with DIVVS AVG. (radiate head l., two standards) and T.A. (seated figure facing, with two children[?]) (Plate I, 8)[8] was issued at about the same date and place as the two *aes* pieces of Tiberius that have just been described. If so, the figures on the reverse are perhaps Livia and her great-grandsons, the twins of Drusus junior, who were, at this same

---

Justinian, who in A.D. 538–9 introduced full-faced busts (Wroth, loc. cit. pp. xvii n. 2, xc f.; cf. Dworschak, *NZ.* 1936, p. 75), increased weights (Wroth, loc. cit. p. lxxx), and inaugurated the dating of his bronze issues (ibid. pp. xvi, xci, cx). Now A.D. 538 was the 600th anniversary of the birth of Augustus, another great landmark in Roman history and one of which the memory is known to have been honoured throughout the centuries of the empire and the Middle Ages (cf. Monteverdi, *Augustus*, pp. 415 ff.). It seems very doubtful whether both of these two coincidences were fortuitous. The Byzantines were no less antiquarian than their Roman predecessors—Heraclius was hailed as another Scipio (p. 153 n. 3)—and Wroth (loc. cit. p. lxxxiv) rightly pointed to the traditional character of their coinage. In A.D. 438, the codification of Theodosius II had coincided with the half-millenary of the birth of Augustus.

1 Severus Alexander: M. & S. IV, 2. p. 118. 601, cf. p. 117. 589 (RESTITVTOR MON.).
2 Cf. Pink, *NZ.* 1935, pp. 1 ff.; Haynes, *NC.* 1941, pp. 33 f.
3 *BMC. Imp.* I, p. 145. 177.
4 Ibid. note (Paris). It is an oak-wreath according to Cohen, I, p. 170. 10; Schulz, loc. cit. p. 15; Wruck, *Die Syrische Provinzial-prägung*, p. 48; *BMC.* loc. cit.; *pace* Strack, I, p. 58 n. 161, Mowat, *Rn.* 1911, p. 430, who call it a laurel-wreath.
5 *BMC. Cyprus*, p. cxx, par. 83; Berlin. Other official coins of Tiberius issued in Cyprus are *BMC.* 5 (rev. IVLIA AVGVSTA, seated priestess), 7–10 (Drusus jun.).
6 The present writer discusses these criteria in *SMACA.*
7 Cappadocia, the choice of Mowat, loc. cit., seems too Easterly. *BMC. Imp.*, Wruck, loc. cit., call the mintage 'uncertain'.
8 Grueber, *NC.* 1904, p. 210 (misread); *FITA.* p. 110.

period, honoured in other provinces and in Rome itself (p. 33). The letters T.A. have elsewhere been tentatively interpreted as T(*iberi*) A(*uctoritate*),[1] the plain use of the *praenomen* being paralleled on a sheath of Tiberian date (FELICITAS TIBERI: p. 45 n. 4) and on countermarks.[2] Such very rare and unusual issues are likely to be 'medallic' (p. 60). But their significance remains conjectural.

(ii) *The half-centenary of the* saeculum *of Augustus*

After various smaller mintages, the Roman mint produced another impressive set of *aes* issues starting in A.D. 34–5 (and no doubt partly composed of the copper which Tiberius had, in the preceding year, obtained by taking over the mines of Sex. Marius).[3] In view of the importance of this date, and the precedent of the foregoing *decennium*, we may conclude that the new coinage commemorated the *vicennium* of Tiberius's principate and of the consecration of Augustus.[4] This series included *sestertii* showing a temple identified as that of Concord;[5] an empty quadriga;[6] Augustus (DIVO AVGVSTO S.P.Q.R.) in an elephant quadriga (*tensa*);[7] and a complex type—with the same inscription—of oak-wreath,[8] two capricorns, globe, and shield inscribed OB CIVES SER.[9] There are also *asses*—sometimes attributed to Lugdunum[10]—with *caduceus*,[11] and others with rudder, large globe (encircled by girdle) and small globe.[12] Sutherland[13] has convincingly attributed to the same period the Divus Augustus

1 *FITA.* loc. cit. But for an alternative possibility, T(*utela*) A(*ugusti*), suggested by resemblance to a type of Vespasian, see below, p. 89 n. 1. Vespasian's issue, struck in A.D. 70–1, seems to celebrate the centenary of the conferment of *ius auxilii*—the ostensible basis of the *tribunicia potestas*—in 30 B.C., and Tiberius's type, if really *Tutela Augusti*, may well belong to c. A.D. 20–1 and to the half-centenary of the same event. The seated figure with two children(?) is common to the coins of Tiberius and Vespasian.

2 E.g. TIB.: *BMC. Imp.* I, p. xxxvi; *FITA.* p. 94; *SMACA.*

3 Following Ritter's emendation of Tac. *Annals,* VI, 19: *aerarias aurariasque*; cf. Sutherland, *American Journal of Philology,* 1945, p. 160; Stein, *PW.* XIV, 1821, etc.

4 Cf. Weber, *Princeps,* I, p. 79* n. 347. Here the celebration is of the vicennial year itself; the decennial coinages had

been issued in the year preceding the *decennium.*

5 Cohen, I, p. 195. 68; cf. *BMC. Imp.* I, pp. 134 n., 137. 116, cxxxviii. It has not been possible to verify recently any piece before A.D. 35–6: but, even if no such piece proved verifiable, the present discussion is substantially unaffected, since the year's time-lag would not be material, cf. above p. 11.

6 *BMC. Imp.* I, p. 134. 103.

7 Ibid. p. 134. 102.

8 Ibid. p. cxxxviii; not laurel, *pace* p. 136.

9 Ibid. p. 136. 109.

10 Cf. Sydenham, *NC.* 1917, p. 85. Some specimens, e.g. Vautier and Collignon (Naville) sale, 1922, no. 212, look very un-Roman; cf. *SMACA.*

11 *BMC. Imp.* I, p. 135. 106; Mowat, *R. it.* 1911, pp. 177, 181 ff.

12 *BMC. Imp.* I, p. 135. 104.

13 *NC.* 1941, p. 102.

Pater *asses* with eagle on globe[1] (a type revived by Nero), and thunderbolt,[2] which share obverse dies.[3]

The two quadriga types—one a *tensa* drawn by elephants, the other an empty *currus triumphalis*—have both been shown by Weber to be relevant to the *funus* of Augustus and to the anniversary obsequies of a *vicennium*.[4] This connection is stressed by DIVO AVGVSTO S.P.Q.R. on the *sestertius*. But while the *vicennium* of his death and consecration was a most significant occasion in itself, it gained in importance by coinciding with the half-centenary of the new *saeculum*, of which the beginning had been so loudly heralded in 17 B.C. Thus the half-centenary of the *saeculum* was, even if it had not coincided with Tiberius's *vicennium*, a considerable occasion; indeed, even its bicentenary was to be thought worthy of numismatic commemoration (p. 110). But—as in the case of so many of these anniversary coinages—it has not apparently been noticed that this half-centenary of the 'Golden Age' is afforded commemoration, and ample commemoration, on the Tiberian issues of A.D. 34–5. Indeed, this applies to no less than six of the eight types that are thus dated:

(1) Empty quadriga. This type had last appeared on a number of *aurei* and *denarii*[5] of Augustus's so-called 'Spanish Mint 2' (it may be Gallic),[6] which had struck them either slightly before, or during, the *saeculares* celebrations of 17 B.C.[7]

(2) Elephant quadriga. Elephants—drawing a *biga*—have only appeared hitherto on the imperial coinage in *c.* 19 or 18 (Rome)[8] and *c.* 17–16 B.C. ('Spanish Mint 2').[9] This type was again to recur half

---

1   *BMC. Imp.* I, p. 142. 155. For a framed 'pseudo-medallion', cf. Mowat, loc. cit. p. 175. For the eagle type (first on *aes signatum*) see id. *Roman Coins*, p. 150; M. & S. I, p. 94; Sittl, *Jahrbücher für classische Philologie*, Suppl.-Bd. XIV, 1884, pp. 42 ff. (and many later writers). For the same theme in Julio-Claudian sculpture, cf. Reinach, *Monuments et Mémoires publiés par l' Académie des Inscriptions*, iii, pp. 39 f.; Strong, *Art in Ancient Rome*, I, p. 170, etc.

    Some scholars stress the 'power' theme and some the 'apotheosis' theme: for both, cf. Bosch, *Die kleinasiatischen Münzen*, II, 1, p. 189 and n. 63. For the globe, see below p. 45 n. 8.

2   *BMC. Imp.* I, p. 142. 157.

3   Sutherland, *NC.* 1941, p. 102.

4   Weber, *Princeps*, I, pp. 79*, 87*; cf. Beurlier, *Essai sur le Culte rendu aux Empereurs Romains*, pp. 73 f. The relevance of the empty quadriga to a 'victory won for, not by, the emperor' (Mattingly, *BMC. Imp.* I, p. cxxxviii) seems more doubtful as regards the issue of Tiberius than in connection with the corresponding issue of Augustus (see next note).

5   *BMC. Imp.* I, p. 68. 390, p. 69. 397.

6   *SWC.*: Lugdunum?

7   Cf. Sutherland, *NC.* 1945, p. 65, etc.

8   *BMC. Imp.* I, p. 7. 36, cf. p. cxii (18 B.C.); for these coinages see above, p. 26 n. 10.

9   Ibid. p. 75. 432, cf. pp. cii, cxii.

a century *after* the issues of Tiberius, likewise with an anniversary intention (p. 94).

(3) Shield with OB CIVES SER., oak-wreath, capricorns, globe. These types had all abounded precisely in *c.* 17 B.C.,[1] and received far greater emphasis then than at any earlier or later date.[2]

(4) *Caduceus.* Apart from an issue of 'joined hands' *quadrantes*, which confirm rather than weaken the anniversary interpretation since they may well be attributable to precisely a quarter of a century before the present issue (p. 28 and n. 2), the Roman coinage had last portrayed the *caduceus* in the hands of the herald-*ludio* of the very same Secular Games of 17 B.C.[3] The *caduceus*, emblem of Mercury and of the distinctive Tiberian qualities *Felicitas*[4] and *Pax*,[5] was in itself a compendious reminder of the *aureum saeculum*.[6] Moreover, Mercury, as well as being a deity with whom Tiberius was sometimes identified in the Western provinces[7] (in which these *asses* circulated), had possessed a very special connection with Augustus (p. 18).

(5) Rudder and globes.[8] These too had last appeared on the *aurei* and *denarii* of 'Mint 2' at about the *saeculares* period.[9] *Fortuna*, whose emblems they are, had likewise been stressed on the coinage of the year or two preceding the 'new age' (cf. p. 26). The reference of the Tiberian *asses* to an Augustan occasion is stressed by the fact that Nerva, when he restored the type in its Tiberian form,[10] was to give it an obverse not of Tiberius but of Divus Augustus.

1   Ibid. pp. 63, 66 f., 70 ff., etc.
2   Sutherland, loc. cit. pp. 66 f.
3   *BMC. Imp.* I, p. 13. 69, p. 74. 431, cf. p. cxii, and Gagé, *Recherches sur les Jeux Séculaires*, p. 66; cf. Mattingly, *JRS.* 1934, p. 87.
4   Cf. Gagé, *Mélanges d'Archéologie et d'Histoire*, 1930, p. 15; id. *Revue archéologique*, 1930, pp. 9, 33; Alföldi, *Röm. Mitt.* 1935, pp. 139 ff.; *APT.* ch. II, sect. iii.
5   Cf. Altheim, *History of Roman Religion*, p. 531 n. 49, and *PR.*; *APT.* ch. II, sect. iv.
6   Rogers, *Studies in the Reign of Tiberius*, p. 12, suggests with some plausibility that the topical significance of the Tiberian type is connected with his generosity after the financial crisis of A.D. 33 (further bibliography of this in de Laet, *Samenstelling*, p. 282 n. 3; cf. id. *Revue de la Banque*, 1940, v).

7   Cf. Chittenden, *NC.* 1945, p. 49 n. 55, p. 53 n. 68 (*CIL.* XIII, 1769).
8   One globe appears to be marine and one terrestrial, as Gardthausen, *Augustus und seine Zeit*, II, p. 13; cf. Last, *Classical Review*, 1943, p. 119, against *BMC. Imp.* I, p. cxxxviii, Rogers, loc. cit. pp. 28 ff. For the globes, see further Alföldi, *Röm. Mitt.* 1935, p. 117; Strong, *JRS.* 1916, pp. 34 f.; Sydenham, *The Coinage of Nero*, p. 33; Brendel, *Röm. Mitt.* 1936, pp. 1 ff.; Boll, *PW.* VII. 1429; Schlachter, *Stoicheia*, VIII, pp. 82 f., 90 f.; Pink, *NZ.* 1946, p. 116. The larger globe is encircled by a zodiacal girdle; cf. Berger, *Geschichte der wissenschaftlichen Erdkunde der Griechen*², p. 458; Boll, loc. cit.
9   *BMC. Imp.* I, p. 62. 344 (with capricorn, cf. Sutherland, *NC.* 1945, p. 60).
10   *BMC. Imp.* III, p. 29. 154; cf. p. 1.

(6) Thunderbolt. This symbol has been related by Mattingly to Vejovis.[1] That divinity was linked, indeed identified, with Apollo,[2] whose prominence at the Secular Games as the god of the new state is well known. Vejovis incorporates Apollo's more funereal attributes,[3] as is appropriate to these *asses* in view of their consecrationary character. It was in *c.* 19–18 B.C. (cf. *Fortuna* in last paragraph) that a thunderbolt had last appeared on the official coinage.[4]

Thus the coinages of Tiberius starting in A.D. 34–5 (they continued unchanged, except for dates, until his death) recall the issues that had heralded the new Age just half a century earlier. The literary sources talk of the last years of Tiberius as a period of unrelieved gloom. This has often been felt to be exaggerated, especially with regard to the general administration;[5] but we have few contemporary records to correct the story. Nor, indeed, do the coins that have been described make any additions to, or subtractions from, our knowledge of the *merits* or otherwise of the government in those years. The catchwords of the Roman government were not necessarily based on supporting facts.[6] Were it necessary to give this degree of credence to official publicity, we should be sorely perplexed about the modern history of not a few countries. No, the information that the coin-types of A.D. 34–5 and successive years have to give us is different, namely that—whatever was going on—the government of the ageing *princeps* did not take a 'defeatist' line in its publicity. On the contrary, it launched a vigorous campaign to remind the people of the great occasion of 17 B.C. on which the Principate had, in public religion, been launched. Implicit in these coin-types is the suggestion by the imperial government that, 50 years after 17 B.C., the *Pax Augusta*, and other blessings conferred by its consecrated founder, were still to hand, if not increased—and that these

---

1 *NC.* 1930, pp. 132 f. For the thunderbolt, see also Alföldi, loc. cit. p. 120; Strong, loc. cit. p. 35 n. 2; von Domaszewski, *Abhandlungen zur römischen Religion*, p. 29, etc.
2 Mattingly, loc. cit. p. 133. For a Republican appearance of Vejovis, *BMC. Rep.* II, p. 290. 585 (L. Caesius); there are also others. For the temple of Vejovis, see Colini, *Bollettino della Commissione archeologica Comunale di Roma*, 1943, pp. 5 ff.; cf. Lugli, *JRS.* 1946, p. 5; Marchetti Longhi, *Capitolium*, 1940, p. 78; *Bullettino del Museo dell' Impero*, 1941, p. 86; *Röm. Mitt.* 1943, p. 27. For the god,

Müller, *Het Reveil van Augustus* (1940) (not seen).
3 Mattingly, loc. cit.
4 *BMC. Imp.* I, p. 64. 362. For the date cf. Sutherland, *NC.* 1945, p. 63. The bolt is in the hand of Jupiter *Tonans*. This seems to be its only appearance since 27 B.C.
5 E.g. Charlesworth, *CAH.* X, p. 642; Kornemann, *Römische Geschichte*, II, p. 197, etc.
6 Cf. Walbank, *Greece and Rome*, 1944, p. 30; Sutherland, *American Journal of Philology*, 1947, p. 48.

solid advantages were what the *populus Romanus* should bear in mind.

Before leaving this theme, reference must be made to the 'twin' series of *dupondii* showing, on the reverse, a small facing bust of Tiberius within a 'medallion', inscribed sometimes CLEMENTIAE[1] and sometimes (with slightly varying type) MODERATIONI.[2] These have been the subject of a survey by Sutherland.[3] The present writer regrets, however, that he cannot accept his attribution of these *dupondii* to *c*. A.D. 22–3,[4] and feels obliged instead to allot them to *c*. 34–7. The reasons for this conviction fall primarily in the notoriously difficult sphere of iconography.[5] The obverse portraits on this series rebel against attribution to *c*. A.D. 22–3, and are far more in harmony with those of the dated gold *quinarii* and *aes* of the last years of Tiberius[6]—the only period, incidentally, in which the obverse legend of the *Clementiae* and *Moderationi dupondii* (TI. CAESAR DIVI AVG. F. AVGVST. IMP. VIII) is otherwise found.[7]

The earlier attribution is perhaps partly based on unusual varieties of both sets of *dupondii*, which have portraits related by Sutherland to the early Tiberian period in which portraits of the reigning *princeps* still followed Augustan models.[8] But these heads are in shape, features and spirit a great deal less close to Augustus than to Caligula (e.g. Plate II, 6)[9]—indeed, they are identical to some of the latter's earliest coin-portraits.[10] It may seem an unorthodox suggestion, but the suggestion must none the less be made that the CLEMENTIAE and MODERATIONI *dupondii* not only started in the last, and not the middle, years of Tiberius, but continued—still

1 *BMC. Imp.* I, p. 132. 85.

2 Ibid. p. 132. 90. The simultaneity of these two series is shown by die-identities, Sutherland, *JRS*. 1938, p. 137. One rare variant reads MODERATIONIS: ibid. p. 129 n. 1; cf. *BMC. Imp.* I, p. 132 n. Was there also a very rare *sestertius?* (Sutherland, loc. cit. p. 134; ibid. Pl. XII. 13; Ars Classica sale, 1930, XV, 1370).

3 Loc. cit. pp. 129 ff.

4 Ibid.; cf. Rogers, loc. cit. p. 38. The present writer must withdraw his remarks on this subject in *FITA*. p. 447 nn. 10 f.

5 The present writer is defending in detail in *SMACA* his use of such criteria in *FITA*.

6 E.g. (CLEMENTIAE or MODERATIONI type first) Sutherland, loc. cit. Pl. XII. 5 = *BMC*.

Imp. I, Pl. XXII. 15; S. Pl. XII. 10 (cf. Levis [Naville] sale, 1925, 280) = Levis 281, Vautier and Collignon (Naville) sale, 1922, 211; S. Pl. XIII. 5 (especially nose) = Vautier and Collignon 212 (mouth and chin) = *BMC*. Pl. XXIV. 11; S. Pl. XIII. 1 (nose) = *BMC*. Pl. XXII. 16.

7 E.g. *BMC. Imp.* I, p. 135. 104 and 106, p. 138. 117 and 120, p. 139. 135 ff.

8 Loc. cit. Pl. XII. 1 (L. A. Lawrence collection); cf. specimens at B.M. and Vienna (casts seen at Oxford).

9 A clearer and even more apparently Caligulan head is that in Sutherland, loc. cit. Pl. XII. 1.

10 E.g. *BMC. Imp.* I, p. 152. 37, etc.

with the inscription of Tiberius—in the first year of Caligula. The literary sources relate some sneers of Caligula at Tiberius, but they also tell of his official approval of his predecessor.[1] But what is more reliable than these post-Tiberian writings is the evidence of the Arval Acts showing that the birthday of Tiberius was still honoured under Caligula;[2] to which must be added the latter's first *aurei* and *denarii*,[3] which, as Mattingly has pointed out,[4] actually show a portrait of Tiberius in anticipation of his expected deification.[5] (Other correctives of the literary tradition are provided by later posthumous honours to Tiberius, including portrait-busts, p. 85.) Under these circumstances it is not so surprising as it seems at first sight for Caligula to have issued a posthumous *aes* coinage for Tiberius, or rather to have momentarily continued the latter's own coinage unchanged except for minor iconographical developments. Mattingly claims a similar phenomenon in Vespasian's coinage for Galba,[5] and there are probable third-century examples of the same practice.[6]

Since Caligula is more likely to have continued a current Tiberian issue than to have revived an obsolete one, the acceptance of these arguments almost necessitates the view that these *dupondii* were still being issued in *c*. A.D. 37. But the multiplicity of their portraits suggests that the issues began rather before that date; and it is natural to think of *c*. A.D. 34–5, the date of the commencement of the large vicennial issues—in which, incidentally, *dupondii* have been lacking, until the CLEMENTIAE and MODERATIONI pieces are imported to fill the gap. We may therefore consider these two types as belonging to those which were produced, first, to honour the *vicennium* (and laud the government) of Tiberius, and, secondly, to celebrate the anniversary of Augustus's death and refer to his *saeculum*.

Much has recently been written of the meaning of the two 'Virtues', *Clementia* and *Moderatio*. Neither of them loses significance when referred to the last, rather than the middle, years of Tiberius. Indeed, Tiberius particularly boasted of his Clemency, and the

1 Cf. Balsdon, *The Emperor Gaius*, pp. 35, 86, 152, 156, 176 f., 214.

2 Henzen, *Acta Fratrum Arvalium*, pp. xlvi n. 1, xlvii, 52, 60; cf. Snyder, *YCS.* 1940, p. 235.

3 *BCM. Imp.* I, p. 146. 1.

4 Mattingly, *JRS.* 1920, p. 37; cf. Smith, *Tiberius and the Roman Empire*, p. 161 n. 163.

5 *BMC. Imp.* I, pp. ccxii f.; II, p. xxviii.

6 E.g. coins apparently struck by Trajanus Decius with the head of Philip, Ensslin, *CAH.* XII, p. 93; and by Aureolus with the head of Postumus, M. & S. V, 2, pp. 328, 577 f. (following Alföldi).

senate celebrated it, after Agrippina's suicide in A.D. 33,[1] and this may be the topical occasion of the coins: it was also almost exactly the time[2] when Valerius Maximus published chapters both on *Clementia*[3] and on *Moderatio*.[4] The unique numismatic appearance of *Moderatio* entitles it to be thought of as the special virtue of Tiberius:[5] the unhappy recollections of his last years are enough to explain its non-recurrence in later epochs, even under such emperors as were likely to value so Republican a quality.[6] *Clementia* too was, before long, to obtain an equivocal reputation as the *virtus regia*,[7] though it survived this as a numismatic type. Augustus had not represented it on his coins, perhaps in view of the too dictatorial CLEMENTIA CAESARIS,[8] and for the same sort of reason as the early *principes* avoided *Liberalitas*.[9] However, *Clementia* was peculiarly associated with the *corona civica*,[10] and one of the four cardinal virtues of Augustus.[11] It 'paired off' with *Virtus* rather than any of the others;[12] and one wonders whether it is not the latter, somewhat comprehensive, quality[13] which the contemporary OB CIV. SER. *sestertii* were intended to represent. At a later date *Clementia* was paired with *Indulgentia*,[14] but the latter's mentions in the early

1   Tacitus, *Annals*, VI, 25; cf. Rogers, loc. cit. pp. 57, 59.
2   Soon after Sejanus's fall in 31: cf. Rose, *History of Latin Literature*, p. 357.
3   V. 1.
4   IV. 1.
5   Rogers, loc. cit. pp. 88, 60 ff., who gives a bibliography. Cf. also the phrase *vis moderandi* quoted by Ciaceri, *Tacito*, p. 158, and *moderator*, Gagé, *Revue historique*, 1936, pp. 322, 327, 334. Walbank, *Greece and Rome*, 1944, p. 30, supports Rogers's distinction between *Clementia* and *Moderatio* (as 'tangential', Rogers, loc. cit. p. 87). For their association, cf. Suetonius, *Jul.* 75; Sutherland, *JRS*. 1938, p. 139, etc. Weber's definition of *moderatio* as referring to Victory (*Princeps*, I, p. 3*) is correct but too narrow; so is Alföldi's interpretation (*Röm. Mitt.* 1935, p. 105) as avoidance of identification with the gods.
6   Claudius prefers *Constantia*, with which the present writer hopes to deal elsewhere.
7   Cf. ten Veldhuys, *De Misericordiae et Clementiae apud Senecam Philosophum Usu atque Ratione*, pp. 86 ff.
8   *BMC. Rep.* I, p. 549. 4176; Mowat, *Rn.*

1911, p. 340; Dahlmann, *Neue Jahrbücher für Wissenschaft und Jugendbildung*, 1934, pp. 17 ff. For its despotic quality, cf. Charlesworth, *Proceedings of the British Academy*, 1937, p. 113. Cf. Antony's funeral speech, Appian, *Bellum Civile* II, 144. 602; von Premerstein, *Vom Werden und Wesen des Prinzipats*, p. 173 and n. 2.
9   Cf. Walbank, *Greece and Rome*, 1944, p. 30.
10   Pliny, *NH*. XVI. 4. 7.
11   Gagé, *RGDA*. p. 146, considers it to have been the special virtue for which the *corona civica* was awarded: Christ, *Tübinger Beiträge zur Altertumswissenschaft*, 1938, XXXI, p. 152, stresses its connection with *Pax*. But there seems no reason to follow Bernhart, *Handbuch zur Münzkunde der römischen Kaiserzeit*, p. 86, in relating the coins of Tiberius directly to Augustus's *corona*.
12   Cf. Liegle, *ZfN*. 1935, pp. 98 ff.; Volkmann ap. von Premerstein, loc. cit. p. 8 n. 1.
13   Cf. Charlesworth, *JRS*. 1943, p. 7.
14   Hadrian: *BMC. Imp.* III, p. 304. 513, p. 305. 518.

empire are limited to a rare semi-medallic issue of Patrae under Caligula.[1]

There is a possibility that the *Clementia*-type was intended to call attention (a little belatedly perhaps, but there are parallels for that [p. 11]) to the tenth or fifth anniversary of one of the two dates (23 and 28) proposed for Tiberius's *ara Clementiae* (pp. 12 f., n. 7). More significant is the analogy of both CLEMENTIAE and MODERATIONI *dupondii* to the six contemporary issues which refer to the half-centenary of the *ludi saeculares* period (p. 44). The 'shields' on both these sets of *dupondii* recall one previous issue and one only, and that consists of Roman *denarii* actually belonging to the immediate aftermath (16 B.C.) of the same Secular occasion:[2]

S.C. OB R.P. CVM SALVT. IMP. CAESAR. AVGVS. CONS. Bust of Augustus, head bare, three-quarters to right, on a round shield inside a laurel-wreath—S.P.Q.R.V.P.S.PR.S. ET RED. AVG., L. MESCINIVS RVFVS III. VIR. Mars standing to left on low pedestal holding transverse spear and *parazonium*.

The reverse legend V(*ota*) P(*ublica*) S(*uscepta*) PR(*o*) S(*alute*) ET RED(*itu*) AVG(*usti*) dates this mintage to 16 B.C.,[3] a year in which the coinage heralding the new *saeculum* strongly persisted.[4] There seems to be a connection between the shields on the *denarii* and the so-called 'medallions' (of very similar appearance) on the *dupondii* apparently issued just about half a century later. Both types look very like *imagines clipeatae*,[5] a form of dedicatory object which began to be very popular in the first years of the Principate.[6] The *imago* on the coin of Augustus is inscribed S(*enatus*) C(*onsulto*) OB R(*em*) P(*ublicam*) CVM SALVT(*e*) IMP(*eratoris*) CAESAR(*is*) AVGVS(*ti*) CONS(*ervatam*). This presumably refers to the presentation to Augustus of an *imago clipeata* in 17 or 16 B.C.[7]—not, therefore, to the *clipeus virtutis* accepted by him in 27 B.C.[8] (the latter had, incidentally,

1 *CMG*.
2 *BMC. Imp.* I, p. 17. 90; Pink, *NZ*. 1946, p. 123. Mowat, *Rn.* 1911, p. 338, notes the parallel with coins of Tiberius.
3 *BMC. Imp.* I, p. xcvi.
4 Cf. Sutherland, *NC*. 1943, p. 45.
5 For recent bibliographies of these, see Sutherland, *JRS*. 1938, p. 137 n. 28; von Premerstein, loc. cit. pp. 92 n. 4, 93 n. 5, 95, 96 nn. 3, 5, 7; cf. also Kollwitz, *Gnomon*, 1941, pp. 222 ff.; Becatti, *Bollettino della Commissione archeologica Comunale di Roma*,

1943, p. 162; id. *Le Arti*, 1942, IV, pp. 172 ff.
6 Cf. Bolten, *Studien zur Geschichte und Kultur des Altertums*, 1937, XXI. 1. pp. 15 ff.; von Premerstein, loc. cit.
7 Bolten, loc. cit. p. 16. Cf. Hadrian, quoted by Charisius (*Grammatici Latini*, ed. Keil, I, p. 122).
8 This is also the view of Mowat, loc. cit. pp. 340 f.; Strack, I, p. 58 n. 157; it is considered as a possibility by Sutherland, loc. cit. p. 137.

been dedicated on a slightly different basis, namely *ob cives servatos*, and may well have borne no portrait of Augustus).[1] The presentation of the *imago* is quite likely to have referred to his health;[2] but, whether it did so or not, this event clearly had some connection with the celebrations of the *saeculum* which dominated all official thought at the time.

Thus the *dupondii* of Tiberius with CLEMENTIAE and MODERATIONI seem to celebrate the half-century of the *ludi saeculares* period, with a special reminiscence of the dedication to Augustus of an *imago clipeata*. But here our deductions must stop. It is quite possible, or even probable, that a similar *imago* was dedicated to Tiberius on the half-centenary of his adoptive father's acceptance of a similar dedication; or even that two *imagines*, and not one, were dedicated to Tiberius—that is to say, one to his Clemency and one to his Moderation.[3] If this is so, it would add further emphasis and meaning to the type of the *dupondii*. But this must remain conjectural. Even without such a conjecture, the coins are significant. Their implication seems to be that 'the state was preserved'—*respublica conservata est*—through Tiberius, and in particular by his inherited *Clementia* and by his own specific quality of *Moderatio*.

So much for the topical theme of the issues of A.D. 34–7, and for the dominant anniversary theme of the *saeculum aureum* which recurs in so many of them. But our discussion of the issues of Augustus (pp. 17, 26) will have prepared us to discover a second anniversary theme as well—namely one inherited from the Republic. We have already met with the *denarii* of M. Plaetorius Cestianus (p. 26), whose coins, attributed to *c.* 70–68 B.C., seem to have influenced those issued just half a century after the latter part of that period. We have now, in *c.* A.D. 33–4, reached the centenary of the same time, and thus of the issues of M. Plaetorius—or the 101st anniversary, which would likewise be a suitable occasion for commemoration (p. 11): and they are duly recalled by no less than three of the types of Tiberius's *vicennium*—a number which, since none of the three types had yet become customary, is seemingly too large for the coincidence to be purely fortuitous. These types (not yet by any means common ones) are the *caduceus*,[4] eagle and thunderbolt.[5]

---

1 *Pace* Bolten, loc. cit. p. 15, etc.
2 Cf. *BMC. Imp.* I, p. cv; Sutherland, *NC.* 1943, p. 45.
3 M. & S. I, pp. 107 n. 2, and f.; Sutherland, *JRS.* 1938, p. 137.

4 *BMC. Rep.* I, pp. 437 ff., 3543 ff.— apparently the first appearance of the *caduceus* as sole type on *denarii*.
5 *BMC. Rep.* I, p. 441. 3596 (eagle on thunderbolt); Mattingly, *RC.* p. 274.

It is impossible to say why both Augustus and Tiberius, or their mint-masters, seem to have been so interested in the coins of this particular moneyer, about whom so little is known.[1] There may perhaps (as so often) be some family reason; but if so we know nothing of it.[2] More probably, as under Augustus, a general reference was intended to the 'good old days' of the Republic, which was, indeed—as the s.c. of M. Plaetorius suggests—in peaceful action in 69–8 B.C., for practically the last time. The same sort of allusion to Republican times is conveyed by another great 'Republican', Trajan, who, with no less regard for the religious significance of earlier coinages and their types, himself revived, or 'restored', many *denarii* of that epoch—apparently likewise on an anniversary occasion (p. 100).

Tiberius, too, was in a number of respects 'Republican' (p. 56 n. 10), and it is in keeping with his character and policy that the traditional themes of his vicennial issues should combine Republican with Augustan motifs. But the most striking evidence of this tendency under Tiberius is provided by the only one of the ten issues starting in A.D. 34–5 to which no anniversary significance, other than that of the *vicennium*, has yet been attributed in these pages. This issue comprises the *sestertii* with temple of *Concordia* (p. 43 and n. 5). A phase of the Augustan theme is there, for this year was precisely the 25th after the probable date (A.D. 10) of the *ara Concordiae Augustae*—itself 50 years after the Treaty of Brundusium (p. 30 n.). This quarter-centenary was of interest to Tiberius, for his special part in the events of Augustus's last decade (p. 26) had included the dedication of the altar of Concord.[3] There are also Tiberian dedications to *Concordia Augusta*.[4]

But what is here particularly noteworthy is the reference to the Republican temples of *Concordia*. The second of those temples was finished in *c.* 216, having been begun in 217 B.C. This latter date was itself the sesquicentenary of the traditional date of the first temple of Concord, 367 B.C.—a coincidence paralleled by other foundations (pp. 3 f.). In the Principate no figure of *Concordia* or of her temple had appeared on official issues until the Tiberian coinage which is

---

1 Cf. *PIR.* III, pp. 42 f.
2 Possibly too the coinage of Plaetorius had itself been of an anniversary character, commemorating the fourth *saeculum* (of 110 years) of the Republic (p. 75 n. 2).

3 'De manubiis'. Cf. Gagé, *RGDA.* p. 165.
4 E.g. *ILS.* 3785; cf. (recently) Koch, *PW.* XV, 1. 1228.

now being discussed: and these *sestertii* seem to have been issued for the quadringenary[1] of the first temple of Concord (four being a figure of special significance [p. 2 n. 3]), and the 250th anniversary (quarter-millenary) of her second temple. In just the same way had Caesar commemorated the centenaries and half-centenaries of great temples (pp. 15 f.), and the practice was to be not infrequently repeated in later reigns (p. 160; cf. p. 3 n. 3).

The selection of this type by Tiberius is significant. The original temple had been traditionally founded by Furius Camillus,[2] whose memory was kept alive in precisely these years in the widely read[3] works of Valerius Maximus (p. 49 n. 2). Moreover, he explicitly associated Camillus with the specifically Tiberian 'Virtue' *Moderatio* which appears to receive its only numismatic commemoration at this very date (p. 47); and he points the moral by linking him with an ancestor of the *princeps*, C. Claudius Nero.[4] At an earlier point in the Principate Livy—who was much concerned with the theme of *Concordia*[5]—had introduced a great deal of topical material into the speech attributed to Camillus on the occasion of the foundation of her temple.[6] There is a close connection between the policy of temple-construction and restoration attributed by Livy to Camillus and that undertaken by Augustus. Recent historians have also decided that Tiberius, though modest in his inscriptions on the subject, was by no means as idle in this respect as our literary traditions have suggested.[7]

All these aspects of the type made it an interesting one in A.D. 34–5, when the empire as a whole (except for a forthcoming Eastern campaign) was enjoying the *Pax Augusta*; whereas the top stratum of the Roman world and its *princeps* were experiencing the aftermath of an attack on Concord made by the conspiracy of Sejanus. It has

1 'Quadringenary' has the authority of the *Oxford Dictionary* and *The Times*, but 'quatercentenary' that of Trinity College, Cambridge, and of leading weeklies. The former is preferred here in order to avoid confusions with 'quarter-centenary'.

2 For a sceptical estimate of the existence of this personage, see Piganiol, *Histoire de Rome*, p. 70. For his continued fame under the empire, cf. Spartian, *SHA. Vita Nigri*, 12. 1; Trebellius Pollio, ibid. *Vita Claudi Gothici*, 1, etc. His temple was reputedly the earliest in honour of any 'personification'.

3 Cf. Rose, *History of Latin Literature*, p. 357 n. 47.

4 IV. 1, 9.

5 Hellmann, *Livius-Interpretationen*; cf. Momigliano, *JRS*. 1943, p. 120. Other recent work on Livy's themes includes *Liviana* (Milan, 1943); Catin, *En lisant Tite-Live*; Zancan, *Tito Livio*, etc.

6 v. 5, 51 f.; cf. Altheim, *History of Roman Religion*, p. 355; Getty, *JRS*. 1947, p. 220.

7 Rogers, *Studies in the Reign of Tiberius*, p. 17, etc.

been suggested independently that the annual festival in honour of *Concordia* was introduced in the principate of Tiberius;[1] and this, like the conspiracy of Sejanus, may have played a part in attaching topical significance to the type.

Concordia had other associations also. The coins show in front of her temple the figures of Mercury and Hercules that were there:[2] we have met with the Augustan manifestations of both (pp. 16, 26). As regards Tiberius, a dedication was made *Herculi Tutatori Aug.* in A.D. 26;[3] and Mercury's *caduceus* is the type of the *asses* issued simultaneously with these *Concordia sestertii* in 34–7 (p. 45). Augustus had in a single year (10 B.C.) set up one altar to Mercury and another to *Concordia, Salus* and *Pax* (see pp. 4 f.);[4] Pliny expressly connects the *caduceus* with *Concordia*,[5] and a large bronze *caduceus* was actually let into the floor of the temple of Concord[6]— which thus gains added significance as a type issued on the half-centenary of the new *saeculum*. *Concordia* also had a marked relevance to the *domus Augusta*—and an urgent one to Tiberius after the real or suspected disloyalties of so many of its members—and it is noteworthy that hers are the attributes allotted by Caligula very shortly afterwards to his favoured sister Drusilla.[7] Closely linked to *Concordia* were *Spes* and *Fides*:[8] *Spes* is relevant to the much disputed steps taken by Tiberius to select a successor, and *Fides* to the financial crisis of the preceding year, as well as (like *Salus*) to the general circumstances of the period following the plot of Sejanus.

Too much, however, must not be made of all these connections. Even people so well versed in public religion as the Romans could hardly be expected to think of them all when they saw these coins. But they could be, and no doubt were, expected to think of some of them (p. 8). Like *Pietas* and *Iustitia* before it (pp. 35ff.), *Concordia* is represented in too general a way for the mint to have intended to stress any one aspect of this concept to the exclusion of the others. But if a dozen educated Romans of A.D. 34–5 had been asked how *Concordia* applied to affairs of state, it is suggested that

1 Gagé, *RGDA.* p. 165.
2 *BMC. Imp.* I, pp. 137, cxxxviii.
3 *CIL.* VI, 343; cf. Snyder, *YCS.* 1940, p. 236.
4 For the connection of *Concordia* and *Pax,* cf. Livy, IX. 19; von Premerstein, *Vom Werden und Wesen des Prinzipats,* p. 126. There is also an echo of ὁμόνοια.

5 *NH.* xxix. 3. 12; cf. *BMC. Imp.* II, p. xxxvii n. 4; Altheim, loc. cit. p. 531 n. 49.
6 Cf. Huelsen, *The Roman Forum,* p. 95; *BMC. Imp.* I, p. cxxxviii n. 4.
7 *BMC. Imp.* I, p. cxlv; cf. Piganiol, loc. cit. p. 264.
8 Cf. Hamberg, *Studies in Roman Imperial Art,* pp. 20 f.; Toynbee, *JRS.* 1946, p. 178.

all the preceding points (and very probably others) would have emerged from their combined replies.

This version of *Concordia*, and the contemporary types, represent a new and climactic development of the anniversary coinages. In complexity and expressiveness they have advanced a step beyond the issues of *c.* A.D. 23. The progress recorded by the latter has been tentatively attributed to Sejanus (p. 41); but he had disappeared, with most of his supporters, before the *vicennium*. Who, then, was responsible for the enlargement of the same conception in A.D. 34–5? We do not know, and will perhaps never know. It may have been one or more of the diminished circle of *amici* of Tiberius, or it may well have been members of his greatly enlarged, though still excellently controlled, secretariat of freedmen and slaves. Or it may have been the *princeps* himself. At all events the development was in keeping with his curious and perhaps morbid attention to the ceremonies and details of public religion.[1]

(iii) *Tiberius: other anniversaries*

In order to sketch the main lines of the Tiberian development of the anniversary coinages, we have, as in dealing with Augustus, deserted exact chronological sequence. The ambitious issues of the *decennium* and *vicennium* of Tiberius have been discussed, but no mention has yet been made of the anniversary coinages which preceded and followed those occasions. This omission will now be rectified, and we shall briefly survey: (1) a Roman *as* of A.D. 15–16; (2) two Eastern *dupondii* and Alexandrian billon of A.D. 20; (3) Romano-Western *asses* of *c.* A.D. 29 or a little later; (4) Eastern *dupondii* and *asses*, and possibly a Roman *sestertius*, of *c.* A.D. 30–1; (5) Eastern *drachmae* of *c.* A.D. 32–4; and (6) Western *sestertii* or *dupondii* of A.D. 37.

(1) The exceptionally rare *as*, dated to A.D. 15–16, which does not show the normal 'seated priestess',[2] but instead of it a chair, above which is an oak(?)-wreath.[3] The present writer must venture to

---

1 Cf. Warde-Fowler, *The Religious Experience of the Roman People*, p. 447 n. 2: see Tacitus, *Annals*, III, 58, VI, 2; Plutarch, *De Defectu Oraculorum*, Ch. XVII, etc. The apparently contrary statement in Suetonius, *Tib.* 69 (*circa deos ac religiones neglegentior*, cf. Thiel, *Mnemosyne*, 1935, p. 260 n. 2) is related to his personal belief in astrology, but the same impression might have been created by his 'moderation' with regard to the worship of Divus Augustus (p. 56 n. 10).

2 *BMC. Imp.* I, p. 128. 65. This type is discussed in *APT*. Ch. III, sect. iv *b*.

3 Paris; cf. *BMC. Imp.* I, p. 129 and n.

doubt the current attribution of this type to 'the transfer of elections from *comitia* to senate'.[1] A more suitable explanation is suggested by Alföldi's researches on the two constituents of the type.[2] The chair is rightly identified by him as curule.[3] Now *sella curulis* and wreath were precisely the most conspicuous public honours paid to recently deceased *divi* and other members of the imperial house. A gilt curule chair had been granted to the divine Julius and shown at the Games,[4] and it appears, with a wreath, on coins of Octavian in his honour.[5] Likewise both chair and gold wreath were awarded to the memory of Marcellus;[6] and after the death of Germanicus, *sellae curules* were adorned by oak-wreaths.[7] It is therefore probable that *sella curulis* and wreath were among the first honours allotted to Divus Augustus also,[8] and that this is the immediate occasion commemorated by the coins.[9] Probably their extreme rarity (in striking contrast to the commonness of the 'seated priestess' type) points to the issue having a private and not a public character. It is conceivable that it was abandoned, before passing the pattern stage, owing to the somewhat lukewarm and unimaginative (though highly correct) character of this tribute to the new divinity. Tiberius was scrupulous in his honours to Divus Augustus, but he was unwilling to allow these to exceed the bounds of reasonableness and equal the wishes of his more emotional subjects.[10] As an alternative to the 'pattern' theory, this type may have

1 Mattingly, *Roman Coins*, p. 170; *BMC. Imp.* I, p. cxxxiii. On that event see (among recent writers) Siber, *Festschrift Paul Koschaker*, I (1939), p. 194; id. *Abh. Leipzig*, XLIV. 2, 1940, pp. 67 f.
2 *Röm. Mitt.* 1935, pp. 10 ff. (wreath), 124 ff. (*sella curulis*); see also Diez, *Wiener Jahreshefte*, XXXVI, 1946, p. 107. On wreaths, see too Schulz, *Die Rechtstitel und Regierungsprogramme auf römischen Kaisermünzen*, pp. 9 ff., 15; Strack, I, pp. 58 n. 157, 59 n. 161, 62 n. 182, etc.
3 Loc. cit. p. 135.
4 Dio 50. 10. 2, 56. 29. 1; cf. Alföldi, loc. cit.
5 *BMC. Imp.* II, p. 405. 76; cf. *BMC. Imp.* II, p. lxxiii n. 4.
6 Alföldi, loc. cit.
7 Tacitus, *Annals*, II, 83; cf. Alföldi, loc. cit. p. 136.
8 Augustus appears to be seated on a *sella curulis* on the Boscoreale cup; cf. Rostov-tzeff, *Social and Economic History of the Roman Empire*, p. 76 = *Storia Economica e Sociale dell' Impero Romano*, p. 94, etc. For curule chair and wreath (*struppus*) on Flavian coinage, see *BMC. Imp.* II, p. lxxiii (Titus).
9 All these 'accession' coinages of Tiberius were somewhat delayed; cf. the impossibility of drawing any historical conclusions from the absence of *aes* in a short reign like Otho's (*pace* Sutherland, *JRS.* 1938, p. 94).
10 See (for example) Gagé, *Revue archéologique*, 1931, pp. 19 ff.; Fink, *YCS.* 1940, p. 159 n. 724; and the caution of Cordier, *Revue de philologie*, 1943, p. 217 (cf. Gelzer, *PW.* x, 1. 525 ff.) regarding the alleged anti-Augustan reaction (on which Rogers, *Transactions of the American Philological Association*, 1940, pp. 534 f.; Syme, *The Roman Revolution*, pp. 383, 408 n. 3, 414 n. 1; cf. Bardon, *Les Empereurs et les Lettres Latines*, pp. 108 ff.).

been felt *ab initio* to be more suitable for private distribution than for mass production.

At all events, it appealed more to a limited class who maintained the old Roman ideas. The type of a curule chair had first appeared on the Roman coinage just 100 years before these *asses*, or before the consecration of Augustus—namely on the *denarii* of P. Furius Crassipes, which have been variously assigned to *c.* 87[1] and *c.* 85 B.C.[2] This centenary allusion—if such it is, and this does not seem unlikely—emphasises that the consecration was not intended to deviate too much from old Republican symbolism. (Indeed, in one sense, 'deification' itself had long been considered common to every man after death: for their souls all joined the *di manes*.[3]) Furthermore, the *sella curulis*, with its suggestion of the curule magistracies, was a symbol of *civilitas*—a quality of which the emphasis under Augustus was reiterated with redoubled force under Tiberius. These very coins, and all other *aes* with his portrait for the first 20 years of his principate, show Tiberius with bare and not laureate head. This is another indication of *civilitas*,[4] and the more marked because, even before his accession, coins had shown him with a laurel-wreath.[5] Tiberius intended some measure of this moderation to extend to his honours for the divine Augustus.

(2) The Eastern *dupondii* of Tiberius with *caduceus* and double *cornucopiae*,[6] and—vastly rarer—the *asses* with *caduceus* and four corn-ears[7] (Plate I, 9), are dated to the latter half of A.D. 20.[8] The former mintage is a major official one.[9] It was apparently issued at more than one mint—probably by Cn. Sentius Saturninus, *legatus*

---

1 Mattingly, *Roman Coins*, p. 280.
2 *BMC. Rep.* I, p. 332. 2604.
3 Cf. Altheim, loc. cit. p. 361.
4 Cf. Sutherland, *NC.* 1945, p. 62.
5 *BMC. Imp.* I, p. cxviii.
6 Ibid. p. 144. 174.
7 Paris: Mowat, *Rn.* 1911, p. 429. 17; cf. *BMC. Imp.* I, p. 144 n.
8 The only verifiable date is IMP. VII. (*sic*) TR. POT. XXII. COS. III, *pace BMC. Imp.* I, p. cxli. The coins are adequately dated by TR. POT. XXII. COS. III; and the vexed question of the eighth *imperator* salutation of Tiberius will not be entered into here.
9 These conclusions (cf. for the Eastern s.c. issues, see below, p. 64) are necessitated by the numbers of specimens observed by

the present writer in the Near East. A period of residence in that area enables one to appreciate that this was a very large coinage intended for circulation throughout the Eastern provinces. Its comparative rarity in Western Europe is due to the infrequency, proportionately speaking, with which coins found in or near Asia Minor reach the West. This consideration, and the fact that little is known of coin-finds in that part of the world, explain why the character of this coinage has generally passed unnoticed. Its 'imperial' scope, however, was realised by Regling, *ZfN.* 1931, p. 292. Many of these pieces bear countermarks, like other major official issues; *BMC. Imp.* I, p. xlii, cf. p. xxxviii. See now Bellinger, *Dura*, VI, pp. 139, 192.

of Syria[1]—and it cannot be limited in mintage or scope to Commagene, or refer only to the annexation of that country in 17.[2] Now the only previous bronze of an official provincial mint to bear a date had been struck on an anniversary occasion (p. 20); and there is reason to believe that the same is true of the next dated pieces of this category (p. 64). Was, then, the present issue also—an equally unusual one—motivated not only by monetary needs, but also by a special, and perhaps anniversary, occasion? Apparently it was; since A.D. 20, when these *dupondii* and *asses* were struck, was the year of the half-centenary of Actium and the fiftieth year of the capture of Egypt by Octavian. Anniversaries of both these occasions received ample commemoration, which, as the *Fasti Amiternini* explicitly testify, was continued under Tiberius:[3] he may have used this occasion to allow African proconsuls numismatic honours,[4] and the cities of Augusta and Tiberias reckoned their era from A.D. 20.[5] The importance of Actium is obvious, and we have good reason to believe that very special attention was also paid to the anniversaries of *Aegyptus capta*.[6] Anniversaries of these occasions were given no less numismatic attention by the successors of Tiberius (pp. 164 f.).

But the anniversary which this Tiberian coinage celebrated was, as in so many other cases, a composite one. The type of the double *cornucopiae* had possessed a Hellenistic history,[7] but its first appearance on the Republican coinage had been on the famous and unprecedented *aurei* of Sulla issued in *c.* 81 B.C.[8] Those *aurei*, and the completion of Sulla's Eastern reorganisation, must be dated precisely 100 years before the present Eastern *dupondii* and *asses* of Tiberius. Thus, the latter celebrate, for the benefit of the Eastern parts of the empire, two great Eastern reorganisations, those of Augustus and

1 Cf. de Laet, *Samenstelling*, pp. 79, 242; *PIR.* III, p. 200. 295.
2 As Mowat, loc. cit. p. 423, who gives a historical survey of the type. Cf. also Cohen, I, p. 190 n. 8. Rollin and Feuardent, *Catalogue*, etc., 1862, p. 654, no. 9592, preferred attribution to Judaea; but this is not very likely.
3 Cf. Gagé, *RGDA.* p. 175: Snyder, *YCS.* 1940, p. 231.
4 *APT.* ch. II, sect. ii (L. Apronius).
5 Cf. Hill, *BMC. Lycaonia*, p. cviii; Head, *Historia Numorum*², p. 802.
6 Taylor, *The Divinity of the Roman*

Emperor, pp. 194 f., 201, 209; cf. Gagé, loc. cit. pp. 157 n. 2, 175 ff.; Snyder, loc. cit. The AEGVPTVS CAPTA type persists at Nemausus long after Augustus (*FITA.* pp. 75 ff.) and is one of the very few Augustan types selected by Trajan for restoration, *BMC. Imp.* III, pp. 1444, xci f. Coins of Augustus may possibly have celebrated the twentieth anniversary of that event: see Appendix I.
7 Mowat, loc. cit. pp. 423 ff. For two accounts of origins of *cornucopiae*, see Ovid, *Fasti*, 5. 115 and *Met.* 9. 85 ff., etc.
8 *BMC. Rep.* II, pp. 463 f.; Mattingly, *Roman Coins*, pp. 25, 36, 47.

of Sulla. It is tempting to consider whether the reference to Sulla does not point to some sympathy felt by Tiberius towards the optimate régime[1] (witness the stress on a mint-master, M. Plaetorius, who was a senatorial protégé [p. 52]). But it is not safe to say more in this connection than that there were considerable resemblances between the Sullan and imperial régimes,[2] that Tiberius had planned the funeral of Augustus so as to resemble Sulla's very closely,[3] and that Tiberius, *pace* a recent theory,[4] was not likely to have any prejudice against a fellow *nobilis*.[5] But the type may also, to some extent at least, be a family compliment.[6] The Cornelii were exceptionally strong in high places under Tiberius, and among them were several Sullae.[6]

The contemporary piece with *caduceus* and corn-ears again celebrates the half-centenary of the Augustan settlement in the East, though not, perhaps, a Republican centenary as well. It is excessively rare—the present writer only knows of a single specimen—whereas the cognate issue, with *caduceus* and double *cornucopiae* accompanying the same inscriptions, must have been an enormous one. We have met with this same contrast in the case of four previous issues also: (1) the very rare pieces with Numa's head, which formed part of a much larger *aes* issue (p. 19); (2) the 'Triumphal' *aes* of Augustus, identical in inscription and moneyers' signatures to vast issues in the ordinary denominations (p. 21); (3) the gold medallion of Augustus with the usual C. L. CAESARES type (p. 23); (4) the *as* of Tiberius with wreath and curule chair, which corresponds exactly in legend and date to the enormous issues of *asses* with the 'seated priestess' (pp. 55 f.).

If we add to this list the Eastern *dupondii* and *asses* of Tiberius, here are five exceptionally rare types occurring simultaneously with very common ones. The rare pieces in question are not only medallic rather than monetary, but every one of them is of an anniversary character. Dr Toynbee has deduced that many medallions were

---

1 For which Sulla's name later stood, even though he was at the time anti-senatorial, Mattingly, *Roman Coins*, p. 36.
2 Cf. Carcopino, *Sylla*, pp. 86, 92, 112, 241, etc.
3 Ibid. pp. 227 ff. See also Poplawski, *Eos*, 1927, pp. 273 ff.
4 de Laet, *Aspects de la Vie Sociale et Économique sous Auguste* (1944); id. *Samen-*

stelling, pp. 251 ff., 261 f., 271 ff.; cf. Ensslin, *Philologische Wochenschrift*, 1942, p. 481.
5 Cf. Nailis, *L'Antiquité Classique*, 1942, p. 152; Gelzer, *Gnomon*, 1943, p. 108; cf. Roos, *Museum*, 1942, pp. 200 f., etc. The answer is that 'Tiberius was not particular about pedigree': Balsdon, *JRS*. 1932, p. 243.
6 E.g. *PIR*². II, pp. 362 ff., 1458 ff., etc.

distributed (in later periods) on special occasions, and particularly on days of annual celebration (pp. 21–2).[1] Probably the same is true of these early, and exceedingly limited, anniversary issues. Dr Toynbee also points out that, though *aes* medallions, as properly understood, did not commence until the second century, certain mounted pieces, and coins with a large flan, seem to have been endowed with a medallic character as early as Augustus and Tiberius.[2] It may, however, be suggested that the principal *aes* medallions of the early principate are the very rare anniversary issues that have been discussed, and others of the same *genre* under Tiberius and his successors (cf. p. 78).

That is to say, in spite of their outward resemblance to coins, these rare pieces were apparently intended for distribution and not for circulation. They were accompanied by vast ordinary issues; and (as regards the *aes* at least) the *senatusconsultum Caesaris auctoritate*, which authorised the public series (p. 28), explicitly or implicitly authorised the small private series also. The recipients of the latter pieces presumably included persons especially connected in some way with the anniversaries, e.g. friends of the dead man, etc. No doubt these were none the less pleased to receive such gifts if the latter partially conformed with well-known types; though (except perhaps in the case of the gold medallions) their artistic value was not as great as that of the Antonine and later medallions.

These conclusions bring us to the contention of Pink and his followers that our knowledge of Roman coinage is confused owing to a failure to distinguish between main series and minor ones.[3] It now appears that many examples of the latter category may be medallic rather than monetary. This applies both to recognisable anniversary mintages (of which we shall meet with several more, equally rare, examples) and also in general to other uncommon types. Nor, of course, need such an inquiry be limited to issues accompanied by simultaneous common series. For example, the gold medallion of Augustus with type of Diana (p. 24) (which is only recognisable as medallic by its size) bears a date not found on the large monetary issues with the same type.

We can now revert to Tiberius, and to his anniversary issues of

---

1 Pp. 73 ff.   2 Pp. 25 ff.
3 *NZ.* 1935, pp. 44 f.; cf. M. & S. IV, 2, p. 11. See also in general, Pink's other

writings in *NZ.* 1933, pp. 17 ff., 1934, pp. 3 ff., 1936, pp. 10 ff.; *Klio*, 1936, pp. 219 ff.; *NZ.* 1946, etc. Cf. *SMACA*.

A.D. 15–16 and 20. We do not know the identity of their distributors. In the former case—if private distribution indeed occurred—this distributor may or may not have been the *princeps* (in honour of his recent accession and of the consecration of Augustus). But in the latter case it was presumably someone in the East. One may conjecture that the pieces with *caduceus* and corn-ears were intended for distribution by Germanicus, who would have been there if he had not died in the previous year. Even if they are not merely patterns, there would be nothing remarkable in the production of a few examples of such an issue notwithstanding his death; Dr Toynbee has identified a comparable time-lag at a later period.[1]

This year (A.D. 20–1) witnessed not only the Eastern *aes* issues of *caduceus* and *cornucopiae*, and *caduceus* and corn-ears, but also the inauguration of official billon coinage at Alexandria (year 7).[2] This consisted of debased tetradrachms,[3] mostly referring to Divus Augustus as well as to the reigning *princeps*.[4] Important monetary innovations often coincided with anniversary occasions (p. 41): and for this very date, A.D. 20, we have a special analogy in the novel *dupondii* and *asses* just discussed. Those seem to celebrate the half-centenary of Actium and *Aegyptus capta*; and so, in all probability, does the revived billon coinage of Alexandria—the first since those events.[5] It seems probable—as in the case of the Eastern *aes*—that the change had been set on foot in the years immediately preceding A.D. 20 by Germanicus, whose interest in Egyptian affairs is well known.[6]

(3) The discussion of the Eastern *dupondii* and *asses* of Tiberius may enable us to reach a tentative identification of two equally rare *aes* issues of uncertain denomination, both with obverse inscription

---

1 Commodus: p. 74.
2 For the Egyptian Regnal New Year of Tiberius, see Pippidi, *Revue Historique du Sud-Est Européen*, 1941, pp. 87 ff. =*Autour de Tibère*, pp. 125 ff., with bibliography; cf. Balsdon, *JRS*. 1946, p. 172.
3 Milne, *Catalogue of Alexandrian Coins in the Ashmolean Museum*, p. xvii, nos. 38 ff.
4 For Livia's lesser prominence on Alexandrian issues under Tiberius than under Augustus, see Kahrstedt, *Klio*, 1910, p. 293 n. 1; cf. Vogt, *Die Alexandrinischen Münzen*, I, p. 6; Kornemann, *Doppelprinzipat und Reichsteilung*, p. 38 n. 1; *APT*. Ch. III, sect. iv.

5 Milne, loc. cit. p. xvi; *FITA*. p. 132. Milne, loc. cit. pp. xvi, xxv, cf. xix, describes the tentative character of the intervening *aes* issues.
6 For a select bibliography of his 'legislation', see Scramuzza, *The Emperor Claudius*, p. 249 n. 17, cf. pp. 64, 246 n. 7; also Kalbfleisch, *Hermes*, 1942, pp. 374 ff.; Siber, *Zeitschrift der Savigny Stiftung für Rechtsgeschichte, Röm. Abt.* 1944, pp. 264 f. For political events in Egypt under Tiberius, see (recently) Allen, *Transactions of the American Philological Association*, 1941, pp. 1 ff.; Momigliano, *JRS*. 1943, p. 117.

DIVVS AVGVSTVS PATER and his radiate head to left, with star above.[1]
One of these pieces shows on the reverse a bare head of Tiberius to
left (Plate I, 10),[2] and the other the veiled bust to left of an aged-
looking lady who can scarcely fail to be Livia (Plate II, 1).[3] In each
case there is an oak(?)-wreath round the reverse, and the two pieces
clearly belong to the same series and occasion. The heads of
Augustus are identical to those on the very common *asses* with
PROVIDENT. and altar;[4] and we may reasonably consider, by the
analogy of the issues of A.D. 15–16 and 20, that these rare pieces
with the portraits of Tiberius and Livia were distributed privately
at the same time as the PROVIDENT. *asses* were released for public
issue. The only surviving example of the coin with the head of
Livia was found at Trier,[5] and we may conjecture mintage in the
same neighbourhood. This is in keeping with the PROVIDENT.
series, for a part (or all) of which a mint in Gallia Comata has
long seemed probable in view of its enormous circulation in that
region and beyond the Rhine.[6] It is, however, also possible that the
piece found at Trier was minted at Rome for provincial distribution.

   The very rare concomitants of the PROVIDENT. series suggest, by
analogy with earlier issues of the same dual kind (pp. 59 f.), that the
whole group, rare and common pieces alike, was issued together,
on an important occasion; but we cannot be sure what this
occasion was. Sutherland has assigned the PROVIDENT. coinage to
the period *c.* A.D. 22/3–30,[7] but it may also have been issued at any
date in that period or indeed slightly after it. Iconographical
considerations favour a date rather after *c.* 23, since the portraits
have evolved since the DIVVS AVGVSTVS PATER issues of that time
(p. 33). The portraiture of the PROVIDENT. coins and their medallic
counterparts closely resembles that of a series of Divus Augustus
dupondii with the type of s.c. in oak-wreath (*corona civica*):[8] the
two groups must be taken together. *Providentia* came into special
vogue after the Sejanus conspiracy of A.D. 31[9] and the altar of

1   The star had already occurred in *c.* A.D.
15–16. On it see Val. Max. *prooem.*; Strong,
JRS. 1916, p. 34.
2   Copenhagen: cf. Sutherland, *NC.* 1941,
p. 104 n. 13.
3   Berlin.
4   *BMC. Imp.* I, p. 141. 146; Lederer,
RS. 1942, p. 11; Cahn, ibid. 1944, p. 69;
Bloesch, *Antike Kunst in der Schweiz*, pp. 68 f.

In the present writer's opinion they are too
late to be accession-issues, as the Tiberius
coin is said to be by Sutherland, loc. cit.
5   Von Sallet, *ZfN.* 1879, p. 62.
6   Cf. *BMC. Imp.* I, pp. xix, xxiii, etc.
7   *NC.* 1941, p. 111.
8   *BMC. Imp.* I, p. 141. 143.
9   E.g. *ILS.* 157, 158; cf. West, *Corinth*,
VIII, 110.

PLATE II

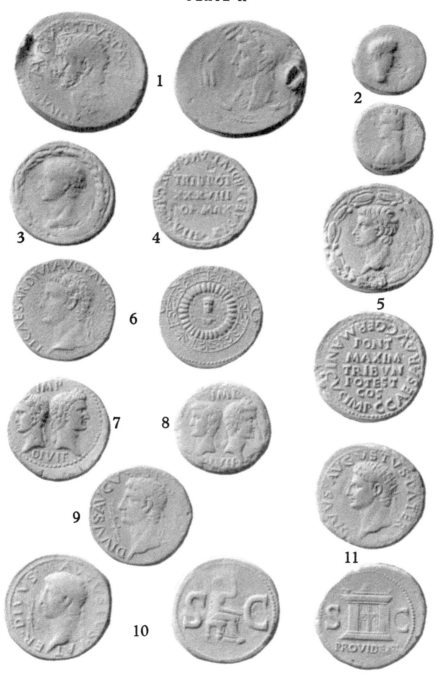

TIBERIUS, CALIGULA AND CLAUDIUS:
RARE AND CONJECTURAL PIECES

Providentia Augusta should perhaps be assigned to that date.[1] The coins could be allotted to the same period. But the altar, or at least its consecration, might be somewhat earlier; and so might the coins and medallions. Without aspiring to certainty, the present writer suggests *c.* A.D. 29.[2] In that year ended the third *lustrum* after the death of Augustus. The same year also witnessed the quarter-centenary of the *adoptio* of Tiberius (A.D. 4). *Providentia* often referred to adoptions;[3] that event was an important one in the *Fasti*,[4] and its anniversaries may perhaps be recorded by certain inscriptions.[5] Furthermore, it was in A.D. 29 that Livia died (we have attributed a *sestertius* to the event [p. 33 n. 6]), and Tiberius no doubt then gained a controlling interest in her copper mines.[6] It seems probable that her portrait on our present 'distribution issues' was engraved after her death rather than before it, since the official coinage of Tiberius in her lifetime had refrained from explicitly portraying her; and her death is a suitable occasion. We may tentatively attribute their distribution to Cn. Cornelius Lentulus Gaetulicus, who became *legatus* of Germania Superior in the very year 29;[7] and their occasion to Livia's death, the *ara*, and the anniversary of the adoption. But this is all conjectural.

Much attention has recently been devoted to *Providentia*.[8] An earlier discussion (p. 36) suggests that the present type is a general one, and that it means to call to mind no single aspect of the personification to the exclusion of its other aspects. *Providentia* had primarily referred to the attitude of the gods to mankind. By an easy transition it came to allude to the attitude to mankind of Divus Augustus. We next think of his forethought in adopting Tiberius, perhaps just a quarter of a century earlier. But other aspects also would occur to those who saw the type. For example, Livia was identified by the

---

1 *CIL.* VI. 2028; cf. Charlesworth, *Harvard Theological Review*, 1936, pp. 111 n. 9, 112; Rogers, *Studies in the Reign of Tiberius*, p. 28.

2 Conceivably the altar was consecrated in *c.* A.D. 29 and dedicated in *c.* 31; cf. above, p. 12 n. 7.

3 Cf. *BMC. Imp.* II, p. lxxv n. 1.

4 Cf. Gagé, *RGDA.* p. 173.

5 Snyder, *YCS.* 1940, p. 236 (*CIL.* XI, 3781). Cf. above, p. 6 n. 1.

6 For *aes Livianum*, see (recently) Korne-

mann, *Grosse Frauen des Altertums*, p. 201; cf. Pliny, *NH.* XXXIV, 3. For Tiberius's failure to pay her legacies, cf. Willrich, *Livia*, p. 79, etc. There was a comparable output of *aes* coinage after the confiscation of mines in A.D. 33 (p. 43 and n. 3).

7 *PIR*². II, 338. 1390; cf. de Laet, *Samenstelling*, pp. 114. 590, 234 etc.

8 E.g. Charlesworth, loc. cit. pp. 107 ff.; Nock, ibid. 1930, p. 266; Rogers, loc. cit. pp. 20 ff.; von Premerstein, *Vom Werden und Wesen des Prinzipats*, p. 126 n. 4, etc.

general public with female personifications and deities.[1] A reference
to her own *Providentia* would not be out of place, especially as a
posthumous compliment. Again, even before the Sejanus conspiracy,
the cult of this 'Virtue' as a quality of the *princeps* himself was on the
increase[2]—with reference both to his good government in general
and, in particular, to his strenuous efforts to provide for the succession. The coin-type is not labelled *Augusti* or even *Augusta*
(though a *municipium* such as Italica can unofficially prefer the
former version).[3] Whatever its relationship to the *ara Providentiae
Augustae* (probably a close one), the coinage was not intended to
specify any particular manifestation of *Providentia*, but rather to
bring this 'Virtue' to the minds of the public, in general terms, as
a guiding principle of the state. The PROVIDENT. type seems to have
been revived on rare issues of Claudius and Nero (pp. 77 n. 2, 80).

(4) The next series with which we have to deal is explicitly dated
to A.D. 30–1. It consists of two bronze denominations with s.c. in
wreath.[4] These are of Eastern origin and circulation; they are the
first of their kind in this principate, and are in direct line of descent
from the similar issues of Augustus.[5] As in the case of the mintages
of that *princeps*, and of earlier Eastern *dupondii* of Tiberius himself
(pp. 57 f.), the Tiberian *aes* issue with s.c. is of greater scope than has
been understood. It is likely to have emanated from more than one
mint,[6] and to have been struck in very large quantities.[7] Probably
the issue was made by the *legatus legionis* (Pacuvius)[8] who deputised
for the absentee governor of Syria, L. Aelius Lamia.[9]

This is the first Eastern s.c. coinage to bear a Roman date. It
stands alone in the principate of Tiberius—apart from the earlier
issue of Eastern *dupondii* and *asses*. Those had been of an anniversary
character, so that an anniversary occasion is not an impossibility for

1   *APT.* Ch. III, sect. iv.
2   Cf. also Charlesworth, *Proceedings of
the British Academy*, 1937, p. 117.
3   Vives y Escudero, *La Moneda Hispánica*,
IV, p. 127. 9; cf. *APT.* Ch. II, sect. v.
4   Wruck, *Die syrische Provinzialprägung*,
p. 178, 15 A and 15 B. See *SMACA*. De
Belfort, *Annuaire de la Société française de numismatique*, 1884, p. 46, quotes rostral wreath.
5   *FITA.* pp. 98 ff.
6   Ibid. p. 100 n. 17 (Antioch is one).
Further varieties in the present writer's
possession; see *SMACA*.

7   The present writer has seen many in
different parts of the Levant.
8   *PIR.* III, 6. 33; cf. de Laet, *Samenstelling*,
pp. 68, 242, 273.
9   *PIR².* I, 34. 200; II, Add. 200; cf. de
Laet, loc. cit. pp. 242, 293 ff.; Marsh, *American
Historical Review*, 1926, pp. 233 ff.; Pippidi,
Athenaeum (Jassy), 1935 = *Autour de Tibère*,
pp. 113 ff., 120 f., n. 5; Seston, *Revue des
études anciennes*, 1943, p. 165. For him
see also Romanelli, *Epigraphica*, 1939,
pp. 99 ff.

these S.C. issues also. An appropriate occasion which occurred at the same date as the coinage is of precisely this character, and is one of the very few anniversary occasions of coinage which have ever been recognised (cf. p. 9). For Wruck[1] has assigned them to the half-centenary of the beginning of the Eastern S.C. series in *c.* 20–19 B.C.

The original issue of Augustus may well have celebrated Tiberius' success in the East in 20 B.C.;[2] and it is no doubt those achievements, even more than the concomitant S.C. coinage, of which the Tiberian issues commemorate the half-centenary. In Augustan publicity, the Eastern events of 20 B.C., and especially the *signa recepta*, took on an enormous significance, and indeed were represented as one of the landmarks in world history.[3] Moreover, in the eyes of many Easterners, it was from that time rather than from any other that the Principate may be said to have begun. Titus was to celebrate similarly the centenary of the same occasion, whereas Hadrian and Severus Alexander were to pay comparable attention to its 150th and 250th anniversaries respectively. There was, then, every reason why the half-centenary of those events should receive numismatic commemoration (just as they had received every form of celebration in the years immediately after they had taken place)—especially in view of Tiberius' part in them.

An isolated Galatian issue,[4] evidently official and the first of its kind since that of Priscus in A.D. 23–4 (p. 35), bears the date 50 (Plate II, 2) and thus commemorates the half-centenary of another aspect of the Eastern events of *c.* 20 B.C., namely the establishment of *provincia* Galatia in that year.[5] A later anniversary of another Galatian occasion was to be celebrated by Vespasian (pp. 91 f. n. 9).

Here, too, may be discussed the Roman *sestertii* with CIVITATIBVS ASIAE RESTITVTIS, showing Tiberius, laureate and togate, seated to left on a curule chair, with *patera* and sceptre (p. 32). These *sestertii* are dated TR. P. XXIIII. (A.D. 22–3), but, as has been pointed out, issues bearing the same date appear to have been struck at least as late as *c.* A.D. 29 (p. 33). This leaves us free to consider to which

---

1 Loc. cit. p. 43. See also his further observations on these issues on pp. 48 ff.

2 *FITA.* pp. 99 f.; cf. *SMACA.*

3 Oltramare, *Revue des études Latines*, 1938, p. 132; cf. Sutherland, *NC.* 1945, p. 64. (Mattingly, *Classical Review*, 1934, p. 161, believes the fourth *Eclogue* to have been revised at about that date.)

4 MHTHP ΘΕΩΝ ΕΤΕΙ N.: Imhoof-Blumer, *Griechische Münzen*, pp. 229, 759.

5 *FITA.* p. 99. The era is presumably the same as that celebrated by Priscus, i.e. it should date from 20 and not 25 B.C., *pace* Imhoof-Blumer, loc. cit.

date within the period *c.* A.D. 22–33 the issue of these *sestertii* can most appropriately be attributed. They commemorate the restoration of Asian cities damaged in recent earthquakes. But the coins were not, in any case, contemporary with the main earthquake, which, followed by a remission of taxes, had occurred in A.D. 17.[1] Nor can the coins have immediately followed even the second earthquake, of A.D. 20.[2] It was in A.D. 23 that the victims of this second disaster, Aegae and Cibyra, received a remission,[3] whereas Sardes celebrated a privilege of the same kind in *c.* 25.[4] The earlier of these two years seems also to have witnessed some resolution by the whole group of cities;[5] so it is at least a *possible* date for our coins.

But it was apparently not until *c.* A.D. 30 that the grateful Asian cities finally established their statuary dedications at Rome[6] and Puteoli.[7] It is to those that the type of the *sestertii* seems particularly relevant. We have seen that it was likewise in 30–1 that Tiberius celebrated—by his great Eastern S.C. issues and the provincial Galatian mintage—the half-centenary of the Augustan successes of 20–19 B.C. which had included the recovery of the standards. Now the events of that period 20–19 B.C., while Augustus was still in the East, had included an extensive reorganisation of the province of Asia. This reorganisation, as the present writer has endeavoured to show elsewhere, comprised *inter alia* the restoration or establishment of a number of cities.[8] It would be in keeping with the general policy of Tiberius for him to select, as a suitable occasion for the dedications and coinage *civitatibus Asiae restitutis*, the half-centenary of the restorations of cities by Augustus. We may tentatively explain the present *sestertii* accordingly, and attribute them to *c.* A.D. 30–1 and to this other aspect of the same anniversary occasion as prompted the Eastern S.C. coinage.

We can scarcely accept Eckhel's view that the seated figure of Tiberius represents him as a divinity.[9] Mattingly[10] and Schulz[11]

1 This is pointed out by Sutherland, *JRS.* 1938, p. 131.
2 Euseb.-Hieronymus 199. 3 (A.D. 19–20); Jacoby, *Fragmenta Historicorum Graecorum*, pp. 847, 1182.
3 Cf. Larsen, *Economic Survey of the Roman Empire*, IV, p. 712.
4 Buckler and Robinson, *Sardis*, VII, 1932, p. 29 nn. 1, 9.
5 *IGRR.* IV, 1514; cf. Rogers, loc. cit. p. 16.
6 Phlegon of Tralles, in Jacoby, loc. cit.;

cf. Rogers, *Studies in the Reign of Tiberius*, pp. 16 f.; Charlesworth, *CAH.* X, p. 651, preferred A.D. 22 as a date.
7 *ILS.* 156; cf. Rogers, Charlesworth, loc. cit.; *Catalogo della Mostra Augustea*, *App. Bibl.* p. 152.   8 *FITA.* pp. 349 ff.
9 *Doctrina Numorum*, I, p. 193; cf. Alföldi, *Röm. Mitt.* 1935, p. 18 n. 1.
10 *BMC. Imp.* I, p. cxxxiv.
11 *Die Rechtstitel und Regierungsprogramme auf römischen Kaisermünzen*, p. 89.

rightly describe his function here as that of the 'civil and religious head of the Roman state'. The type is not comparable to the seated figure of Augustus on coins of c. A.D. 22–3, for Tiberius is laureate and not radiate; he is seated on the curule chair of *civilitas* (cf. p. 57) and not a throne; he has no altar beside him; and he carries a half-length sceptre instead of a long one.[1] It is probably somewhat misleading to emphasise the Jovian character of his attitude;[2] though even if the Jovian analogy were intended, this might be due to too faithful reproduction of the statue dedicated by the Asian cities, or to a reminiscence of the Augustan half-centenary, rather than to deliberate official policy of Tiberius. The type, though expressive of the *statio principis*, is not incompatible with the carefully emphasised mortality of Tiberius.

(5) Our next issues are the first Latin *drachmae* of an Eastern mint which is plausibly assigned to Caesarea in Cappadocia. They show heads of Tiberius (laureate) and Drusus junior (bare), and are dated to A.D. 32–3 and 33–4.[3] The reference to the *decennium* of the death of Drusus is rather obvious. Nor is it surprising, especially in the light of the well-attested posthumous publicity for Drusus.[4] It is unnecessary to detect any special reference to the discovery of Tiberius, from A.D. 31, that Drusus had been murdered by Sejanus.[5] The immediate occasion for the issues may well have been military, since operations were impending in the East.

The Roman *asses* of Drusus bear his head and the reverse inscription PONTIF. TRIBVN. POTEST. ITER. round S.C. (p. 32 n. 11). Are certain Italian scholars right in considering these *asses* posthumous?[6] Local coinages with imitated portraits do not assist us to determine this point.[7] The only other official coin portraits of Drusus—other than undatable ones in Cyprus[8]—are provided by coins of Cyrene showing his head and those of his children, probably before his death.[9] The Cyrenaic portraits, however, show only a travesty of his real features, and there is no need to consider them imitations of

1 Cf. Alföldi, loc. cit. p. 115 n. 2.
2 Ibid. pp. 18 n. 1, 110.
3 *BMC. Imp.* 1, p. 144. 171, etc. The Paris specimen quoted there is of the earlier date, *pace* p. cxli of the same work. Cf. also Sydenham, *The Coinage of Caesarea in Cappadocia*, p. 31. 43 ff.
4 See especially Rogers, loc. cit. p. 153; cf. Stuart, *Classical Philology*, 1940, pp. 64 ff.

5 Conjectured by Cohen, cf. Laffranchi, *R. it.* 1918, p. 183, Mattingly, loc. cit. p. cxli.
6 E.g. Pietrangeli, *Civiltà Romana*, VII, 1938, pp. 60 f.
7 Cf. now *SMACA.*
8 *BMC. Cyprus*, p. 74. 8.
9 *BMC. Cyrenaica*, p. 121. 49 ff.

those on the Roman *asses*. It is true that Drusus enjoyed his second tribunician year for at least several months before his death,[1] but, as has been said, he was also commemorated for many years after his death. It must therefore be considered possible that these *asses*, like the *drachmae*, commemorate the tenth anniversary of that occasion. They might, however, equally signalise the *quinquennium* of his death, like posthumous coinages in honour of later personages (p. 99 n. 2). Or they might have been issued partly for the *quinquennium* and partly for the *decennium*, for the portraits vary.[2] If one had to choose between the two anniversaries, the former (A.D. 27–8) would perhaps be preferable, since the style of most portraits seems as close to A.D. 22–3 as to 34–7; but this point cannot be insisted upon.

(6) The last issue of Tiberius, apparently a *dupondius*, shows his bare head to left, the field being encircled by a laurel-wreath; on the reverse is TI. CAESAR DIVI AVG. F. IMP. VIII. round the edge, and TRIB. POT. XXXVIII. PONT. MAX. in field (Plate II, 3, 4).[3] It was issued in A.D. 37, and in style, type, and extreme rarity, it closely resembles two coins issued by Caligula after his accession in the same year (Plate II, 5).[4] The unusual feature of the wreath round the obverse seems to link the issue with the no less rare commemorative issues (or medallions) which have been tentatively attributed to a *legatus* of one of the Germanies (p. 63). Our present issue of Tiberius might have emanated from the same authority—perhaps again from Cn. Lentulus Gaetulicus (it does not look Eastern and we must reject Mowat's attribution to Cilicia).[5] It must, however, be borne in mind (as for the gold medallions of Augustus, and for medallic *aes* of Claudius) that, wherever it was distributed, the place of issue may possibly have been Rome.

Its character was probably commemorative: and the year A.D. 37–8 witnessed the centenary of one of the greatest occasions in the Roman *Fasti*, namely the birth of Augustus.[6] The epigraphic sources

1　Rogers, *American Journal of Philology*, 1940, pp. 457 ff.; id. *Studies in the Reign of Tiberius*, p. 132. But Blanchet, *Rn.* 1943, p. xlix, is in any case wrong in attributing the Roman *asses* to a date as early as A.D. 21.

2　The Cambridge collection has two coins with portraits that are suggestively different from the norm; but see *SMACA*.

3　Paris: Mowat, *Rn.* 1911, p. 429. 19; cf. *BMC. Imp.* I, p. 145 n.

4　*BMC. Imp.* I, p. 397. 108 *bis*; Mowat,

Rn. 1911, pp. 431. 20, 432. 21 (the latter with obverse titulature C. CAESAR GERMANICI F.M. AGRIPPAE N.).

5　Loc. cit. p. 431.

6　Cf. Snyder, *YCS.* 1940, p. 227, Fink, ibid. p. 159 n. 730; Gagé, *RGDA.* pp. 181 f. On the *natales* of *divi*, see especially Beurlier, *Essai sur le Culte rendu aux Empereurs Romains*, p. 73; Schwartz, *Revue des études anciennes*, 1944, pp. 266 ff. (p. 277 n. 3 Augustus).

emphasise the honours which anniversaries of that event received, in the principate of Tiberius[1] and long after.[2] Moreover, this centenary especially recommends itself as the occasion of the present issue in view of its equal appropriateness for celebration (in the same year) by the successive *principes*, Tiberius and Caligula, who issued these similar pieces in a single year.[3] Perhaps it also especially recommended itself to the *legatus* on the Rhine since it coincided with the half-centenary of the Western reorganisation of Augustus in *c.* 14–13 B.C.—the true commencement of the Principate for the Western provinces.[4] It is fitting that the anniversary coinages of Tiberius should conclude with one which celebrates the birth of Augustus and a great event of his reign.

Some time during the last years of the principate of Tiberius there was a varied, though exceedingly rare, *aes* issue by one Basila, a *legatus* of Galatia who has been identified as T. Helvius Basila.[5] Both the previous *aes* issues by Tiberian governors of Galatia have appeared to be of an anniversary character (pp. 35, 65), so that there is reason to expect the same to be true of Basila's coinage. The occasion, however, cannot be certainly identified. It may have been the fifteenth or twentieth anniversary of the consecration of Augustus and accession of Tiberius.[6] If, however, Ramsay is right in attributing this governorship to *c.* A.D. 37,[7] then Basila's coinage, like that of Cn. Lentulus Gaetulicus (?), possibly commemorates the centenary of the birth of Augustus.

1 List given by Snyder, loc. cit. p. 228, cf. p. 193 n. 937; cf. Gagé, *Revue archéologique,* xxxiv, 1931, p. 25; Henzen, *Acta Fratrum Arvalium,* pp. xxxvi, 51.
2 Cf. Snyder, loc. cit. p. 191 n. 925; Gagé, loc. cit. Cf. the coinage of Carausius, and perhaps even Justinian (see above, p. 41 n.).
3 Unless Caligula issued them both? Cf. perhaps Caligulan portraits of Divus Augustus (Plate II, 9, 10): cf. also *SMACA.*

4 According to Balsdon, *The Emperor Gaius,* p. 106, the situation in Germany in the last years of Tiberius was bad—thus necessitating propaganda.
5 *FITA.* pp. 328 n. 3, 354 n. 9, 399.
6 For the attribution to *c.* 30, see de Laet, *Samenstelling,* p. 243. 532, and n. 1, doubted by Cadoux, *JRS.* 1946, p. 201.
7 *The Social Basis of Roman Power in Asia Minor,* p. 114.

CHAPTER IV

CLAUDIUS AND NERO

(i) *Claudius*

It will be argued elsewhere[1] that, under Caligula, certain colonies, notably Nemausus (Plate II, 7, 8) and Patrae, issued coins or medallions for the combined occasions of his accession and their own half-centenary; and that another, Cnossus, issued a large coinage for the *vicennium* of the death of Germanicus (A.D. 39). An isolated Caesarean drachm of Germanicus with Divus Augustus,[2] and an even rarer and more isolated silver issue attributed to Antioch,[3] may commemorate the same occasion; but in general the official issues of Caligula—mainly dynastic—came into being too promptly for occasions other than the accession to be identifiable (but see pp. 68 f.).

It is a very different matter with Claudius, under whom anniversary types seem to have attained a new degree of complexity. It is to be expected that this antiquarian *princeps* should not neglect the now fully established traditionalist institution of the anniversary coinages. Indeed, inscriptional evidence indicates that Claudius was attentive to anniversaries and, not least, to the combination of them on single occasions. An instance is provided by the deification of Livia. This occurred in the year A.D. 42, which was the centenary of her birth (cf. p. 5). The day of the year selected for it was that of the eightieth anniversary of her marriage,[4] and incidentally also the day of the *Ludi Palatini* (a function which at a much later date appears to have witnessed commemorative issues, p. 156).[5]

The great year of anniversary coinage in this principate is A.D. 41–2. Perhaps the most striking, because the most complex, instance is provided by *aurei* and *denarii,* starting in that year, inscribed PACI AVGVSTAE.[6] The type accompanying that legend is a winged female figure, which advances to right. In her left hand

1 *CMG.*
2 *BMC. Imp.* I, p. 162. 105.
3 Paris: Wruck, *Die syrische Provinzial-prägung,* p. 180. 17, who attributes it to Syria.
4 Cf. Weber, *Princeps,* I, p. 101*.
5 The occasion was signalised by the issue of

dupondii (with the portrait of Divus Augustus and a figure of DIVA AVGVSTA as Ceres: *BMC. Imp.* I, p. 497. 224; cf. Sydenham, *NC.* 1917, p. 272); and also perhaps by Plate II, 9, 10 (cf. Sutherland, *NC.* 1941, Pl. I, 8–9).
6 *BMC. Imp.* I, p. 165. 6.

she holds a *caduceus*, and she bends her right arm upwards to draw a part of her robe up across her face. In front of her, rearing up from the ground, is a snake. In a discussion elsewhere[1] the present writer has endeavoured to substitute for earlier interpretations the view that, whereas the figure is *Pax* and her wings and *caduceus* symbolic of *Victoria* and *Mercurius-Felicitas* respectively, the gesture with her right arm indicates *Pudor-Pudicitia*.[2] But what concerns us here is rather the fact that the snake would undoubtedly suggest, to the majority of Romans who studied this type, *Salus*. "Several interpretations of this snake have been suggested,[3] but the most relevant one to Peace has not been recognised; and it happens also to be the same interpretation as demonstrably applies to at least 90 per cent of the numerous other appearances of the snake on imperial coinage, including a number well before the end of the first century.[4] All of these associate the snake with another 'Blessing'[5] with its roots deep in Roman antiquity, namely *Salus*. This is usually translated as 'Health', but I prefer to render it 'Well-Being'; for it referred in the first instance, from very early times, to the Common Weal, whereas the allusion to personal health only came in through second century B.C. Greek influences. Both versions may be read into the snake on our coin, for both had a meaning for Claudius. On the one hand his health had always been feeble; and on the other hand this antiquarian emperor took a deep interest in the primitive significance of *Salus*, as is shown by his revival, a few years later, of a most ancient and solemn ritual in which *Salus* was identified with the prosperity of the State, the *augurium salutis*.[6]

"Now the essential feature of this ceremony was that it could only be held in a profound state of Peace;[7] so it is easy to see why on our coin, as on an altar found in Eastern Spain,[8] it is with Peace that the

---

1 *PR.* = *Univ. of Edinburgh Journal*, 1949, pp. 229 ff., to which acknowledgments are due for the quotation starting at the foot of this page (pp. 238 f.).
2 Not, as is often supposed, Nemesis; reasons for this proposed change are offered in *PR.*; cf. also *CSNM*.
3 Nemesis, Minerva *Victrix* (*BMC. Imp.* I, p. cliii), Egypt (Rostovtzeff, *Journal of Egyptian Archaeology*, 1926, p. 25 and n. 2). A snake on *orichalcum* coinage of Caesar should have been mentioned in *FITA*. p. 7: it may have the same meaning as here.

4 *BMC. Imp.* I, p. 361. 265 (Galba), II, p. 47. 264 (Vespasian), p. 237. 84 (Titus).
5 Cicero, *De Legibus*, II, 11, 28; *PR.*
6 Tacitus, *Annals*, XII, 23; cf. *ILS.* 9337.
7 Dio 37. 24.
8 Deubner, *Röm. Mitt.* 1930, p. 37. This is the snake-staff of Aesculapius, whose relation to *Salus* was extremely close (Pliny, *NH.* xxix. 72; Vitruvius I, 2, 7; *CIL.* VI, 20, 30983). *Salus* is also linked with the other divinities symbolised by this type, Mercury (Cornutus, *Theol. Gr. Comp.* 16), *Felicitas* (Henzen, *Acta Fratrum Arvalium*, pp. 71 ff.,

snake of *Salus* is associated. The same two words are joined by Caesar;[1] and then, in 10 B.C., between the establishment of his great Altar of Peace and its dedication, Augustus founded an additional joint cult in which *Pax* and *Salus* were worshipped together.[2] Ovid[3] tells us that the same cult included Janus, a Roman god of remote and obscure antiquity who was likewise indissociably linked with Peace, for when wars came to an end the gates of Janus's temple were solemnly closed; and when peace was first established after the deaths of Antony and Cleopatra, the orders went out simultaneously for the closure of this temple of Janus and for the equally peaceful ceremony of the *augurium salutis*.[4] So Peace, *Salus* and Janus must be regarded as linked in the closest possible way.

"I want you to bear in mind this close connection while I point out to you a peculiar set of coincidences of certain dates. The coinage of Claudius which is my subject was initiated in A.D. 41. Now the year in which Augustus had inaugurated the joint cult of Peace, *Salus* and Janus was 10 B.C.—and this, bearing in mind that there was no A.D. 0, was exactly, to the nearest year, half a century earlier. Secondly, the earliest *augurium salutis* identifiable in historical times took place in 160 B.C.[5]—exactly 150 years earlier than Augustus's cult, and exactly 200 years before our coins of Claudius. This is striking enough, but it is not all. For here is a third peculiar coincidence. The first recorded temple of Janus, the partner of Peace and *Salus* in this pagan Trinity, was founded precisely 100 years earlier still—in 260 B.C.[6] This is all highly relevant to our coins of Claudius; for it means that they coincided exactly with the tercentenary of the temple of Janus, and equally exactly with no less than two further anniversaries based upon it—the second centenary of the earliest recorded *augurium salutis*, and the half-centenary of the joint cult of these two deities with Peace. In view of the historical and religious connections between these ideas, there are overwhelming odds

---

84 f., 168), and *Victoria* (*CIL.* VI, 30975 [A.D. 1])—who, like *Pax* (Curtius, *Ges. Abh.* II, 190), may originate from Athena (cf. Plutarch, *Pericles*, 13).

1 *Bellum Civile*, III, 57, 4.

2 Dio 54.35.2. Also *Concordia*, whose temple contained a *caduceus* (see above,

p. 54); for a link with *Salus* see *FITA.* p. 271. In the same year 10 B.C. an altar was dedicated to Mercury, *ILS.* 92.

3 *Fasti*, III, 881.

4 Dio 51.20.4.

5 Liegle, *Hermes*, 1942, pp. 249 ff.

6 Tacitus, *Annals*, II, 49; cf. above, pp. 4 f.

against the three coincidences to which I have referred all being due to mere chance (cf. pp. 3 f., 15 f., 52 f., 160)."

This is, then, a highly complex type, more so than the Augustan *Pax-Iustitia* (p. 39). "Such borrowings, and the intentional mixtures of identities and ideas that result from them, became a most characteristic feature of Roman thought also. Such combinations seem to the modern mind somewhat arid and artificial, but they came more easily to the Greek, and more easily still to the Roman, who spent a great deal of his time worrying that his prayers might not be directed to the right divinity or to a sufficient number of interested divinities, or even that he might not be addressing them by the right names; thus a dedication to Peace seemed much more likely to be effective, and her representation more likely to evoke a response from public opinion, if she were linked with as many kindred conceptions as possible."[1]

Back to Augustus again, but now to the part played by the father of Claudius in the Augustan principate, look the *aurei*, *denarii* and *sestertii* of Nero Drusus (NERO CLAVDIVS DRVSVS GERMANICVS IMP.),[2] the half-centenary of whose death fell in the second year of the reign of Claudius.[3] Dobiaš notes, though without comment, that 50 years elapsed between his death and this coinage[4] (cf. p. 9). Possibly an important monetary reform at Alexandria in the same year[5] was likewise intended to honour Nero Drusus, father of its benefactor Germanicus (p. 61). Anniversaries of the death of Nero Drusus had been kept alive even before his son became emperor;[6] an Augustan inscription records the *vicennium* of his first victories (p. 4 n. 9). The centenary of the death of Nero Drusus was apparently to receive commemoration from Domitian (pp. 96, 178).

By another anniversary coinage Claudius recorded his own connection with an important Augustan occasion. For an exceptional

1 *PR.*; cf. *CSNM.*

2 *BMC. Imp.* 1, p. 178. 95 ff., p. 186. 157; Stuart, *The Portraiture of the Emperor Claudius*, pp. 36 f. n. 188. The *aurei* and *denarii* are not Augustan, as tentatively Hill, *Historical Roman Coins*, p. 162; cf. Newby, *Numismatic Commentary on the Res Gestae of Augustus*, p. 73 n. 102.

3 For honours by Claudius, cf. Kornemann, *Gestalten und Reiche*, p. 277, etc.

4 *Transactions of the Numismatic Congress of* 1936, p. 161.

5 Cf. Milne, *Catalogue of Alexandrian Coins in the Ashmolean Museum*, p. xx.

6 Cf. Beurlier, *Essai sur le Culte rendu aux Empereurs Romains*, p. 73 n. 4; Pippidi, *Recherches sur le Culte Impérial*, pp. 196 f.; Abaecherli, *Studi e materiali di Storia delle Religioni*, 1935, p. 157. For the iconography of Nero Drusus, see Picard, *Revue des études Latines*, 1941, p. 274, etc.

Lugdunese *quadrans* (without P.P.)[1] revived the Altar of Lyons type and the inscription ROM. ET AVG., both obsolete since the early days of Tiberius.[2] This issue has been convincingly attributed to the fiftieth birthday of Claudius,[3] which very shortly followed his accession in A.D. 41. Claudius was born on 1 August 10 B.C.: and the very same year had probably witnessed the dedication (after a somewhat earlier consecration) of the great *Ara Romae et Augusti* at his birthplace, Lugdunum (pp. 12 f. n. 7). Nero repeated the ROM. ET AVG. type, and Carausius was to revive it on the tercentenary of the Altar (pp. 82 n. 3, 145).

Contemporary with these birthday pieces of Claudius, and comparable to them in anniversary purpose, was a series of common Roman *sestertii* with the new type of SPES AVGVSTA S.C., and Hope standing with flower.[4] This likewise refers to the birthday of Claudius, which fell on the same day of the year as the annual vows to *Spes*. It was, moreover, to *Spes* that Germanicus, the brother of Claudius, had dedicated a temple about 24 years earlier, in A.D. 17[5]— an occasion of which this coinage may celebrate the quarter-centenary year. There may well also be a topical allusion to the birth of the imperial heir, Britannicus, which occurred in 41 or 42.[6] *Spes* was to have a numismatic future devoted to such themes of heirship.

Another of the coinages that began in *c.* A.D. 41-2 was the large issue of *asses* with LIBERTAS AVGVSTA S.C.,[7] and a figure of that deity ('Blessing'), new to imperial coinage and last seen under Brutus.[8] This characteristic blend of innovation with tradition emphasises the official view that *libertas* was not irreconcilable with the Principate.[9] This needed stressing after the autocratic behaviour of Caligula; and in the days when, after his death, the future of the Principate hung in the balance, the watchword given by the consuls had been *Libertas*.[10] Claudius did not refrain from recording on his coinage that the

---

1 I.e. early; *BMC. Imp.* I, p. 196. 227.

2 Ibid. p. 62 and n. But the current attribution of the Tiberian cessation to as late a date as the Sacrovir-Florus revolt is very doubtful: see *APT.* Appendix 8.

3 *BMC. Imp.* I, p. clx. In honour of his birthday Claudius probably added an element to the ceremonies of 1 August, cf. *YCS.* 1940, p. 125. For the importance of imperial birthdays, see above p. 1 and n. 5.

4 *BMC. Imp.* I, p. 182. 124.

5 Cf. ibid. p. clvi.

6 For the day, see Schwartz, *Revue des études anciennes,* 1944, p. 275. Stuart, loc. cit. p. 55 n. 294, quotes *IGRR.* IV. 559 as commemorating the occasion.

7 *BMC. Imp.* I, p. 185. 145; cf. Scramuzza, *The Emperor Claudius,* p. 63.

8 *BMC. Rep.* II, pp. 480 ff., 71 ff.

9 On *libertas,* see *FITA.* pp. 324, 401 ff. (with references).

10 Cf. Piganiol, *Histoire de Rome,* p. 249.

senate had had little hand in his accession;[1] but these *asses* represent a gesture indicating that his principate intended to provide no less advantages than would have accrued from a restoration of the Republic.

This interpretation is given added point by the unrecognised anniversary character of the issue. According to tradition, A.D. 41–2 or 42–3 was the 550th year of the expulsion of the kings and foundation of the Roman *libertas*;[2] and according to one reckoning (p. 2 n. 7), 550 years was just five *saecula*. This anniversary was relevant to the Claudian version of the events of A.D. 41. Almost exactly 200 years later (though the precise date cannot be fixed within a year or two), another constitutionalist emperor, Gordian III, was to bring *Libertas* back to the coinage after all his immediate predecessors had refrained from using the type. The government of Claudius had surely also considered the anniversary to give added point to the type—as it does.

The remaining coinage of the 40's includes further anniversary issues, though it is difficult to identify all of them with accuracy. A possible example is provided by various pieces issued in honour of Germanicus, namely an extensive series of Roman *asses*,[3] an exceptionally rare Roman piece of *sestertius* size,[4] and a number of provincial issues. The last-named include an equally rare *as* (?) of Antioch, which has a Claudian portrait and appears to accompany a plentiful output of Antiochene *aes* of Claudius.[5] Germanicus was much honoured by Claudius and might therefore have received numismatic honour at any time during his reign. But the Roman *sestertii* and *asses* in his late brother's honour always attribute to Claudius the title P.P., and are unlikely, then, to have been issued before *c.* 43–4 at the earliest.[6] It is therefore by no means improbable that they should be assigned to the quarter-centenary of the death of Germanicus, which must have been celebrated in precisely that year.

---

1 IMPER. RECEPT. and PRAETOR. RECEPT. (*BMC. Imp.* I, p. 165. 5, p. 166. 8); cf. Sutherland, *JRS.* 1941, p. 72, etc.

2 The traditional date was 510–508 B.C.: Polybius III, 22. 1; cf. Varro, Beloch, *Römische Geschichte*, pp. 35 f. Pliny, *NH.* XXXIII, 19, and Cn. Flavius give 507 B.C.

3 *BMC. Imp.* I, p. 193. 215.

4 Ibid. no. 214.

5 Wruck, *Die syrische Provinzialprägung*, p. 61, p. 180. 24 ff.

6 Cf. Sutherland, *Reports of the Research Committee of the Society of Antiquaries of London*, XIV, 1947, p. 158 n. 5.

This interpretation of the issues as emanating from an anniversary occasion is in keeping with the extreme rarity of the Roman and Antiochene Germanicus pieces of *sestertius* and *as* (?) size respectively. They may well have been 'money-medallions' intended for private distribution only: the *sestertius* appears to provide an early example of the practice by which these special distribution pieces were to be of unusual artistic distinction.[1] The scarce, but not unusually rare, Claudian *sestertii* of Agrippina senior[2] may possibly be attributed to the same occasion, unless they refer rather to the *decennium* of her death, which must have been commemorated in c. 43.[3] The *decennium* of the death of another imperial lady, Antonia the mother of Claudius, is honoured by one of the first *aes* issues of Caesarea ever to bear an imperial portrait;[4] but this is apparently local.

Another feature of the numismatic history of this principate is the fine issue, attributed to Ephesus, of tetradrachms bearing the inscription COM. ASI., ROM. ET AVG. These represent the Asian temple of Rome and Augustus, apparently with Claudius standing in armour within it.[5] In the later years of the century, multiple Asian and Caesarean drachms with Latin legends were to be almost exclusively of an anniversary character (pp. 83 f., 92). There is little difficulty in conjecturing a similar occasion for the present issue. Among the greatest festivals in public religion were the commemoration days of Actium (31 B.C.) and of the capture of Egypt (30 B.C.). The 75th anniversaries of those events fell in A.D. 45 and 46 respectively. Still more relevant—in view of the inscription COM. ASI.—is the new organisation received by the *Commune Asiae* in 29 B.C.,[6] and first commemorated by tetradrachms issued by Augustus on the occasion of its first *decennium*.[7] Claudius's coinage

1 Cf. Toynbee, p. 212.

2 *BMC. Imp.* I, p. 194. 219; cf. Vulpe, *Dacia*, I, p. 213, Marcea-Berciu, *Apulum*, I, 1939–42, p. 199 n. 30, for finds.

3 No conclusion can be drawn from the alleged restoration of Agrippina senior's *sestertii* by Nerva, for such pieces are false; cf. Mattingly, *BMC. Imp.* III, p. l. These forgeries seem first to have been published in *Periodico di Numismatica e Sfragistica*, 1868, p. 50.

4 Sydenham, *The Coinage of Caesarea in Cappadocia*, p. 35. 61; *BMC. Galatia*, etc.

p. 46. 13 (Antonia and Octavia standing). For Caesarea under Claudius see also Stuart, *The Portraiture of the Emperor Claudius*, p. 12 n. 90.

5 *BMC. Imp.* I, p. 196. 228, cf. *SWC*. Alföldi interprets the imperial figure as *proconsul* (*Röm. Mitt.* 1935, p. 47, Abb. 5). See also for this figure Bernoulli, *Römische Ikonographie*, II, 1, pp. 329 f.; Stuart, loc. cit. p. 37.

6 Cf. *FITA*. p. 377.

7 *BMC. Imp.* I, p. 114. 705; cf. *SWC*.

at this Asian mint (no doubt through the proconsul, whose name is unknown) seems to have signalised anniversaries of these occasions. The only tetradrachm known of Vespasian—with closely corresponding types—was to commemorate the centenary of the same events (p. 88). Another 75th anniversary (A.D. 48–9),[1] that of the *restituta respublica* in 27 B.C.—which continued to be a great day in *Fasti* and *Ferialia*—may possibly be the occasion of a very rare revival of Tiberian DIVVS AVGVSTVS PATER 'Altar' *asses*, with Claudian portraits (Plate II, 11).[2]

The rare Claudian official issues in honour of Germanicus have, in conjunction with the common Roman *asses*, been ascribed to the quarter-centenary of his death (p. 75). Another anniversary is very likely to be the occasion of equally rare *aes* mintages in honour of Agrippina junior and Nero, and of commoner *aurei* and *denarii* that are seemingly of the same date.[3] The rare *aes* issues of Nero include a *sestertius*[4] and *dupondius*[5] both of Balkan provenance, and the former is paralleled by *sestertii* of Agrippina junior from the same part of the world.[6] Likewise, there are scarce Ephesian tetradrachms both of mother[7] and son,[8] the former being accompanied by her husband Claudius. The commencement of these issues is attributable to *c.* A.D. 51, to which some of them are actually dated.[9] Now the *decennium* of Claudius occurred, and was celebrated, in precisely that year: nor was he likely to deviate from the practice of his predecessors, who had always signalised their *decennia* by important mintages (pp. 19 ff., 31 ff.).

But what was new to such coinages was the vigorously dynastic character of these decennial issues, which present a contrast to the complex traditions evoked by the corresponding coinages of Augustus and Tiberius. Caligula had not lived to celebrate even a *quinquennium*; so it was left to the government of Claudius, and to the influence of Agrippina junior, to prompt this innovation[10]—and,

1 For religious events of 48–9 see Scramuzza, *The Emperor Claudius*, p. 237, cf. n. 113; Nock, *CAH.* x, p. 499.

2 E.g. illustrated by Sutherland, *NC.* 1941, ibid. Pl. III, 13 (?), 18; cf. 19 (ibid. p. 112 n. 21: head r., Vienna), and 7.

3 *BMC. Imp.* I, p. 174. 72, p. 175. 79, p. 176. 82 and 84, p. 177. 89.

4 Ibid. p. 195 and n. (Paris and Berlin).

5 Ibid. p. 397. 242 *bis*; Toynbee, p. 29 n. 7; Alföldi, *Röm. Mitt.* 1935, p. 24 n. 3.

6 *BMC. Imp.* I, p. 195 and n. (Berlin and Sofia).

7 Ibid. p. 197. 231 and 234.

8 Ibid. p. 198. 236.

9 Ibid. p. clx. Cf. a Caesarean issue, *BMC. Galatia*, etc. p. 47. 14 (ET. I; Mount Argaeus).

10 Claudius's marriage with Agrippina seems to have stimulated the output of his statues as well; cf. Stuart, loc. cit. p. 41. For her iconography, see Fuchs, *Die Antike*, 1938, pp. 265 ff., etc.

apparently, to the governors of Asia and Moesia, as well as to the mint coining gold and silver at Rome, to carry it out. The former of these governors may have been P. Memmius Regulus, P. Suillius Rufus or L. Pedanius Secundus,[1] whereas the governor of Moesia was probably C. Terentius Tullius Geminius[2] or Flavius Sabinus.[3] But the *aes* issues, even if intended for Moesian distribution, may conceivably have been issued at Rome: the same *caveat* has been entered for medallic pieces of Augustus (p. 24) and Tiberius (p. 62), for whom, incidentally, an earlier governor of Moesia may already have struck an anniversary issue (p. 42).

The rare *sestertius*-sized pieces of Agrippina junior and the young Nero seem to be the successors of similar anniversary 'money-medallions' of the early Principate (p. 60), and the forerunners of medallions proper. At Rome (as in the case of the Germanicus *sestertius*) such rare pieces sometimes still bore the symbol s.c., to indicate that they were explicitly or implicitly authorised by a *senatusconsultum* authorising a major issue. In the provinces, the *legati pro praetore* of Tiberius and Caligula had already made similar private issues, not necessarily connected with any accompanying issue or *senatusconsultum* (p. 68). But Caligula had started a new custom by doing the same thing even at Rome. His ADLOCVT. COH. *sestertii*[4] do not bear the letters s.c. or s.p.q.r. They may have been issued as additional pay for the praetorian guard:[5] at so early a date the absence of s.c. seems to imply some closer connection with the *princeps* than other issues possessed.[6] The exceptional Germanicus *sestertii* of Claudius, by including s.c. and accompanying a large series of *asses*, exhibit a return to orthodoxy in this respect. Nero was to repeat the Caligulan innovation, but the Flavians reverted to the more conservative practice.[7]

1 Cf. de Laet, *Samenstelling*, p. 240, nos. 682, 794, 719.
2 Between A.D. 47 and 54: Stein, *Dissertationes Pannonicae*, I. 2, 1940, p. 28; between A.D. 47 and 50 according to de Laet, loc. cit. p. 236.
3 De Laet, loc. cit.
4 *BMC. Imp.* I, p. 151. 33.
5 Balsdon, *The Emperor Gaius*, p. 34; Toynbee, p. 28 n. 4; cf. Dio 59. 2. 1.
6 Cf. Toynbee, p. 28 cf. n. 4. But on the approximate equivalence of s.p.q.r. to s.c. see above, p. 20. But, even under Augustus, ROM. ET AVG. coins had lacked s.c. or s.p.q.r.

7 The last identifiable anniversary coinage of Claudius is represented by a strange colonial *aes* piece (Lederer, *NC.* 1943, pp. 92 f.: coll. Scheyer, Lugano; second specimen in present writer's possession). It shows portraits of Nero (not yet *princeps*) and Britannicus, and is African in style. The colony calls itself C.H., which might be either Hippo Diarrhytus or Hadrumetum; Lederer attributed it to Hippo Diarrhytus. This is one of the *coloniae Iuliae* of whose foundation we do not know the exact date (*FITA.* p. 461). It may have occurred at any time between the battle of Thapsus in 46 and the end of 28 B.C.

(ii) *Nero*

The year of Nero's accession coincided with the beginning of the fifth *decennium* since the consecration of Augustus. It is not surprising that so signal an occasion is noticed by the coins—especially as there was, from this time, a second imperial *divus*, in the person of Claudius, to accompany the divine Augustus. The first *aurei* and *denarii* of the new principate (with a new deference to the senate indicated by the legend EX S.C.) are programme issues for Agrippina junior and for Nero (in that order of emphasis);[1] but immediately thereafter the three themes to which reference has been made—accession, deification and anniversary—appear blended on the coinage. But the anniversary motif is dual. For the next *aurei* and *denarii* of Nero and Agrippina (A.D. 55) show the two deified emperors[2] (or possibly Augustus and Livia)[3] in an elephant quadriga; whereas the contemporary, or almost contemporary, pieces of DIVVS CLAVDIVS AVGVSTVS show an empty quadriga.[4] These two quadrigae, with divergent details, were precisely the types of the *sestertii* of Tiberius (p. 44) which had commemorated the twentieth

---

If, however, it was founded by Caesar immediately after the battle of Thapsus, then the last year of Claudius (Jan.–Oct. A.D. 54)—under whom this piece was struck —was the 100th year of the colony, and thus a suitable date for such an exceptional issue. The local custom of issuing centenary coinages was not yet dead in Africa: for the 100th anniversary of the Mauretanian colony of Babba seems to have been signalised by a coinage under Nero (*FITA.* pp. 222 f.). Hippo Diarrhytus does not, incidentally, appear to be one of the colonies of which the foundation had been commemorated by contemporary coinage, and this omission would be not unexpected in the case of a *deductio* in 46 B.C.: for no local foundation coinages of a date before *c.* 45 B.C. have been identified (ibid. p. 308).

Hippo Diarrhytus, in its dynastic zeal, represents Britannicus as well as Nero (for dedications to the former see Stuart, loc. cit. pp. 14, 18, 25, 42, 55 nn.; Collart, *Z. f. Schweizerische Archäologie u. Kunstgeschichte,* II, 1940). There was nothing new in a colonial coinage commemorating heirs once or twice removed, as well as the heir apparent

(*FITA.* pp. 268, 320). It may be added that Augustus, who had figured on the earlier coinage of this city (ibid. p. 224, cf. n. 5), had been dead for exactly 40 years in A.D. 54, and that anniversary too may have played its part in inspiring so exceptional an issue. Possibly the governor who authorised it was Curtius Rufus (de Laet, *Samenstelling,* pp. 72, 115. 604; *PIR².* II. 394. 1618), and possibly the coins were intended for private distribution rather than for circulation. See also *CMG.*

1 *BMC. Imp.* I, p. 200. 1, cf. p. clxxi.
2 As M. & S. I, p. 145 n. 10; *BMC. Imp.* I, p. clxxii; Stuart, loc. cit. p. 38.
3 As Cohen, I, p. 275. 3; Sydenham, *The Coinage of Nero,* p. 46 n. 2. Id., p. 47 n., expresses disagreement with attributions to Claudius and Messalina.
4 *BMC. Imp.* I, p. 200. 4; cf. p. clxxiii, and Grether, *American Journal of Philology,* 1946, p. 247 n. 153. On Divus Claudius in general, see Charlesworth, *JRS.* 1937, p. 57; Stuart, loc. cit. p. 41; and for issues in his honour at Caesarea and other mints, see below, p. 83.

anniversary of the death of Augustus. Their recurrence on its fortieth anniversary was no doubt deliberate.[1]

Augustus, Tiberius and Claudius had laid great numismatic emphasis on the *decennia* of their principates, and Nero does the same. His *decennium*—to which Laffranchi has detected a reference in the Arval *Acta*[2]—was particularly significant since it coincided with the half-centenary of the death of Augustus. In the present writer's opinion this combined anniversary was the occasion of Nero's great revival of *aes*—involving its reissue after a suspension of nearly two decades—which, on independent grounds, is assigned to A.D. 64.[3] Many emperors selected important anniversary occasions for their revivals and reforms of *aes* coinage (p. 41). It would appear to be strange if, with these analogies, the coincidence of Nero's reform with so important an anniversary[4] were due to mere chance—particularly since Nero had expressly named Augustus as his model.[5]

Furthermore, the reformed coinage of Nero includes a number of individual types which tell the same story. The issues in question are the following: (1) the common *aurei* and *denarii* with Vesta and her temple;[6] (2) the *dupondii* and *asses* with Victory types,[7] many of them equally common; (3) the rare variants of those coins lacking S.C.;[8] (4) the exceedingly rare *as*-sized pieces with types of PROVIDENT. and altar;[9] (5) Eagle on globe;[10] and (6) Neptune;[11] and (7) the *aurei* and *denarii*, of medium scarcity, with AVGVSTVS AVGVSTA and the figures of an emperor and empress[12] (p. 83).

With regard to (1), which is, on grounds regardless of anniversaries, attributed to A.D. 64 or soon after,[13] the last temple of Vesta to appear previously on the coinage (p. 34) had commemorated the

1 On the other hand an isolated gold *quinarius* issued by Nero in A.D. 55–6 may possibly commemorate the centenary of Julius Caesar's death: see Appendix I.
2 *Atti e Memorie dell' Istituto italiano di Numismatica*, 1921, p. 58. For the connection between *Adventus* and anniversaries, cf. below, pp. 140, 151 f.
3 Toynbee, *NC.* 1947, pp. 131, 135; cf. Sydenham, *The Coinage of Nero*, p. 15.
4 No political turning-point can be assigned to the year: Toynbee, loc. cit. p. 130, against L'Orange, *Apotheosis in Ancient Portraiture*, p. 57.
5 Suetonius, *Nero*, 10. 1.

6 *BMC. Imp.* I, p. 213. 101 ff.; cf. Brown, *Numismatic Notes and Monographs*, xc, 1940, p. 20 n. 19.
7 *BMC. Imp.* I, p. clxxxi; Sydenham, loc. cit. pp. 103 f.
8 *BMC. Imp.* I, loc. cit., etc.
9 *BMC. Imp.* I, p. 276 n.; Sydenham, loc. cit. p. 114.
10 *BMC. Imp.* I, Sydenham, loc. cit.
11 *BMC. Imp.* I, loc. cit.; Sydenham, loc. cit. p. 115.
12 *BMC. Imp.* I, p. 208. 52; Sydenham, loc. cit. p. 128.
13 *BMC. Imp.* I, p. clxxxv; Sydenham, loc. cit. p. 105.

tenth year after the death of Augustus. Likewise, similar types in the future were to be almost completely restricted (except for personal allusions to empresses) to centenaries and half-centenaries of that same occasion (pp. 91, 135). (2), the Neronian type of 'Victory', a type closely connected with *vota* (p. 21), was carefully imitated from Tiberian pieces commemorating the *decennium* of Augustus's death (p. 34) (the type was to recur on contorniates apparently commemorating the 350th anniversary of the same event). The inauguration of Nero's Victory coins, and of their rare variants without s.c.—like similar rare variants of other common Neronian *aes*[1]—has been attributed on stylistic grounds to the anniversary year A.D. 64 or thereabouts.[2] This consideration, and the simultaneous reappearance of framed 'pseudo-medallions',[3] remind us of the custom, inherited from earlier emperors, by which extensive coinages on anniversary occasions were sometimes accompanied by small issues intended for private distribution only (p. 60).

Among his issues inaugurated in *c.* A.D. 64, Nero may also have included pieces of medallic appearance (sometimes accompanying common or fairly common issues of the same types) *with* s.c.[4] These presumably emanated, directly or indirectly, from a *senatusconsultum Caesaris auctoritate* authorising *aes* coinage. It seems certain that so important a reform as that of *c.* A.D. 64 originated from a special *senatusconsultum*, particularly as Nero's reign had hitherto witnessed no regular Roman *aes* issues. But such *senatusconsulta* had already under Tiberius become infrequent and comprehensive (p. 33); and the single Neronian decree may well, without repetition, have authorised all the remaining vast *aes* coinage of his reign.

As regards Nero's pieces lacking s.c., Caligula too had issued a Roman *sestertius* (p. 78) without that mark; but this step does not seem to have been repeated—except possibly for Claudian issues which, even if struck at Rome, were intended for Moesia (p. 78)—until it now recurs, on a considerable scale and accompanied by other

---

1 *BMC. Imp.* I, p. clxxix n. 1; cf. Toynbee, p. 29 nn. 10, 11; Sydenham, loc. cit. pp. 38, 103; Gnecchi, III, pp. 4 ff.
2 Sydenham, loc. cit. p. 104, etc.
3 Toynbee, p. 26, cf. n. 3.
4 For the doubtful Levis collection piece,

see *BMC. Imp.* I, pp. 217 n., clxvi; Sydenham, loc. cit. p. 103. 44, cf. n. 2, and for the equally questionable Walters collection piece with the harbour of Ostia, *BMC. Imp.* I, p. 222 n.; Sydenham, loc. cit. p. 108. 4; Toynbee, p. 26 n. 3.

novelties, in the decennalian year of Nero.[1] Perhaps this, the fiftieth year after the death of Augustus, witnessed a breach of his precedent, namely a considerable diminution in the direct connection between *senatusconsulta* and individual *aes* mintages. Did the former, from now on, authorise coinage not only for an indefinite period, but also within such wide limits that this or that issue could be sponsored, without the senatorial countersign, by the imperial secretariat? At all events the earlier method for authorising official *aes* coinage, based on a series of *senatusconsulta*, is showing signs of decline; perhaps now each one gave the *princeps* of its day something like *carte blanche*.[2]

Another of the vagaries of Nero's *aes* series is provided by the exceptionally rare pieces (4) to (6) above, with types revived from *asses* issued respectively in *c*. A.D. 29(?) (p. 62), 34–7 (p. 44), and the late 30's or early 40's.[3] The last-named of those prototypes was in honour of Agrippa, but the other two had commemorated Augustus; and it is very probable that all these pieces were, like other issues, reminiscent of the half-centenary of the latter's death. Doubt is attached to the theory that they were emergency issues from the mint of Lugdunum made after the fire of A.D. 65.[4] On stylistic grounds it seems rather more probable that they emanated from another Western mint unknown to us. Possibly they were issued privately by a *proconsul* or *legatus*—perhaps the former in view of the appearance of s.c., omitted by the *legatus* of Moesia (?) (p. 78)—to commemorate the anniversaries that occurred in the year 64.

The *aurei* and *denarii* with AVGVSTVS AVGVSTA, (7), are left to the end because their attribution to this occasion is even more

1 This phenomenon implies a minor qualification of Toynbee's description of the revival of 64 as 'a return to Roman numismatic tradition' (*JRS*. 1948, p. 161; *NC*. 1947, p. 131).
2 Possibly in due course a *senatusconsultum* to this effect was incorporated in the *lex de imperio* of each *princeps* on accession. On *ILS*. 244, sometimes considered to be the *lex de imperio* of Vespasian, see especially Last, *CAH*. XI, pp. 406 ff. (references on p. 897), ibid. XII, pp. 352 ff.; also Levi, *Rivista di Filologia*, 1938, pp. 1 ff.; *Athenaeum*, 1938, pp. 85 ff.; Piganiol, *Histoire de Rome*, p. 285. The present writer cannot accept all the conclusions on this subject of Magdelain, *Auctoritas Principis*, pp. 90 ff.

3 For the date of the original Agrippa *aes* with the type of Neptune see *CMG*., where A.D. 37 (Caligula) is proposed. Nero's revivals also included the ROM. ET AVG. Altar type (*BMC. Imp.* I, p. 279 n.; Sydenham, loc. cit. p. 115), but not apparently for an anniversary occasion (as far as can be determined at present), unlike the revivals of the same type by Claudius and Carausius (p. 145).
4 As Sydenham, loc. cit. It is doubtful whether they are from Tiberian dies, as Sydenham, ibid., cf. M. & S. I, p. 177. They are clearly not hybrids, though other Tiberius-Nero hybrids exist (M. & S. loc. cit.).

tentative. But these coins, too, seem to belong to *c.* A.D. 64–5 rather than a later date;[1] and, even if the personages represented are indeed Nero and Poppaea[2]—not Statilia Messalina—rather than Augustus and Livia, the form of the legend implies a significant reference to the latter couple.[3] For the male is radiate; and though Nero was the first *princeps* to use the radiate crown on coinage of his lifetime[4] (i.e. on *aes* from *c.* 64 onwards), yet it was fitting that this innovation should coincide with the half-centenary of the award, on deification, of the radiate crown to Augustus, its holder *par excellence*.[5] The female figure appears as *Concordia*, and this is a divinity which had been thought suitable for a coinage commemorating the *vicennium* of the death and consecration of Augustus (p. 52).

Seven coinages have been selected as possibly including specific references to the half-centenary of those events, and to the *decennium* of Nero.[6] Some of these attributions may meet with disagreement, but even if only a few are accepted the link between the monetary reform of *c.* A.D. 64 and the joint Augustan and Neronian anniversaries is probable. The same joint occasion is perhaps responsible for the fact that, in this year, A.D. 63–4, the official mint of Alexandria produced an enormous output of tetradrachms—more than twice as large as in any previous year.[7] Attributable to the same occasion are Nero's drachms (with Latin inscriptions but Greek dates), apparently of the official mint of Caesarea in Cappadocia, dated, like the Alexandrian series, to his tenth year (A.D. 63–4).[8] The commemorative character of these is stressed by the fact that they are Nero's only dated silver issues made at Caesarea. Mention should be made here of some further drachms and didrachms—at Caesarea and perhaps other mints[9]—of Nero and Divus Claudius.[10] These

---

1 Cf. M. & S. I, p. 147 n. 1.
2 As Alföldi, *Röm. Mitt.* 1935, p. 109, C.P., *Bullettino del Museo dell' Impero Romano*, 1941, p. 115, against Nicodemi, *Catalogo del Museo Sforzesco*, s.v.
3 Cf. Toynbee, *NC.* 1947, p. 139.
4 Mommsen, *Römisches Staatsrecht*, I³, pp. 428 f.; Piganiol, *Histoire de Rome*, p. 452; Alföldi, loc. cit. pp. 139 f. n. 2 (bibliography).   5 Alföldi, loc. cit.
6 Possibly Corinth too may provide an issue in *c.* A.D. 63–5, signed by L. Rutilius Piso and P. Memmius Cleander (West, *Corinth*, VI, p. 23), just before its 100th anniversary (i.e. they are not *quinquennales*);

but this is too conjectural to be given detailed attention here.
7 Cf. Milne, *Catalogue of the Alexandrian Coins in the Ashmolean Museum*, p. xx.
8 *BMC. Galatia*, etc., p. 47. 14; cf. Sydenham, loc. cit. p. 157.
9 For the stylistic distinctions, see *BMC. Galatia*, etc., p. 171 n., where they are ascribed to Antioch. *BMC. Imp.* I, p. clxxxiv, attributes them to Caesarea, and Imhoof-Blumer, *Abh. München*, 1890 = *Griechische Münzen*, pp. 687ff., Head, *Historia Numorum* p. 384, to Crete.
10 *BMC. Imp.* I, p. 282. 413 ff., p. 283. 418 ff.

may well be contemporary and attributable to the same half-centenary;[1] the Caesarean mint had already shown an interest in anniversaries under Tiberius (p. 67) and Claudius (p. 76 n. 4), and was to revert to the same themes later in the century (p. 92).

The death of the first *princeps* does not appear to have been the only Augustan event which received anniversary commemoration under Nero. The latter's third year (A.D. 56–7) had already witnessed a revival of official tetradrachms at Alexandria.[2] These were the first tetradrachms to have been struck for ten years, and the issue was a larger one than had been made in any year of the preceding principate. Most similar monetary reforms and revivals at Alexandria were due to an anniversary occasion (p. 41 n. 5), and this seems to be no exception.[3] For in A.D. 57 began the 100th year after the conferment of *imperium* on Augustus in 43 B.C. That was a date to which great prominence had been given in the early imperial *Fasti*, and this emphasis continued at least as late as Constantius II (p. 152). The bicentenary of the same occasion was to be signalised by Antoninus Pius with a dedication and coinage. The conferment of *imperium* in 43 B.C. is the only one of his various awards of that power which Augustus chooses to mention in the *Res Gestae*.[4] This had its effect on later emperors and scholars to whom, unlike Augustus, *imperium* was a synonym for the Principate. Thus it was from 43 B.C. that Victor[5] and Eusebius[6] were to calculate the beginning of the rule of Augustus; and at an earlier date the *Lex Narbonensis* had likewise attached especial importance to that year.[7] Augustus himself may have noted, or arranged, the coincidence of the *vicennium* of 43 B.C.[8] with a great administrative reform.[9]

The concluding period of Nero's principate witnessed further anniversary issues. One of these is provided by the same official mint

---

1   *BMC. Imp.* I, p. 282 n. 2. The type had already appeared near the beginning of the reign.
2   Milne, loc. cit.
3   There was also a topical military occasion, ibid. p. xxv.
4   Cf. *FITA*. p. 418. On Augustus's emphasis on this date, see Gagé, *Revue historique*, 1936, p. 280.
5   *Epitome de Caesaribus*, I, 30; cf. Snyder, *YCS*. 1940, p. 231 n. 13.
6   Ed. Schoene, II, p. 138; cf. Snyder, loc. cit.
7   *ILS.* 112; cf. Hoey, *YCS.* 1940, p. 193 n. 937 (for recent discussion and bibliography,

see Riccobono, *Fontes Iuris Romani Ante-justiniani*², I, 1941, pp. 199 ff.). Whether the *Feriale Duranum* did likewise is uncertain: Fink, *YCS.* 1940, p. 67.
8   In considering anniversaries of 43 B.C. it cannot usually be determined with certainty which of the great occasions of that year is being celebrated: for *Fasti* honour not only the conferment of *imperium* but also that of the *imperator* title and consulship (Gagé, *RGDA.* pp. 163, 171 f., 178). Perhaps sometimes the death of Caesar also plays a part.
9   On 23 B.C. see now *AC*.

of Alexandria. For that is the only possible explanation of the billon tetradrachms of Nero's thirteenth year with the head of Tiberius, duly inscribed ΤΙΒΕΡΙΟΣ ΚΑΙΣΑΡ.[1] This is the first appearance of Tiberius at Alexandria since his lifetime; this thirteenth year of Nero's reign (A.D. 66–7) is also the year of the *tricennium* of the death of Tiberius. The suggestion that this occasion was celebrated by Nero need not be considered any more surprising than the evident fact that the official issues of Alexandria under that emperor represented Tiberius at all. In reality, neither of these points should surprise us; nor, indeed, should any other posthumous reference to Tiberius during the first century.[2] His reputation remained high throughout that period. Caligula had already accorded him numismatic and other honours (p. 48), and Claudius honoured him also;[3] a number of statues of Tiberius are of Claudian date.[4] Vespasian (whose so-called *lex de imperio* duly mentions Tiberius) was to repeat the latter's *Iustitia* type on its half-centenary (p. 91), and later anniversaries of other Tiberian coinages are also celebrated (p. 97, cf. n. 4). Not only Vespasian and his sons, but Nerva and even Trajan, restore his types;[5] and Tiberius still appears in a Smyrna temple in the time of Caracalla.[6] There is inscriptional evidence of much other posthumous celebration,[7] and Nero, being himself a Claudian, was not likely to refrain from taking his part in this.[8] The evils of the reign of Tiberius had not yet been magnified out of proportion by a number of special circumstances; and he naturally had his place in the Caesareum at Alexandria.[9]

---

1 Milne, loc. cit. pp. xxv, xxxv, 7.

2 Tiberian reminiscences on the coinage are commented on by Toynbee, *NC*. 1927, p. 291; *BMC. Imp.* III, p. xc; M. & S. II, p. 304.

3 Cf. Dio 60. 10.

4 A.D. 45–6 (*Africa Italiana*, 1940–1, pp. 76 f., 91, Abb. 76, 77; Schweitzer, *Röm. Mitt.* 1942, p. 105; Poulsen, *Acta Archaeologica*, 1946, p. 47). Cf. the posthumous silver bust (Merlin, *Revue archéologique* [*L'Année épigr.*], 1941, p. 330. 105); cf. others cited by Curtius, *Röm. Mitt.* 1935, p. 270 (but see Poulsen, loc. cit. p. 13); Poulsen, loc. cit. p. 9 and n. 32 (but it may have been adapted to another person, ibid. n. 31).

5 Toynbee, *NC*. 1927, p. 291, etc.

6 *BMC. Ionia*, p. 288. 403.

7 E.g. his cult in Lycia (Fougères, *De Lyciorum Communi*, p. 105), the names of months at Aphrodisias, Prusa, etc. (Beurlier, *Essai sur le Culte rendu aux Empereurs Romains*, p. 160).

8 A portrait-bust of Tiberius (conceivably adapted to another person) seems to be Neronian (end of n. 4). Seneca(?), *Apocolocyntosis*, 1, 2, is complimentary about him (*ad deos isse*); cf. Vittinghoff, *Der Staatsfeind in der römischen Kaiserzeit*, p. 87 n. 382. For Nero as a reincarnation of Tiberius in a pejorative sense, cf. Schwartz, *Revue des études anciennes*, 1944, p. 275.

9 On this, see Bell, *Jews and Christians in Egypt*, pp. 35, 60.

A second anniversary issue of the last years of Nero's principate consists of *denarii* with *aquila* and two standards on the reverse.[1] These are convincingly attributed to early A.D. 68.[2] The type had been absent from the coinage for a very long time; but now it reappears, not only on Nero's coins, but on the almost exactly contemporary *denarii* of L. Clodius Macer in Africa. There it is accompanied by the inscriptions LEG. I. MACRIANA LIB.[3] and LEG. III. AVGVSTA.[4] The reminiscence of Antony's legionary *denarii* is unmistakable: and the most probable date for the inauguration of the latter (*c.* 33–2 B.C.[5]) was precisely 100 years before the *denarii* of Nero and Macer. (Moreover, one of these *denarii* of Macer, with type of lion's scalp,[6] seems—though this cannot be considered equally certain—to look back to an isolated legionary *denarius* of Octavian,[7] again of *c.* 33–2 B.C.,[8] with the rare type of a lion, which also appears on official Mauretanian *aes* of the same date.)[9]

That the century interval between Antony and Macer did not fail to influence the latter's types is confirmed by the facts that the next revival of Antony's legionary *denarii* occurred in *c.* A.D. 165–9, just 200 years after the original issue (p. 107), and that its third centenary likewise witnessed one of the few subsequent revivals of legionary issues (p. 137). Under these circumstances it cannot be agreed that the coincidence between Antony's and Macer's types is fortuitous.[10] It is just possible that the latter honoured this centenary because Antony's *denarii* were the last coins previously struck by an opponent of the Julio-Claudian house. It is also possible that Nero responded with the almost identical type in order to show that it was rather he, as a descendant of Antony, who could claim the type as his; for descent from Antony had already become a factor of which an earlier

1 *BMC. Imp.* I, p. 214. 107. Of about the same date seems to be a centenary issue, apparently of *colonia* Babba, with AVGVSTVS DEDVCTOR (*FITA.* p. 222).
2 *BMC. Imp.* I, p. clxxv; Sydenham, *The Coinage of Nero*, p. 130.
3 *BMC. Imp.* I, p. 286 n.
4 Ibid. p. 286. 3 f.
5 *BMC. Rep.* II, p. 526 n. 1.
6 *BMC. Imp.* I, p. 286. 3; p. clxxxviii, Mowat conjectures that this was the old badge of *Legio III Augusta*.
7 *BMC. Rep.* II, p. 417; Willers, *NZ.* 1902, pp. 80, 83; Ritterling, *PW.* XII, 1376

(LEG. XVI). The mintage is uncertain; it might be African.
8 *FITA.* p. 60 n. 7 argues for its pre-Actian date: its titulature (IMP. CAESAR DIVI F.) is that of Mauretanian *aes* (see next note) of *c.* 33–1, a period to which (since this titulature was short-lived) the *denarius* also should be assigned.
9 Charrier, *Description des monnaies de la Numidie et de la Mauretanie*, p. 165; *FITA.* p. 60.
10 As *BMC. Imp.* I, p. clxxxviii; Proskey and Mabbott, *Numismatic Review*, I, 1 (June 1943), p. 32.

princeps, Caligula, was not ashamed.[1] But Macer seems to echo legionary coinage of Octavian as well as of Antony; and probably the main motive behind these centenary issues of Nero and Clodius Macer was a more general one, namely the great popularity and fame of Antony's issues, especially among the legions themselves. They were still in circulation long after this date.[2] The type was repeated, with the addition of prows, by Galba[3] and Vitellius.[4]

1 Cf. Balsdon, *The Emperor Gaius*, pp. 207 f.

2 E.g. the Bristol hoard: Mattingly and Pearce, *NC*. 1938, pp. 86, 98.

3 *BMC. Imp.* I, p. 334. 153, p. 335. 156, etc. There is also a possible anniversary issue bearing the head of Galba, ibid. p. 357. 255 (HONOS ET VIRTVS; repeated by Vitellius, ibid. p. 375 n.). *Honos* had not appeared since Augustus; and A.D. 68, the accession year of Galba, marked the tercentenary of the vowing by Q. Fabius Maximus Verrucosus of the temple of *Honos ante portam Capenam* (Wissowa, *Religion und Kultus der Römer*[2], p. 595). But even if this coincidence is intentional (and Antoninus Pius likewise seems to commemorate *Honos* on an anniversary), the coin portraying Galba possibly was not issued until the principate of Vespasian (*BMC. Imp.* I, pp. ccxii ff.; not accepted by C.P., *Bullettino del Museo dell' Impero Romano*, 1941, p. 115); if so, its commemoration of the anniversary is not immediate but delayed. For other 'pseudo-anniversary' issues see p. 128 n. 2.

4 *BMC. Imp.* I, p. 383 (Imhoof-Blumer coll.). The coinage attributed to the years A.D. 68–70 needs reconsideration and may yield further anniversary types: for the epoch see now Hohl, *Philologische Wochenschrift*, 1939, pp. 307 ff.; Zancan, *Pubblicazioni della Facoltà di Lettere e Filosofia della R. Univ. di Padova*, XVI, 1939; Siber, *Abh. Leipzig*, XLIV, 2, 1940, p. 82; Wickert, *Klio*, 1941, pp. 137 f., etc.

CHAPTER V

FROM VESPASIAN TO COMMODUS

(i) *Vespasian and Titus: Augustan centenaries*

Vespasian modelled his policy to a considerable extent on that of Augustus, especially in the sphere of public religion[1] with which the coinage is so indissolubly linked. His monetary output recalls the first *princeps* in two main respects: first, by the use of a dozen Augustan types,[2] not apparently issued on any anniversary; and secondly, by commemorating the centenaries of great Augustan occasions. The 100th anniversary of Actium fell in A.D. 70, that of the annexation of Egypt in 71, and that of the *restituta respublica* in 74. Vespasian followed his predecessors Tiberius, Claudius and Nero in according numismatic celebration to these centenaries. This is one of the very few anniversary groups which have been recognised as such, apparently first (in part) by Laffranchi.[3] (See Appendix III.)

The centenary coinage of Actium and *Aegyptus capta* includes an exceedingly rare Asian tetradrachm (= 3 *denarii*) of A.D. 70,[4] the only known piece of this denomination between Claudius (p. 76) and Domitian (p. 98). The events of 31–30 B.C. had inspired new 'eras',[5] and their centenary did likewise: for early issues of Vespasian from Antioch and Cyprus bear the inscription ETOYΣ NEOY IEPOY.[6] At Rome, on the same occasion, is found a *denarius* with an *adlocutio* type,[7] recalling an Octavianic issue of the years immediately preceding Actium.[8] Probably some very rare DIVVS AVGVSTVS *aurei* were issued in Spain at the same time.[9]

The most unusual of Vespasian's centenary coinages comprises rare *dupondii* of A.D. 70(?) and 71 inscribed TVTELA AVGVSTI S.C., and

---

1 Cf. Piganiol, *Histoire de Rome*, pp. 274, 282. For Vespasian as financier, see now Homo, *Mélanges Radet* (*Revue des études anciennes*, 1940), pp. 453 ff.

2 Cf. Mattingly, *NC.* 1920, p. 181 n. 6; id. *BMC. Imp.* II, pp. xxxviii f.; Laffranchi, *R. it.* 1911, pp. 430 ff.

3 Loc. cit. p. 428; cf. Mattingly, *NC.* 1920, p. 181, *BMC. Imp.* II, p. xxxviii; von

Schroetter, *Wörterbuch der Münzkunde*, p. 582.

4 *BMC. Imp.* II, p. 94. 449; cf. p. lxvi.

5 Cf. Gagé, *RGDA.* p. 157 n. 2.

6 Cf. Laffranchi, *R. it.* 1911, p. 428 n. 1.

7 *BMC. Imp.* II, p. 8. 47, cf. p. xxxiv.

8 *BMC. Imp.* I, p. 100. 611.

9 Ibid. p. cxcvii; cf. (with slight divergence of dating) p. 304 nn., p. 305. 58 ff.; *BMC. Imp.* II, p. xix.

showing a woman (*Tutela?*) seated, placing her right hand on the head of one small figure and her left hand on the shoulder of another.[1] *Tutela* was a popular Flavian conception.[2] It may conceivably have appeared on a coin of Tiberian date (Plate I, 8; p. 43 n. 1).[3] Its next occurrence[4] is just 200 years after the present coin (under Tetricus, p. 138); and its only subsequent appearance, under Carausius, was to commemorate an Augustan tercentenary (p. 146). The coins of Tetricus coincided with the tercentenary of the sole rule of the first *princeps*. This corroborates the general presumption that the issue of Vespasian celebrated the centenary of those events[5] (in which case the two small figures on the *dupondii* seem to represent the *populus Romanus* rather than the emperor's sons).[6] This presumption is increased by the fact that others of Vespasian's issues of the same date were, as Laffranchi and Mattingly have pointed out, precisely of this anniversary nature. It may therefore be concluded that the *dupondii* with TVTELA AVGVSTI commemorated the 100th anniversary of the sole rule of Augustus.

Von Premerstein[7] has described the importance of the *Tutela* idea in the Augustan principate. He was probably wrong in believing that a formal *cura et tutela* was one of the legal bases of that principate;[8] but, on the moral, philosophical and social planes, the *tutela* by Augustus over his empire played a great and variegated part. It comprises, for example, his 'protection' of the *patria* (Rome and Italy),[9] of Republican institutions,[10] and even *legum suarum et morum*;[11] and there is a strong cliental connection.[12] Von Premerstein was obliged by his theory of the 'legalised' *cura et tutela* to date its

---

1 *BMC. Imp.* II, p. 112. 527, p. 129. 596. C. Kraay doubts the former.
2 Material in *BMC. Imp.* I, p. xliv, n. 3; von Premerstein, *Vom Werden und Wesen des Prinzipats*, p. 129 n. 1; Weber, *Josephus*, pp. 260 ff.
3 A piece with the same legend attributed to Vitellius is probably false: *BMC. Imp.* I, pp. 383, ccxxvii.
4 The Nerva pieces with TVTELA ITALIAE are probably false: *BMC. Imp.* III, pp. 21 n., xlix. They were published by Merlin, *Rn.* 1906, pp. 298 ff.   5 Cf. *AC.*
6 *BMC. Imp.* II, p. xliv and n. 3, considers both alternatives.
7 Loc. cit. pp. 117 ff. Cf. Sachers, *PW.* XIV (1943), 1497 ff.

8 Cf. (with references) *FITA.* pp. 452 f. n. 5.
9 E.g. Ovid, *Fasti,* I, 531; Horace, *Odes,* IV, 14. 42, *Epistles,* II, 1. 1–4; cf. von Premerstein, loc. cit. pp. 123, 150.
10 Cf. Riccobono, *Annali del Seminario Giuridico di Palermo,* 1936, p. 506; von Premerstein, loc. cit. p. 119 n. 4.
11 E.g. Ovid, *Tristia,* II, 233 f.; cf. von Premerstein, loc. cit. p. 130 n. 2.
12 Von Premerstein, loc. cit. p. 131 n. 4; cf. Suetonius, *Tib.* 6; Horace, *Epistles,* I, 1. 103. Von Premerstein, loc. cit. p. 126 n. 4, rightly distinguishes from such usages dedications to *Tutela* as the protection *over* the emperor (sc. by the gods).

inception from 27 B.C.[1] But on the more admissible non-legal plane
it was appropriate to earlier periods also, and not least to the events
of 31–30 B.C., in the centenary year of which these *dupondii* were
struck.

But the special appropriateness of this particular date A.D. 70 is
perhaps only discernible if we glance at the complicated constitutional history of the Augustan period. The present writer has
attempted elsewhere[2] to trace the development of the *tribunicia
potestas* during the first years of the Principate, and in particular to
estimate the importance of the dates 36, 30 and 23 B.C. in its evolution.
In that discussion it was argued that, whereas the *raison d'être* of the
'conferment' of 36 B.C. was *sacrosanctitas* based on inheritance from
Julius, and whereas the year 23 witnessed the inauguration of the
executive machinery of the Principate, the importance of the grant
of 30 B.C. lay (as is expressly suggested by Dio) in the *ius auxilii*.[3]
This, then, is the grant of which Tacitus is thinking when he
describes the *princeps* as *se ferens ad* TVENDAM *plebem tribunicio
iure contentum*.[4] The connection with *Tutela* is clear, and it is not
fortuitous that this rare type appears on the centenary of the adjustment of *tribunicia potestas* in 30 B.C.[5]—and that it recurs on the
tercentenary of the same occasion.

In honouring the centenary of the *tribunicia potestas*, Vespasian
seems to have selected 30 rather than 23 B.C. as his starting point.[6]
But, from the point of view of that power, 30 B.C. had been of largely
propagandist importance, whereas 23 had witnessed the inauguration
of the process *tribunicia potestas—Caesaris auctoritas—senatusconsultum* on which the whole Augustan administration hinged.
Tacitus was to realise the fictitious character of the 30 B.C. reform,
but neither he nor our other literary authorities (least of all Dio)
were interested in the significance of the 23 measure—a significance
which was obsolete even before they were born. The same point is
brought home to us by Vespasian's *dupondii*. These select for centenary celebration the date at which publicity was given to the
Tutela of Augustus (30 B.C.), not the date at which he adjusted his
administrative system (23 B.C.). Probably, too, they intend to

1 Loc. cit. p. 128.
2 *FITA*. pp. 449 ff.
3 Ibid. pp. 451 ff.
4 *Annals*, I, 2; cf. *FITA*. p. 449 (n. 2,
modern references).

5 Cf. *AC*.
6 Though an isolated gold *quinarius* of
A.D. 75–9 might conceivably celebrate the
centenary of the reform of 23 B.C.; see
Appendix I.

commemorate in a more general sense the decisive character of the former year (cf. p. 88).

Features of the other great centenary, that of the *restituta respublica* of 27 B.C., include types of oak-wreath,[1] IVSTITIA AVG.[2] and a temple of Vesta[3]—probably *Vesta in Palatio*.[4] The last-named type recalls that the same temple, closely associated as it is with Augustus, had appeared under Tiberius (p. 34) and Nero (p. 80) on anniversaries of the death of the first *princeps*—and in the former case just half a century before the present issue. Under later emperors precisely the same phenomenon was to occur (pp. 123, 135). The oak-wreath seems to refer directly to the *corona civica* awarded to Augustus just 100 years earlier—Vespasian and Titus may themselves have received one on the centenary occasion[5]—and the *Iustitia* type likewise alludes to the inclusion of this personification among the four cardinal 'Virtues' of the *clipeus virtutis* presented to Augustus at the same date (27 B.C.). But the only coins that had ever commemorated *Iustitia* by name before had been the *dupondii* of Tiberius issued exactly half-way between the Augustan occasion and the Flavian centenary (p. 34). The celebration by Nero of the *tricennium* of the death of Tiberius (p. 85) has reminded us that the latter's posthumous reputation remained high for many years; so the present honorific implication under Vespasian—if, as seems probable, there is one—need not surprise us. Vespasian's son Domitian was to revert to this theme, and, when we do likewise, reference will be made to the causes which led to the ultimate downfall of the reputation of Tiberius (p. 97 n. 4).

The *denarius* of Vespasian which commemorates the Tiberian half-centenary and Augustan centenary of *Iustitia* is a very rare one and may have been intended for private distribution only. It is believed to have been issued at Narbo[6] or possibly Nemausus.[7] This issue shows *Iustitia* with abnormal attributes[8] and commemorates some occasion now unidentifiable.[9]

---

1 *BMC. Imp.* II, p. 20. 101, etc.

2 Ibid. p. 75; *Revue Belge de Numismatique*, 1882, p. 402. This is scarcely likely to be a hybrid but is ignored in accounts of the *Iustitia* type, e.g. by Lange, *Zeitschrift der Savigny Stiftung für Rechtsgeschichte, Röm. Abt.* 1932, p. 297. It is undated.

3 *BMC. Imp.* II, p. 151. 664, p. 155. 674 (Titus), p. 144. 648 (Domitian), cf. p. 21 etc.

4 Cf. Brown, *Numismatic Notes and Monographs*, XC, 1940, pp. 40 ff.

5 *BMC. Imp.* II, p. xxxvi.

6 Ibid. p. lvii.

7 Blanchet, *Rn.* 1932, p. 112.

8 Corn-ears (or branch?) and sceptre.

9 Under Tiberius the province of Galatia had joined in the numismatic commemoration of anniversaries (pp. 35, 65), and in the same

Titus, on accession to the Principate, reverted to another early imperial theme, namely that of the much celebrated Parthian settlement of 20 B.C. Its half-centenary had been honoured numismatically by Tiberius (p. 64): the centenary occurred in A.D. 80–1. It is no doubt to the latter occasion that Titus's issues of Asian tetradrachms,[1] and Caesarean bronze dated to his third year,[2] should be ascribed. Asian tetradrachms, in their previous appearances under Claudius (p. 76) and Vespasian (p. 88), had commemorated anniversary occasions, and this will continue to be the case under Domitian (p. 98). Likewise the mint of Caesarea had shown a marked concentration on anniversary themes (pp. 67, 76, 83). We know that Titus honoured the memory of Augustus;[3] and the Eastern reputation of Titus himself made the issue a particularly relevant one to him. Hadrian was to celebrate the next half-centenary of the same Augustan occasion, and Severus Alexander its quarter-millenary. Titus also showed his traditionalism in another direction, by his unprecedented and explicitly named 'restoration' series.[4]

Equally unusual are the circumstances attaching to the exceedingly rare pieces of *sestertius* size with two different portraits of Britannicus.[5] Mattingly has recently reattributed these from the principate of Claudius[6] to that of Titus, pointing out that the latter emperor had been a close friend of Britannicus in his youth.[7] Furthermore,

territory a colony (which had also apparently issued anniversary coinage in his reign) maintained the practice under Vespasian. This is Antioch in Pisidia—now in Cappadocia—of which a coin (the only one known of Vespasian at that city) is dated to A.D. 76 (Ritterling, *ZfN.* 1928, p. 57). In that year fell the centenary of the annexation of the kingdom of Galatia in 25 B.C. by M. Lollius (cf. *FITA.* p. 250), and this anniversary suggests an occasion of the issue. The new Galatian era had started in 20 B.C., when the province was founded, and that had been the occasion from which the Tiberian half-centenary issue was calculated (p. 35). But during the previous five years (25–20 B.C.) the country had been in Roman hands: it was *redacta in potestatem*, and not yet *in formam provinciae* (cf. Strack, II, pp. 223 ff. and n. 949; *BMC. Imp.* III, p. cvi; Moesia and Mauretania each passed through a similar stage). Thus the centenary of 25 B.C. was, for this region, at least as important an occasion as that of

20 B.C. Possibly, too, Pisidian Antioch was commemorating privileges of its own received in the former year, though it does not appear to have been colonised until somewhat later (cf. *FITA.* p. 250). But the issue probably has a topical significance also, connected with the reorganisation of central Anatolia by Vespasian (Syme, *CAH.* XI, p. 140).

1 *BMC. Imp.* II, p. 252. 149 (Titus) and 150 (Domitian and Divus Vespasianus).

2 *BMC. Galatia*, etc. p. 49. 27 (A. Caesennius Gallus).

3 Cf. Gagé, *Revue historique*, 1933, p. 12 n. 3.

4 *BMC. Imp.* II, pp. lxxvii ff., 281 ff. Possibly they are timed for the same anniversary (cf. Trajan [p. 100]).

5 *BMC. Imp.* I, p. 196. 226; II, p. 293. 306.

6 To which they are ascribed in *BMC. Imp.* I, pp. clii, clix.

7 *BMC. Imp.* II, p. lxxviii; *NC.* 1930, pp. 330 ff.

the reverse of this issue, Mars with s.c., is, in style and in composition, out of keeping with the Julio-Claudian period and reminiscent of Flavian coinage.[1] These historical and numismatic points link up with the fact that the quarter-centenary of the untimely death of Britannicus (14 February A.D. 55) fell in A.D. 80, during the principate of Titus. That, apparently, is the occasion which these pieces commemorate; and it may be partly for the same reason that his 'restoration' issues include the *Spes* type of Claudius,[2] referring to Britannicus's birth (p. 74).

The *sestertii* with heads of Britannicus were perhaps intended for private commemoration only, and, if so, fall in the direct line of succession to those Julio-Claudian issues of which the medallic character is visible from their extreme rarity and unusualness rather than from any structural feature. Of the Julio-Claudian pieces, some had been issued alongside a large and common series resembling them in some way, whereas others had not (p. 60). These *sestertii* of Britannicus apparently fall in the latter category. Likewise, some of the Julio-Claudian coins had borne s.c. while others had omitted it: the Britannicus pieces, herein differing from only one *sestertius* of Titus,[3] display the letters. So do certain other *sestertii* of the Flavian emperors[4] and Nerva[5]—and indeed of later emperors[6]—which have an equal claim, through rarity and unusualness, to be considered medallic, though, unlike other pieces of the Flavian

1 It originated with Vitellius, *BMC. Imp.* I, p. 378. 58, cf. p. ccxv. For Flavian repetitions of the type, ibid. II, p. 136. 621, p. 188. 777 ff., etc. For the Flavian Mars, see Magi, *I Rilievi Flavi del Palazzo della Cancelleria*, pp. 73 f. (p. 73 n. 1, bibliography). For the origins of the cult, see recently Dumézil, *Jupiter-Mars-Quirinus, Horace et les Curiaces*, etc.
2 *BMC. Imp.* II, pp. lxxviii, 289. 297.
3 Ibid. p. 254. 152, cf. p. lxxvii; ibid. III, p. xciii; Strack, I, pp. 9 ff., 62 ff.: a reversion to the occasional practice of Caligula and Nero?
4 E.g. Vespasian (*BMC. Imp.* II, p. 123 = Pl. 22. 7, p. 124. 576, and some of the *sestertii* struck posthumously for Galba), Titus (ibid. p. 260. 188, p. 261. 189), Domitian (p. 364 = Pl. 71. 6, p. 407 = Pl. 80. 12), etc.
5 E.g. *BMC. Imp.* III, p. 24. 132, etc.
6 The situation changed under Trajan,

when proper *aes* medallions began to be struck. But even thereafter very rare *sestertii*, etc., did not cease to be issued (even in the midst of very common coinages), and some of these may have retained a medallic, i.e. non-monetary, character until quite late in the third century (e.g. at the end of the *aes* series, those of Aurelian, etc.). Mention has been made (p. 60) of the insistence of Pink and Elmer that a broad distinction exists between common, regular issues and rare irregular ones: some recurring types remain common and others remain rare for long periods at a time. Particular attention must be focussed on this phenomenon during the first century, when *aes* medallions, as usually described, did not exist; for their place was taken by the various categories of 'abnormal' *aes*, of one of which the Britannicus '*sestertii*' provide a good example.

dynasty,[1] their structure is normal. The mark s.c. here either denotes a special decree by the senate in honour of the quarter-centenary of Britannicus, or, more probably, it has no great significance, and is intended vaguely to connect these pieces with contemporary *aes* issues, which are likely to have been authorised by a single *senatus-consultum* not long after the accession (p. 82).

(ii) *Domitian*

The anniversary issues of Domitian divide naturally into two main categories: (1) an important and complex series of A.D. 85; (2) isolated mintages of A.D. 83, 87, 88, 91, 92 and 95.

The issues of A.D. 85 included the first silver medallions (as far as is known at present) that had ever been struck at Rome.[2] They are inscribed IMP. VIII. COS. XI. CENS. POT. P.P., and the types are *Germania*[3] and Minerva,[4] the latter reverse reproduced also in base metal.[5] The same year witnessed a second, and equally remarkable, development, namely the most ambitious issue of *sestertii*[6] that had ever appeared in a single year or indeed in a single principate. This great series includes types strongly reminiscent of the great years 18–16 B.C.—elephant quadrigae,[7] Apollo and lyre,[8] 'Victory',[9] and *Virtus*.[10] That period, already recalled by the half-centenary issues of Tiberius (p. 44), had terminated with a year (16 B.C.) which was not only exactly 100 years before Domitian's *sestertii* of A.D. 85, but which, like the latter year, had witnessed an unparalleled output of coin-types.[11]

It is due to more than mere chance that Domitian's unprecedented series of *sestertii* of A.D. 85 occurred 100 years after the no less

---

1 E.g. of Vespasian (*BMC. Imp.* II, p. 180=Pl. 31. 1, p. 198. 805; Mattingly, *Roman Coins*, Pl. XXXIV. 5); cf. perhaps an impressive piece of Galba (*BMC. Imp.* I, pp. ccxvi f., 359. 260).

2 This is on the assumption that the Vienna silver piece with DIVVS AVGVSTVS IMPER., OCTAVIA (Cohen, I, p. 214. 1; Kahrstedt, *Klio*, 1910, p. 296) is false. It is not mentioned by Dr Toynbee (though Regling considered it to be genuine).

3 *BMC. Imp.* II, p. 317. 85; cf. pp. xiv, lxxxiii n. 1, lxxxvi; Toynbee, pp. 127, 195.

4 *BMC. Imp.* II, pp. 316. 83, lxxxvi; Toynbee, loc. cit.; Gnecchi, III, p. 13. 1.

5 *BMC. Imp.* II, p. 316. 83 n.; Gnecchi,

III, p. 13. 2 (no reverse inscription): *BMC. Imp.* II does not refer to the *aes* piece (Gnecchi, III, p. 13. 1), which may therefore be false.

6 *BMC. Imp.* II, pp. 362 ff., xcii ff.

7 Two quadrigae on arch: ibid. p. 364 n.; Paris, cf. p. xciii and n. 2.

8 Ibid. p. 367. 318. Ibid. p. xciv points out the Secular reference, which no doubt applies to the *ludi* of Augustus as well as to the forthcoming ones of Domitian. For an exceptional gold *quinarius* celebrating Domitian's games, see Appendix I.

9 *BMC. Imp.* II, p. 375. 355.

10 Ibid. p. 366. 313.

11 Cf. Sutherland, *NC.* 1943, pp. 40 ff.

unprecedented series of Augustan *aurei* and *denarii* of 16 B.C., and indeed echoed a number of the types introduced by the coinage culminating in that year. Both the mintages of 16 B.C., and Domitian's reminiscent types just a century later, were intended to record topical events of great importance—in the case of Augustus the first year of the new *saeculum*, and in the case of Domitian—who is known to have honoured Divus Augustus[1]—his own German victories. In further imitation of Augustus, Domitian was going, in A.D. 88, to celebrate *ludi saeculares*.[2] Just as the *saeculum* of Augustus had been heralded, three years in advance, by a military event to which unparalleled importance had been attached (p. 65), so Domitian's new *saeculum* was timed to start three years after his own equally publicised military commemoration. A further feature of the coinage of A.D. 85 is the traditionally 'composite' character of the anniversaries which it commemorates. For one of its types[3] comprises the oblong shields previously encountered only on the coins struck by Claudius in honour of Nero Drusus (p. 73), of whose first victories[4] A.D. 85 was the 100th year. The anniversaries of these victories are known to have been celebrated after the latter's death (p. 4).

These points may be considered in conjunction with another series of issues by Domitian, namely his large silver medallions[5] and *aes* medallions[6] of A.D. 92. The former constitute only the second known issue of silver medallions in Rome's history, the previous one also being of Domitian, having been struck in A.D. 85 on an anniversary occasion (p. 94). We may compare the only three gold medallions which had apparently so far appeared. The two Augustan ones had commemorated anniversaries (pp. 23, 24), whereas Domitian's coincided with his new *saeculum*.[7] With these analogies, comprising (as far as we know—though no deduction can be surely based on the hazardous *argumentum a silentio*) the sum total of medallions in the precious metals that had so far appeared, there is a presumption that some special occasion, and not improbably an anniversary one, must be found for his silver medallion of A.D. 92.

1 Cf. Gagé, *Revue historique*, 1933, p. 12 n. 3.

2 *BMC. Imp.* II, p. 326. 130; Charlesworth, loc. cit. p. 26. Cf. pp. 5, 110.

3 *BMC. Imp.* II, pp. 366. 311, 373. 351 f.

4 Cf. Syme, *CAH.* x, p. 349. For the work of Nero Drusus in Germany, see Vollgraff,

Mélanges Radet (*Revue des études anciennes*, 1940), pp. 686 ff.

5 *BMC. Imp.* II, p. 337. 191; Toynbee, p. 127; Gnecchi, *R. it.* 1898, p. 44.

6 *BMC. Imp.* II, p. 411; Gnecchi, III, p. 14. 5 f.: Paris.

7 *BMC. Imp.* II, p. 324. 117 n., formerly in Paris coll. (4- or 5-*aureus* piece).

Now in precisely the same year occurred the centenary of the death of Nero Drusus. Claudius had already commemorated its half-centenary (p. 73); and Domitian himself had borrowed the type of Claudius for an issue which, it has been concluded, is very likely to have been occasioned by the centenary of the first victories of Nero Drusus. Probably, then, the centenary of the latter's death produced the issue of the silver medallion of A.D. 92. The same occasion may well have inspired the first of the 'Nome' coinages of Alexandria, a city devoted to the memory of Nero Drusus' son Germanicus (cf. p. 61 and n. 6).[1]

Relevant to that medallion is the fact that, in A.D. 91, the year preceding its issue and the 100th year after the death of Nero Drusus, Domitian's title *Germanicus*[2] was given unusual emphasis by its appearance unabbreviated on *aurei*.[3] This recalls the practice of Vitellius (p. 5). That emperor, however, had intended to celebrate Germanicus rather than Nero Drusus; but it was not unnatural that Domitian should commemorate the latter, whose centenaries coincided with his own wars.[4] This is all the more probable since Domitian paid marked attention to the other great campaigner in Germany of the time of Augustus, namely Nero Drusus's brother Tiberius. Domitian was an admirer of Tiberius and a careful student of his memoirs.[5] The elephant-quadriga on the coinage of A.D. 85 (p. 94 n. 7) recalls that this type, introduced by Augustus 100 years earlier, had been repeated by Tiberius at a date almost exactly equidistant between the issues of Augustus and Domitian (p. 44).

Similarly, one of Domitian's earliest motifs is SALVS AVGVST.,[6] another inscription now reappearing just half a century after the period in which Tiberius may have employed it (p. 33 n. 6): here the connection with Tiberius is the more marked since it was the latter who had introduced the type to the coinage.[7] Moreover, an exceptional *quinarius* of A.D. 83,[8] in which began the 100th year of the *saeculum* of Augustus,[9] repeats for its sole type the *caduceus* which had likewise

1 See Appendix II.
2 Conferred in A.D. 83 according to Asbach, *Westdeutsche Zeitschrift für Geschichte und Kunst*, 1884, p. 17, but could be somewhat later, cf. Blanchet, *Rn.* 1941, p. 10 n. 10.
3 *BMC. Imp.* II, p. 334. 171 ff.
4 However, Domitian 'restores' an *as* in honour of Germanicus: *BMC. Imp.* II, p. 416. 511.

5 Cf. Charlesworth, *CAH.* XI, p. 23.
6 *BMC. Imp.* II, p. 309. 54; cf. p. lxxxv. It might be as late as *c.* A.D. 84 but could easily be an 'accession' issue.
7 Domitian varies it by giving the type an agricultural character.
8 *BMC. Imp.* II, p. 305. 38.
9 For the habitually anniversary character of *quinarii*, see Appendix I.

been the sole type (for the first time in imperial history) of the *asses* of Tiberius issued for the half-centenary of that *saeculum* (p. 45).[1]

In A.D. 87 Domitian issued a very rare and unusual piece of *as* size[2] reviving the custom, obsolete for over 40 years except on 'restoration' coinages, of devoting the whole reverse type to S.C., surrounded by an inscription. This custom had reached its full development under Tiberius. Now it was in precisely the year 87 that the half-centenary of the death of Tiberius occurred. At first sight it may seem strange to see that occasion receiving commemoration so long afterwards, but it is made less so by certain considerations. First, Domitian was a keen student and imitator of Tiberius; and among the latter's *asses* which he 'restored' was one with this very type.[3] Secondly, the posthumous reputation of Tiberius stood very high, and he received much commemoration (pp. 48, 85), until—based perhaps to some extent on Domitian's admiration for him[4]—a reaction set in at about the turn of the century. Thirdly, and in particular, a precedent had been established by Nero, who commemorated the *tricennium* of the death of Tiberius on his coinage of Alexandria (p. 85). It seems fairly clear that Domitian's *as* was prompted by some special occasion, and such an anniversary provides a suitable one.

But this issue might, alternatively or as well, have celebrated another anniversary. The type S.C. seems to indicate some topical occasion relating to the senate. But the complimentary effect is somewhat qualified by the fact that this is the first and only coinage of Domitian which bears the significant title CENSOR PERPETVVS in full;[5] it appears on the reverse, with S.C. The connection of the perpetual censorship with the senate is obvious. But the archaistic type recalls the early Principate; and the year 87, when this *as* was issued, may have been the 100th year after a revision of the senate by Augustus—possibly his third and last *lectio*,[6] or perhaps a separate

1 This same occasion of A.D. 83 might have prompted the "restorations", which are early, *BMC. Imp.* II, p. xcvi.

2 *BMC. Imp.* II, p. 387. 398, cf. p. xciv.

3 Ibid. p. 415. 509.

4 Other causes included: (1) the preservation of the works of hostile pamphleteers (cf. de Laet, *Samenstelling*, p. 295; Carcopino, *Aspects mystiques de la Rome païenne*, pp. 109 ff.); (2) the posthumous increase of the figure of Germanicus by the later Julio-

Claudians and Vitellius, and consequent creation of a suitable hero for talented writers like Tacitus to set against Tiberius. On the posthumous repute of Tiberius, see Pippidi, *Ephemeris Dacoromana*, 1938 = *Autour de Tibère*, pp. 11 ff., p. 20 n. 1.

5 There may be some significance in the occasional statement *in full* of titles that are generally abbreviated, e.g. A. VITELLIVS GERMANICVS IMP. (see p. 5 n. 7).

6 Cf. Stuart Jones, *CAH.* x, p. 149.

recognitio.[1] This was precisely the task which Domitian had set himself as a permanent feature of the Principate as he conceived it. He had been *censor perpetuus* since about the end of A.D. 85;[2] but the present pointed type may refer to a measure of 87, perhaps the first important one based on his recently acquired *potestas*. Possibly, in commemoration of such a measure, these pieces were distributed privately to selected senators.[3] This would be no more surprising, or tactless, than the demonstrable emphasis on the title itself.

Domitian issued an Eastern tetradrachm in A.D. 95,[4] the first for some years and the first dated one since 82. An array of precedents created by earlier tetradrachms will have prepared us for an anniversary occasion. In particular, the only known tetradrachm of Vespasian had celebrated the centenary of Actium or *Aegyptus capta* (p. 88). That issue was struck just a quarter of a century before Domitian's tetradrachm of A.D. 95, which may therefore be ascribed to the 125th anniversary of the same victories.

(iii) *Trajan and Hadrian*

It has been shown, in connection with the Julio-Claudian emperors, that early imperial anniversary series were closely linked with the origins of the *decennalia* and of their coinage (p. 19). Issues for *decennalia*, *vicennalia*, etc., had habitually been designed to celebrate, not only the tenth or twentieth anniversary of the current reign, but simultaneously some centenary, or its subdivision or multiple. In the second century, however, the two types of coinage become, with a few exceptions, distinct, and we may therefore, at this stage, bid farewell to the *vota* issues—as decennalian, and soon quinquennalian,[5]

---

1 Cf. von Premerstein, *Vom Werden und Wesen des Prinzipats*, p. 163. See also Schulz, *Mnemosyne*, 1937, pp. 161 ff.

2 Charlesworth, *CAH*. xi, p. 24, cf. n. 2.

3 How far the allusions to Augustus and Tiberius can be pressed in comparison with each other, it is difficult to say; but Domitian admired both, and the Roman world was by now accustomed to 'combined' anniversary coinages. We know little (except from coins) of the steps taken by Domitian (if any) to present to the people, in the favourable light of publicity, his own innovations, such as the *censoria potestas perpetua*. But his known admiration for Tiberius, and the fact that

commemorations of that *princeps* were still by no means unfashionable, make it not unlikely that he was glad to quote the Tiberian principate as forerunner of his own. But, failing further evidence (which study of the coins may perhaps produce), the whole subject must be treated with considerable reserve.

4 *BMC. Imp.* II, p. 352. 253, cf. p. xciv; Gnecchi, III, *Tavola di Supplemento*, No. 2. For a IOVI VICTORI type of this year see *Museum Notes*, II, 1947, pp. 21 ff.

5 Cf. Pearce, *NC*. 1937, p. 117. For a new theory of the etymology of *lustrum*, see Müller, *Het Reveil van Augustus*, p. 87.

mintages come to be called. Such mintages now revive,[1] and hereafter continue with the same regularity as under the first emperors, and with an added explicitness;[2] whereas the anniversary coinages that form the principal subject of this book, namely those issued on the centenaries, etc., of the great Republican and early imperial occasions, seem to pursue a separate course.

The first three decades of the second century seem to have been a period in which anniversary coinages did not enjoy a great vogue. Trajan presumably preferred to build up his own corpus of coin-types from great contemporary events; and it may possibly have been felt that the traditional institution of the anniversary issues, like other features of the first century A.D. (such as the good reputation of Tiberius who had been so closely connected with such issues), had been somewhat discredited by the uses made of it by Domitian.[3] But there are at least two anniversary mintages of Trajan. Mars had become a common type on the coins, but his specific description as MARS VICTOR on *aurei* of A.D. 112–14[4] is arresting since no coin had

1 As regards numismatic commemoration, Vespasian and Domitian seem to have devoted comparatively little attention to their *decennalia*: but the former's Caesarean silver and *aes*, on which year dates are 'nine' (*BMC. Galatia*, etc., p. 48. 20) and 'ten' (ibid. p. 47. 18), might belong to that category. The fact that an issue of Titus (as Augustus) at Caesarea may have borne the date 10 (ibid. p. 48. 23) interestingly recalls the manner in which the *respublica restituta* of Augustus—i.e. the dynastic era —had continued to be honoured after his death by Tiberius. Cf. Hadrian, who may have coined at Alexandria for the *tricennium* of Trajan (see Appendix II).
2 They continue (as under Tiberius and Nero) as commemorating *decennia*, etc. as commemorating the consecration of the previous *princeps* as well as the accession of the current one. E.g. at the very outset of this period, the *Commune Bithyniae* issues coins for Divus Nerva on an occasion identified by Bosch (*Die Kleinasiatischen Münzen*, II, I, p. 189) as the first *quinquennalia* of Trajan. Mention may also be made of the possibility that Hadrian's *aurei* with DIVIS PARENTIBVS, despite their (usually earlier) obverse inscription HADRIANVS AVGVSTVS P.P., were issued for or near his *vicennium* (cf. *BMC.*

Imp. III, pp. cxvii, cxxxvi, cxli). Incidentally the emperors of whose consecrations the anniversaries were honoured in this way were not necessarily the latest in date, or even the last to have been deified. E.g. Antoninus Pius may perhaps commemorate the half-centenary of Nerva's death (Appendix II); Severus, possibly on the *quinquennium* of the death of Commodus, coined for that emperor (Divus Commodus: M. & S. IV, I, p. 99. 72A); and some of the issues in honour of Divus Claudius Gothicus may perhaps be attributable to the *decennium* of his death and to the reign of Probus (M. & S. V, I, p. 203) (though others struck on behalf of the same *divus* should be ascribed to the intervening emperor Aurelian [p. 140 n. 5]). In other cases, naturally, the same occurs when the intervening emperor or emperors have not been deified, e.g. Severus Alexander strikes for 'Divus Antoninus Magnus' (Caracalla) (M. & S. IV, 2, pp. 128, 717 ff., cf. n. to 720), again apparently on the *decennium* of the latter's death.
3 Though, against the vilification of Domitian in favour of Nerva and Trajan, see Syme, *JRS.* 1930, pp. 63 ff.; *Philologus* 1936, pp. 238 ff.
4 *BMC. Imp.* III, p. 262. 258.

displayed the name of this deity for some 40 years. This exceptional usage is very likely to be connected with the half-millenary of the original temple of Mars, and quarter-millenary of his second temple, two occasions which coincided in A.D. 113 (p. 4). In thus commemorating the anniversaries of early temples, Trajan is at once living up to his reputation as the most Republican of emperors,[1] and copying a precedent dating at least from Caesar (pp. 15 f.). He also seems to celebrate the sesquicentenary of the latter's death:[2] for A.D. 107 is the most probable year for his so-called 'restoration' *aurei*,[3] in which figure prominently four for Julius Caesar (as against only two for Augustus[4] and his successors), once as DIVVS IVLIVS,[5] once as C. IVLIVS CAES. IMP. COS. III,[6] and twice as CAESAR.[7] This is an appropriate tribute from one great conqueror to another, and its emphasis is unusual (p. 133).[8]

The anniversary references on Hadrian's issues seem to have been more numerous. A feature of his principate is a group of three silver medallions of Roman workmanship, with reverse inscription PONT. MAX. TR. POT. COS. III. Two of these show *Felicitas* (or *Pax?*) standing with *caduceus* and *cornucopiae*,[9] and the third shows Jupiter (the Zeus of Phidias) enthroned with 'Victory' and sceptre.[10] Such issues of silver medallions seem only to have occurred in one previous reign, namely that of Domitian (at least only his have survived), and they had all been of a commemorative character (pp. 94 f.). Two of his three issues had celebrated not topical events but anniversaries; and the legends of Hadrian's silver medallions indicate attribution to *c.* A.D. 119[11]—the 150th year after the battle of Actium. The half-centenary and centenary of that occasion had been commemorated numismatically by Tiberius (p. 58) and Vespasian (p. 88) respectively, and Hadrian's exceptional medallic

---

1 Cf. M. & S. II, p. 304; Mattingly, *Roman Coins*, p. 169.
2 Cf. perhaps Nero and Valerian, 100th and 300th: see Appendix I.
3 *BMC. Imp.* III, pp. lxxxvii ff. On this series see also Cesano, *Bollettino del Circolo Numismatico Napoletano*, July–Dec. 1939.
4 Whereas Nerva's 'restoration' *aes* had stressed Augustus exclusively, *BMC. Imp.* III, pp. 28 ff.
5 *BMC. Imp.* III, p. 142. 697.
6 Ibid. p. 142. 696.
7 Ibid. p. 141. 30 f.

8 Possibly there is also some thought of 43 B.C., as a decisive year in the foundation of the Principate (p. 84). Perhaps, too, Trajan's first 'Nome' coinage (A.D. 109–10) celebrates the sesquicentenary of the first *ovatio* of Augustus: see Appendix II.
9 *BMC. Imp.* III, p. 281. 327, cf. Toynbee p. 128: 7-*denarius* piece (*BMC.* loc. cit. n.: 7½-*denarius* piece).
10 *BMC. Imp.* III, p. 281. 326, cf. Toynbee, p. 128. 213 f.: 8-*denarius* piece.
11 Cf. *BMC. Imp.* III, pp. cxvi, cxxix.

issue seems to fulfil a similar purpose just half a century later.[1] The celebration of Rome's great Eastern 'settlement' was a significant theme in the circumstances of A.D. 119. It was at Antioch that Hadrian had been saluted emperor, and he spent much of his life in the East: A.D. 119 may have been the only whole year that he spent in Rome during the first 16 years of his reign.[2]

These large silver medallions have the long obverse inscriptions and the style characteristic of the first years of Hadrian's principate. At some date between A.D. 122 and c. 125 these inscriptions and this style were superseded, and immediately replaced by the entirely new features of the great HADRIANVS AVGVSTVS series.[3] This new series is described by Mattingly:[4] 'we find a gracious style of Greek character, new idealisation of the imperial portrait, a simplification of title and legend—all of which remind us involuntarily of Augustus. The new imperial style *Hadrianus Augustus*—occasionally, even more notably, *Augustus Hadrianus*[5]—proves that Hadrian consciously intended to set himself beside the founder of the Empire.' This last theme is pursued further by Strack,[6] who attributes these remarkable developments to the sesquicentenary of the *respublica restituta* of Augustus (A.D. 123–4).[7] Strack is thus one of the very few numismatists who have detected the anniversary character of any series other than those celebrating *decennia* and *saecula* (p. 9); he is also unique among numismatists in attributing to an anniversary occasion one of the great monetary innovations or reforms of the empire. His argument is supported by our interpretation of other such innovations, at many dates during the whole Principate— including a date in the later years of Hadrian himself (p. 104)—as timed to coincide with anniversary occasions (p. 41). No anniversary occasion yielded in popularity and importance to the centenaries and half-centenaries of the *respublica restituta*.

In this same connection should be noted a remarkable group of

---

1 Hadrian's first 'Nome' coinage at Alexandria (A.D. 121–2) may well commemorate the sesquicentenary of *Aegyptus capta*; see Appendix II.

2 Cf. Weber, *CAH*. XI, p. 319, cf. p. 303.

3 Strack, II, pp. 12 ff.; *BMC. Imp.* III, pp. cxv, clxvii, *pace* M. & S. II, pp. 320 ff.

4 *BMC. Imp.* III, p. cxxxiv, cf. p. cxvi.

5 Ibid. pp. 293 n., 382 n., 443, 467 n., 480 n., 529 n., 563, cf. p. 393.

6 II, pp. 12 ff.; cf. *BMC. Imp.* III, pp. cxvi n. 3, cxxxiv (here Strack is misquoted as attributing the series to the 150th anniversary of *Actium*).

7 *BMC. Imp.* III, pp. cxvi, cxxxiv, also associates the innovations with Hadrian's intended return to Rome (125 or 126; 125 according to Weber, *CAH.* XI, p. 319; Piganiol, *Histoire de Rome*, p. 306; but see *BMC. Imp.* III, p. cxii n. 5).

eastern tetradrachms issued a few years later, in c. A.D. 128–32.[1] These display the obverse legend IMP. CAESAR AVGVSTVS and a portrait that is evidently intended to represent Augustus. The reverse inscription, accompanying the Augustan type of Diana, is HADRIANVS AVG. P.P. REN. This might mean either of two things: (1) REN(*ovavit*), the coins being mostly overstruck on tetradrachms of Antony and Augustus,[2] and *renovatio* being a current religious idea especially connected with the contemporary temple of Venus and Rome (p. 127);[3] or (2) REN(*atus*), with reference to Hadrian's initiation at Eleusis,[4] after the example of Augustus, later followed also by Gallienus.[5] There is also an allusion to the Νέος Θεός idea, the relevance of which to the coinage the present writer has endeavoured to describe elsewhere.[6]

Mattingly now prefers the latter of these interpretations (*renatus*).[7] We, too, may accept it in view of the coincidence of A.D. 131—the year of Hadrian's third and last visit to Athens, when his initiation may have been completed[8]—with the 150th anniversary of the Augustan success in the East in 20 B.C. (*signa recepta*). The half-centenary of that great occasion had been previously commemorated by Tiberius (p. 65) and its centenary by Titus (p. 92). The latter's issue had, like Hadrian's, consisted of tetradrachms, a favourite medium for anniversary commemorations. The bicentenary of the same events was to be celebrated by a gold medallion of Severus Alexander. It was precisely in 20–19 B.C. that Augustus had probably been initiated into the Greater Mysteries at Eleusis,[9] so that this anniversary occasion was a fitting one for Hadrian's description of himself as the new or reborn Augustus. Hadrian compared himself to Augustus, and it is in that capacity that he portrayed Diana on *aes* medallions as well as on these and other coins.[10] He also recalled Augustus by introducing Romulus to the coinage (p. 128 n. 2). The

1 *BMC. Imp.* III, p. 395. 1094, cf. pp. clvii, clxi.
2 Ibid. p. clvii.
3 Cf. Gagé, *Annuaire de l'Institut de Philologie et d'Histoire Orientale de l'Université libre de Bruxelles*, 1936, p. 151.
4 Cf. Graindor, *Athènes sous Hadrien*, pp. 7, 118 ff.; Guarducci, *Bullettino del Museo dell' Impero Romano*, 1941, pp. 149 ff.
5 Cf. Alföldi, *25 Jahre Römisch-Germanische Kommission*, pp. 12 ff.; id. *ZfN.* 1928,

pp. 174 ff. Id. *Dissertationes Pannonicae*, 1937, p. 56, points to the connection with Augustus.
6 *FITA.* p. 358.
7 Loc. cit. p. clxi; cf. Herzfelder, *NC.* 1936, p. 17.
8 Graindor, loc. cit. p. 119; for the date, cf. Piganiol, loc. cit. p. 306.
9 Graindor, *Athènes sous Auguste*, pp. 19, 21 ff.
10 Cf. Toynbee, p. 140.

Eleusinian reference is of interest in the history of second century religious thought. It could scarcely have been expressed in this way by any of Hadrian's predecessors, though they mostly anticipated his desire to be considered a second Augustus; this is Hadrian's peculiar variant of the 'restoration' coinages issued by all his predecessors since Titus.

Equally relevant to Augustus is a later Hadrianic example. This is provided by coins[1] and *aes* medallions,[2] inscribed TELLVS STABIL., of *c.* A.D. 134–6.[3] These inscribe the name of the goddess *Tellus* on the official coinage for the first time.[4] Now it was during these very years (actually in A.D. 134) that the 150th anniversary of the *ludi saeculares* occurred: and Horace's *Carmen Saeculare* had contained a special reference to *Tellus*,[5] with the quarter-millenary of whose temple it may very nearly have coincided (p. 4 n. 8). Strack,[6] though he does not see the anniversary occasion, is right in connecting the *Tellus* type of Hadrian with ideas of the *saeculum aureum*. Trajan had maintained, or revived, the custom of celebrating numismatically the centenaries of ancient temples (p. 100); Antoninus Pius, too, was to be particularly active in this respect. It is, then, not improbable that Hadrian's type commemorates the quadringenary of the temple of *Tellus* as well as the sesquicentenary of the Augustan *saeculum*. This type has considerable relevance to Hadrian's principate, in which agrarian reform played so large a part.[7] Possibly the issue occurred in the first year after the anniversary, A.D. 135, but this need not affect its commemorative character (p. 11). Quadringenaries perhaps had an importance of their own (p. 4 n. 3).

If the TELLVS STABIL. issues celebrate the 150th anniversary of the Augustan *saeculum aureum*, or the first year after that anniversary, it is difficult to avoid the same conclusion as regards the whole of the great 'Province' coinage of Hadrian. This comprises, *inter alia*, the great series with ADVENTVI AVG...., EXERCITVS... and RESTITVTORI

---

1 *BMC. Imp.* III, p. 332. 737, etc.

2 Toynbee, p. 93.

3 *BMC. Imp.* III, p. cxliv. Ibid. pp. cxvii f. somewhat prefers A.D. 135 to 134 for the beginning of the series, but this is uncertain. Weber, *CAH.* XI, p. 319, likewise prefers A.D. 135 (Strack prefers A.D. 136) for Hadrian's return to Rome, with which the new issues may well be connected (*BMC. Imp.* III, pp. cxliv, clxxi).

4 Her unnamed figure, however, may possibly be identifiable on an issue for Domitian's Secular Games: *BMC. Imp.* II, Pl. 78. 7; cf. Toynbee, *The Hadrianic School*, p. 140 n. 4. For another, doubtful, appearance under Hadrian, ibid. p. 143, cf. n. 3.

5 Ll. 29 f.

6 II, p. 183; cf. Toynbee, loc. cit. p. 142 n. 2.

7 Cf. Weber, *CAH.* XI, p. 317.

AVG....[1] These series are closely connected with, and as it were summed up by, the TELLVS STABIL. type;[2] they are also, again like the latter, related to the 'Golden Age' motif.[3] This conclusion gains further interest from the entirely novel and remarkable character of the 'Province' series.[4] Ten years earlier Hadrian, like many of his predecessors and successors, seems to have timed his first great monetary innovation to coincide with a notable anniversary, in this case the sesquicentenary of the *respublica restituta* (p. 101). It is in keeping with this that his second great innovation should be arranged to coincide with the sesquicentenary of the *saeculum aureum*. This adds point to the important 'Province' series and throws new light on Hadrian's deliberate reminiscence of Augustus.[5]

It is just possible that an isolated Alexandrian mintage, of 'Nome' types and dated to A.D. 127–8, celebrates an anniversary of yet another *princeps*, namely the *tricennium* of the accession of Trajan.[6]

(iv) *The Antonines*

The activity of Antoninus Pius in the field of anniversary issues is represented by at least six groups of issues, comprising the following types:[7] (1) *Iuventas* (A.D. 140–4);[8] (2) *Honos* (A.D. 140–4);[9] (3) Janus (A.D. 140–4);[10] (4) the Capitoline Triad (medallions)[11] and their birds—owl, eagle, peacock (*quadrantes*)[12] (*c.* A.D. 140–2);

1 *BMC. Imp.* III, pp. clxxi ff. etc.; Strack, II, pp. 139 ff.; Toynbee, loc. cit. pp. 24 ff. Cf. also some possible medallions: Gnecchi, III, pp. 18 ff.

2 Cf. *BMC. Imp.* III, pp. clxxxii (cf. clxxxi), clxxvi; Strack, II, pp. 153 ff. The 'Province' series seems to come at the beginning of the A.D. 134/5–8 issues (as *BMC. Imp.* III, p. cxviii; cf. Toynbee, *NC.* 1936, p. 330) and not near their end (as Strack, II, pp. 17 ff.).

3 Cf. Strack, II, pp. 181 ff.; *BMC. Imp.* III, p. cxlv.

4 *BMC. Imp.* III, pp. cxlii, clxxi.

5 *Colonia* Pella, coining in this principate (Gaebler, *Die Antiken Münzen Nordgriechenlands*, III, 2. p. 99. 30)—apparently for the first time for about a century—may well be commemorating the 150th anniversary of its foundation in 30 B.C. (*FITA.* p. 283).

6 See Appendix II. In a similar manner the regnal era of Vespasian had been used by Titus. Aurelian was to date his tribunician power from the accession of Claudius Gothicus.

7 This list excludes the last of the 'Nome' issues of Alexandria, an isolated mintage which may commemorate the half-centenary of the death of Nerva (see Appendix II). Septimius Severus also seems to have celebrated Nerva's anniversaries.

8 *BMC. Imp.* IV, pp. 268 ff. 1397 and 1047 ff. (Aurelius).

9 Ibid. p. 40. 263, and p. 225. 1395 (Aurelius).

10 Ibid. p. 210. 1317, and p. 220. 1369 (TR. POT. COS. III. [S.C.]).

11 Gnecchi, II, p. 16. 66.

12 *BMC. Imp.* IV, p. 224. 1392 (COS. III. S.C.).

(5) Aesculapius (A.D. 156–7);[1] and (6) TEMPLVM DIV. AVG. REST. COS. IIII (A.D. 157–8).[2]

The type of *Iuventas*, issued for the young Marcus Aurelius, is her first known appearance on Roman coinage.[3] The date of issue, though generally considered to have been *c.* A.D. 140–1, need not have been earlier than *c.* 143–4, in which fell the 350th anniversary (multiples of seven having a special significance [p. 2 n. 3]) of the date (207 B.C.) on which the temple of *Iuventas* had been vowed by M. Livius Salinator.[4] *Honos* too—another type for the youthful Aurelius—occurs but rarely on coins; it was over 70 years since her last appearance, and that had probably celebrated a temple anniversary (p. 87 n.). The present coins with *Honos* belong towards the end of the period 140–4.[5] We may therefore see a deliberate coincidence with the 350th anniversary (in A.D. 142–3) of the rededication of the temple of *Honos* by M. Claudius Marcellus in 208 B.C.[6] Janus is an equally unusual type for imperial issues,[7] and the fourth centenary of his temple (*c.* 260 B.C.),[8] which likewise fell within this period (in *c.* A.D. 140–1), is surely the occasion of the coinage, just as a Claudian issue apparently commemorated its tercentenary (p. 70): for independent reasons Mattingly,[9] in correction of Strack,[10] prefers an early rather than a later date within the period A.D. 140–4 for this issue. Centenary mintages for temples go back to Caesar (pp. 15 f.).

This brings us to (4), for *Iuventas* and Janus were closely connected with the Capitoline deities.[11] Monetary issues in honour of the three divinities of the Capitol are very unusual (though this was not an entirely new type for medallions).[12] The present series coincides with the 650th anniversary of the great temple of those deities.[13] Its seventh centenary was likewise to be celebrated by Commodus (p. 111). The Aesculapius type, also, though again not

---

1 Ibid. p. 343. 2034 (Aurelius: TR. POT. XI. COS. II. S.C.).
2 Ibid. p. 79. 550, p. 135. 916 (dated: A.D. 157–8), p. 140. 938 (of A.D. 158–9), etc.; cf. Strack, III, p. 85.
3 *BMC. Imp.* IV, p. lviii; Strack, III, pp. 44 ff. For the dynastic policy of Pius, see Vogt, *Gnomon*, 1940, pp. 381 ff.
4 Livy, XXXVI, 5–6; cf. Platner and Ashby, *Topographical Dictionary of Ancient Rome*, p. 308.
5 Cf. *BMC. Imp.* IV, loc. cit.
6 Cf. Platner and Ashby, loc. cit. p. 259.

7 For the cult, see recently Altheim, *Italien und Rom*, II. p. 48; id. *Wörter und Sachen*, pp. 41 ff.; Huth, *Janus*; Lambrechts, *Mélanges Heuten* (*Latomus*, 1946), pp. 327 f.; Grimal, *Lettres d'Humanité*, 1945, IV, pp. 15 ff.; Calza, *Notizie degli Scavi*, 1939, pp. 361 ff.
8 Cf. Platner and Ashby, loc. cit. p. 277.
9 Loc. cit. p. lxxx.
10 III, p. 77.
11 Cf. Lambrechts, loc. cit. pp. 325, 327.
12 Toynbee, pp. 137, 204.
13 Beloch, *Römische Geschichte*, p. 35; Piganiol, *Histoire de Rome*, p. 38.

unprecedented on medallions,[1] may represent the début of that deity on the coinage;[2] and this innovation occurs in the 450th year of the most probable date for the arrival of Aesculapius's cult in Rome,[3] his next appearance being on its half-millennium (p. 119).

It is in keeping with the policy of Antoninus Pius that he should have honoured these great Republican centenaries and even half-centenaries. He showed conservative and antiquarian tendencies in matters of religion.[4] One may compare his *aes* medallions commemorating a wide range of subjects from Rome's traditional past.[5] Antoninus resembled his forerunners Augustus, Claudius and Domitian in this taste for the past and for anniversary coinages, just as, like them, he celebrated Secular Games. It was in his principate, too, that Appian wrote about ancient events, and Pausanias about ancient temples, such as those commemorated on the official coinages.

The last Roman piece of Antoninus to require consideration here refers to his restoration, not of coinage—for like Hadrian he preferred his own variants to this Flavian and Trajanic custom—but of the temple of Augustus and Livia.[6] The issue was made in *c.* A.D. 157–8; and Antoninus, with his historical bent, must have been aware that the later of those years witnessed the second centenary of the *imperium* of Augustus in 43 B.C.—an occasion already apparently honoured with centenary coinage by Nero (p. 84). Like Nero 100 years earlier, Antoninus Pius, in timing coinage (and perhaps the restoration of the temple also) to coincide with the bicentenary of Octavian's first *imperium*, intended to commemorate not merely one of a number of Augustan anniversaries but the date on which the essential power of the *Imperatores* had first been conferred. The reference to Augustus, though not the same anniversary motif, is paralleled on *aes* medallions of Antoninus, on which *Felicitas Augusti* carries a capricorn,[7] and on coins of that emperor inscribed ROMVLO AVGVSTO.[8]

---

1 Cf. Toynbee, pp. 138, 160; Mattingly, *BMC. Imp.* IV, p. xcv; Gnecchi, II, p. 9. 1 ff., III, p. 21. 108.

2 It is uncertain whether a large *aes* issue of Galba (*BMC. Imp.* I, p. 359. 260) represents Aesculapius or Apollo, and whether it is monetary or medallic (p. 94 n. 1).

3 293 B.C.; cf. Piganiol, *Histoire de Rome*, p. 89, etc.

4 Ibid. p. 295. For the religion of the period, see Swoboda, *Klio*, 1939, p. 232.

5 Toynbee, p. 143, etc.; id. *Archaeological Journal*, 1942, pp. 33 ff., *Classical Review*, 1925, pp. 170 ff.; *BMC. Imp.* IV, pp. xciv f.

6 *BMC. Imp.* IV, p. lxxiii, p. 135. 916 (TEMPLVM DIV. AVG. REST. COS. IIII.); cf. Grether, *American Journal of Philology*, 1946, p. 251, etc.

7 Cf. Toynbee, p. 100 n. 1.

8 Ibid.; *BMC. Imp.* IV, p. 206. 1286, p. 215. Another allusion to Augustus occurs at *colonia* Olbasa, which during this principate

As regards the reign of Marcus Aurelius, the technique which has been used in this book may facilitate a partial solution of two numismatic problems. The first of these is provided by the 'restoration', inscribed ANTONINVS ET VERVS AVG., of a legionary *denarius* of M. Antonius.[1] The second problem is constituted by the issues of A.D. 172–3 with RELIG. AVG. and types of Mercury, with or without his temple.[2] The first of these coinages is isolated and has been considered inexplicable.[3] But its background becomes clearer when one recalls that the probable date of issue (*c*. A.D. 165–9)[4] coincides with the second centenary of Antony's legionary *denarii*; that the only intervening legionary piece (of L. Clodius Macer) had been issued on the centenary of the same *denarii* (p. 86); that, although legionary coinage in general is far from frequent, their tercentenary was to be commemorated in the same way (p. 137); and that they enjoyed a very wide circulation until the period of the Severi at least (p. 87 n. 2). Such was the fame of Antony's coinage in spite of the defeat, so soon afterwards, of the legions that he had honoured. But the reason why Aurelius and Verus single out *Legio VI Ferrata* for this honour—for this they do—must remain unexplained.

The coins with RELIG. AVG. and Mercury, dated to A.D. 172–3, have been related to the incident of the 'rain miracle' which attracted so much attention at the time.[5] This 'miracle' has been dated to A.D. 174. But the allusion of these coins has been held to point to an earlier date;[6] in a recent study of the rain incident, Roos has

inaugurates its coinage with his portrait inscribed AVGVSTVS OLBASENORVM (Head, *Historia Numorum*², p. 709; Ruge, *PW*. XVII, 2. 2398). If, as is probable, Olbasa was founded after *c*. 13 B.C. (Ramsay, *JRS*. 1916, p. 86, etc., favours *c*. 6 B.C. but this is now disputed; the whole matter seems to need setting out afresh)—the coins of Antoninus Pius might commemorate its 150th anniversary. The same is true of *colonia* Comama, which likewise makes its first issues in his principate. Two other colonies, Cremna and Parlais, seem to inaugurate their issues under Aurelius (*BMC*. *Lycia*, etc., p. 216. 5, *BMC*. *Lycaonia*, etc., p. xxvi), conceivably for the bicentenary either of the annexation of Galatia in 25 B.C. or of its era of 20 B.C. (p. 91 n. 9).

1 *BMC*. *Imp*. IV, p. 456. 500, cf. p. cxxiii.
2 Ibid. p. 469. 583 (IMP. VI. COS. III.), p.

471. 601 (Aurelius), p. 628. 1441 (temple), p. 631. 1461; p. 472 n. (doubtful) reads IMP. VII. (or VIII.) COS. III.

3 According to *BMC*. *Imp*. IV, p. cxxiii, the coinage might be partly due to the similarity of the names Antonius and Antoninus.

4 Ibid. p. cxxiii n. 2: the eagle and standards reverse occurs at Alexandria in A.D. 165–6 (Vogt, *Die Alexandrinischen Münzen*, pp. 140 f.). The Roman issues may have been as early as *c*. 165; it is very likely that the moneyers of Aurelius did not know the exact date of the legionary. *denarii* of Antony (cf. p. 128 n. 2).

5 Cf. Toynbee, *NC*. 1940, p. 209; Nock, *CAH*. XII, p. 413 n. 1, etc. (Arnuphis).

6 Cf. *BMC*. *Imp*. IV, p. cxxxix; Piganiol, loc. cit. p. 368; Guey, *Mél. d'Arch. et d'Hist*. 1948, id. *Rev. de Phil*. 1948, p. 42.

denied that the coins have anything to do with it;[1] and the matter can only be left as unproven. The Roman tendency to remember anniversaries, which applies to the Antonines as much as to any other period, suggests a new approach. The year 173–4 was the bicentenary of the *restituta respublica* of Augustus. Anniversaries of that occasion had received scrupulous attention throughout the first century, and such celebrations were to continue until long after the time of Aurelius (p. 141).[2] The word RELIG(*io*) which appears on this coinage[3] could apply to honours paid by an emperor to the memory of the first *princeps*. Its occurrences are rare, and the next of them, under Valerian, was to coincide with another great anniversary, the tercentenary of the deification of Julius (p. 133). Mercury is a very suitable god for representation on a memorial coin of Augustus. Recent research has shown the extent to which, in popular religion at least, he was identified with that deity: Mrs Chittenden has compared the temple on these coins with the Farnesina stucco relief on which the figure of Mercury is labelled OCTAVI.[4]

An objection to the present interpretation might be made on the grounds that the Mercury temple of these coins has a semicircular pediment, considered to be of Egyptian origin, which did not reach Roman official religion until long after the life of Augustus.[5] But the history of the anniversary coinages supports Mrs Chittenden's contention[6] that such a motif need not necessarily indicate a specifically Egyptian significance for this Mercury.[7] For, in the first place, allusions are often of a highly composite character. Secondly, a deity of whose temple or altar the centenary is celebrated is often represented neither in a purely traditional guise nor for purely antiquarian reasons. However ancient the temple or occasion that is commemorated, the god or goddess is frequently endowed with a modern or topical significance and appearance, far removed from ancient Roman orthodoxy. A further example of this practice will

---

1 *Mededeelingen der Koninklijke Akademie van Wetenschappen, Afd. Letterkunde, Nieuwe Reeks*, 6, 1, 1943, p. 28.
2 An issue of silver *quinarii* in A.D. 163–4 may well celebrate the sesquicentenary of the death of Augustus: see Appendix I.
3 For *religio*, see Warde-Fowler, *The Religious Experience of the Roman People*, p. 192 n. 5; Altheim, *History of Roman*

Religion, p. 355 (short bibliography); Kerényi, *La Religione Antica (Storia delle Religioni*, XIV, 1940), pp. 64, 98 ff. etc.; de Sanctis, *Rivista di Filologia*, 1940, pp. 201 ff.
4 *NC.* 1945, pp. 50 ff.
5 Roos, loc. cit. p. 28 n. 93.
6 Loc. cit. pp. 54 f.
7 As Guey, *Rev. de Phil.* 1948, p. 18.

be found in the new character given to Jupiter by Commodus. As regards Mercury, many exotic manifestations of that divinity in the second century could be cited.[1] But the Egyptian temple-shape, if not selected as a compliment to the 'rain-bringer' Arnuphis,[2] may well refer (like crocodiles on many coins) to the capture of Egypt which inaugurated Augustus' régime. Like other emperors before and after him, Marcus Aurelius may use the occasion of an anniversary coinage to 'bring up to date' a divinity whose traditional aspect is relevant to the anniversary occasion.

Commodus is not behind Aurelius in combining antique anniversary occasions with references to the philosophical and religious tendencies of his own day. Both these motifs may be discerned in the legend SAEC(uli) FEL(icitas) on his decennalian coinage of A.D. 184–5.[3] This inscription, though later the commonest of clichés, was still very unusual in the time of Commodus. (Indeed, its only previous appearance, as far as is known, had been on coins of Faustina junior;[4] and this can hardly be regarded as a complete precedent, since the types of the Antonine and later empresses form a self-contained system that is quite distinct from the main imperial trends.)[5] The theme was, of course, appropriate to the *decennalia*, but its topical allusion was of wider scope. Commodus called himself the 'refounder' of Rome (and in a very few years he was to announce the beginning of a new *saeculum*).[6] But the allusion was not only to the present or future, for this issue coincided with the bicentenary of the *aureum saeculum* of Augustus (17 B.C.).[7] Such an anniversary was a fitting occasion for reference by the coinage to the forthcoming gestures of Commodus, who, like Augustus, described his new era as Golden.[8]

1 Besides the articles of Chittenden, Roos, and Guey, recent published work on Mercury-Hermes in general includes that of Festugière, *La Révélation d'Hermes Trismégiste*, I (1944); Kerényi, *Albae Vigiliae*, NF. 1, 1944; Bober, *Harvard Theological Review*, 1946, pp. 75 ff.; Rose, *JHS.* 1944 (1946), p. 110; id. *Classical Review*, 1946, pp. 91 ff.; etc.

2 Epit. Dio, 71, 8–10; cf. Chittenden, *NC.* 1945, p. 55, Guey, loci cit.

3 *BMC. Imp.* IV, p. 719. 166, p. 799 (P. M. TR. P. X. IMP. VII. COS. IIII. P. P., VOT. DE.; Victory).

4 Ibid. p. 161, p. 403. 136, p. 534. 936, p. 542. 991.

5 Cf. Pink, *NZ.* 1933, p. 19 n. 5. For a special study of the coinage of the Antonine empresses, see Laffranchi, *Numismatica*, 1938 (May–June). Their types seem to refer to anniversaries less often than those of other coinage.

6 Cf. especially Aymard, *Revue des études latines*, 1936, pp. 350 ff.; p. 351 for *Felicitas*.

7 For the centenary under Domitian, see above, pp. 94 f.

8 Cf. Ensslin, *CAH.* XII, p. 358.

The same year witnessed the issue of *denarii* and *asses* with CONC(*ordia*) MIL(*itum*).[1] This is not a very common type,[2] and it is here making its début as far as the issues of Commodus are concerned. This début occurs just 150 years after Tiberius had introduced the temple of *Concordia* to imperial coinage on the half-centenary of the Augustan *saeculum* (p. 52); it is also the 550th anniversary (end of fifth *saeculum* of 110 years) of that temple, and the quadringenary of the *aedes Concordiae in arce* (pp. 3, 2 n. 7). The government of Commodus is unlikely to have been unaware of these facts. But we are used to anniversary issues being given a topical 'twist', and there is nothing strange, especially at this date, in the selection of the soldiery as the body whose Concord is specially celebrated.

An unusual type on coins and medallions beginning in A.D. 189 is APOLLINI PALATINO.[3] Apollo *Palatinus* is indissolubly connected with the memory of Augustus; and the Palatine shrines had attained their greatest development on the inauguration of the temple of Vesta *in Palatio*, when Augustus created one of the bases of the Principate by becoming *pontifex maximus* in 12 B.C. The coins and medallions of Commodus were surely issued on the second centenary of that occasion, just as Domitian had held Secular Games on its centenary (pp. 5, 95 n. 2). So, in all probability, were two entirely isolated gold medallions of the same year A.D. 189, the first known representatives of this *genre* since Domitian (p. 95). These have types of FORT. FELI.[4] and PACI AETER.[5] The former was probably issued on 1 January.[6] The gold medallions of Domitian and Commodus, the only known issues in this medium between Augustus and Severus Alexander, were just 101 years apart. They commemorated the 100th year and bicentenary respectively of the same event.[7]

Among the more extraordinary types of the last year or two of the life of Commodus are I(*ovi*) O(*ptimo*) M(*aximo*) SPONSOR(*i*)

---

1 *BMC. Imp.* IV, p. 717. 159, p. 801 (P.M. TR. P. X. IMP. VII. COS. IIII. P.P.).
2 *Concordia* occurs most frequently on the coinage of empresses.
3 *BMC. Imp.* IV, p. 739. 271, p. 740. 276, p. 743. 292, p. clx (cf. p. 720), p. clxvii. Some of these are later than A.D. 189, but Mattingly ascribes the beginning of the type to that year and to a return by Commodus to the imperial residence.

4 *BMC. Imp.* IV, p. clxxxi; Gnecchi, I, p. 3. 1.
5 *BMC. Imp.* loc. cit.; Gnecchi, I, p. 3. 2.
6 Cf. Toynbee, p. 89.
7 Another noteworthy type of the same year (? perhaps non-Roman) is ROMVLO CONDITORI (*BMC. Imp.* IV, p. 740: Paris). It is possible that this type too, under Commodus as under other emperors, carries an Augustan allusion.

SEC(*uritatis*) AVG(*usti*) (coins[1] and medallions[2]) and IOVI DEFENS(*ori*) SALVTIS AVG(*usti*).[3] These are both dated to A.D. 191, and it is the first time that Jupiter has appeared in such a guise. The new and almost monotheistic character attributed to Jupiter by Commodus and his contemporaries is well indicated by references, on a further set of coins, to IOVI EXSVPER(*antissimo*).[4] This, as has been rightly said,[5] is God himself; so unrecognisable has the traditional poly- theism become. But, even if this Jupiter is not also Commodus himself, the connection of such a deity with Commodus-Hercules is not hard to see.[6] As Nock remarks about Commodus, there was a 'new directness of concentration upon his person'.[7]

These developments, however, can only be seen against their true and Roman background by recalling that the date (A.D. 191) selected for the commemoration of Jupiter as O.M. SPONSOR SEC. AVG. and DEFENSOR SALVTIS AVG. is that of the traditional seventh centenary (seven being a number of special significance) of his great Capitoline temple (p. 160). Many emperors besides Com- modus commemorated the foundations of ancient temples, and Antoninus Pius had celebrated in this very manner the 650th anni- versary of the same building (p. 105). But the issue of Commodus has a special significance owing to the deliberate conflation of the newest and most antique manifestations of Jupiter *Optimus Maximus*. Moreover, the original temple had signalised the beginning of the Roman Republic and of the Capitoline era; and Commodus- Hercules too, under the auspices of all-powerful Jupiter, had now refounded Rome and introduced a new *saeculum*.

1   *BMC. Imp.* IV, p. 754. 347, p. 833. 678, cf. p. clxix.

2   Ibid. p. clxxxii; Gnecchi, III, p. 183.

3   *BMC. Imp.* IV, p. 754. 349, p. 833. 679, cf. p. clxix.

4   Ibid. pp. 728, 808, 812, cf. p. clxxv.

5   Piganiol, *Histoire de Rome*, p. 300; cf. especially Alföldi, 25 *Jahre Römisch-Ger- manische Kommission*, 1930, p. 20; Cumont, *Archiv für Religionswissenschaft*, 1906, p. 323; Peterson, *Forschungen zur Religion und Literatur des Alten und Neuen Testaments*,

NF. LIV. 1926; id. *Der Monotheismus als politisches Problem*, etc.

6   A century later the link between Jupiter and Hercules was formalised by their position as patrons of Diocletian and Maximian; cf. Mattingly, *CAH.* XII, p. 329. For recent research on Jupiter, see the various works of Dumézil (e.g. *Jupiter-Mars-Quirinus*) and Lambrechts, *Mélanges Heuten (Latomus*, 1946), pp. 321 ff., on Jupiter-Janus-Vesta.

7   *CAH.* XII, p. 416, cf. p. 438, and Weber, ibid. XI, pp. 388 f.

CHAPTER VI

FROM PERTINAX TO VALERIAN

(i) *The emperors of* A.D. *193–4 and Severus*

Pertinax, in his short reign (A.D. 193), showed himself no less inclined to numismatic innovation than his predecessor; but the types which he introduces are popular ones[1] originating solely from the old Roman religion, without the exotic ingredients inserted by Commodus. For example, a *denarius* of Pertinax is inscribed MENTI LAVDANDAE[2] and appears to represent *Mens Bona*.[3] This deity had appeared on municipal coins of Paestum under the Republic[4] but not, it seems, on any official issue before the present one.[5] Her suitability to a régime in reaction against the novelties of Commodus is obvious. But probably the innovation is at least partly due to a tercentenary of the restoration of her temple falling at this time. This restoration had been performed by M. Aemilius Scaurus, and 107 B.C. (after the Cimbrian campaign) has been proposed as its date as an alternative to that of his consulship (115 B.C.).[6] Such a blend of topical relevance with antique occasion is in the normal tradition of the anniversary coinages.

But the same year, A.D. 193, also witnesses a new development of this theme. No sooner was the rule of the Antonines ended than its earlier part began to be regarded in much the same golden light as the days of Augustus: thus too its anniversaries, and particularly the anniversaries of its coinages, began to be celebrated.[7] The transitional emperors Pertinax, Didius Julianus and Pescennius Niger provide no less than four pointed reminiscences of the early

---

1 Cf. Mattingly, *Numismatic Review*, July 1946, p. 103.

2 M. & S. IV, 1, p. 8. 7. We have now entered a period for which the forthcoming *BMC. Imp.* V (not seen) will need to be taken into consideration.

3 M. & S. IV, 1, p. 4. Mattingly, *Numismatic Review*, loc. cit. p. 104, renders 'with praiseworthy intent'.

4 Cf. *FITA.* p. 324 (references).

5 Cf. M. & S. IV, 1, loc. cit.

6 Platner and Ashby, *Topographical Dictionary of Ancient Rome*, p. 339.

7 The fact that these commemorations specially apply to the anniversaries of coinages rather than to the anniversaries of events (cf. pp. 8, 161 ff.) may explain why the *Feriale Duranum* and comparable sources supply little analogy or complementary information (the literary sources never take much note of anniversary years—except *saecula* and *decennia*: see Introduction).

coinages of Antoninus Pius: (1) OPI DIVIN[AE] (Pertinax),[1] (2) SECVRITAS P.R. (Didius Julianus),[2] (3) HILAR. TEMPOR. (Didia Clara[3] under Didius Julianus), (4) ROMAE AETERNAE (Pescennius Niger).[4] The fact that each of these types directly recalls the great issues of Antoninus Pius of A.D. 140–4 is hardly likely to be an accident, especially as A.D. 193 and 194 represented the half-centenaries of dates within that period.

Before the OPI DIVIN. of Pertinax, the only numismatic appearance of *Ops* had been in that very series of Antoninus (OPI AVG.),[5] towards the end of the period A.D. 140–4.[6] The topical reference of Pertinax (whose *Ops*—unlike the *Ops Consiva* of Antoninus— holds ears of corn)[7] is to the reforms resulting from his own expert knowledge of agriculture.[8] The anniversary occasion, on the other hand, is no doubt related to the impression that Pertinax would resume the policy of the earlier Antonines.[9] One of those emperors, Marcus Aurelius, had introduced Pertinax to the senate,[10] and the latter had owed his earliest important commands to Antoninus Pius himself.[11] The successors of Pertinax did not repeat the type of *Ops* until Carausius, just 100 years later.

As has been said, Pertinax himself had repeated it from an issue of Antoninus, on the half-centenary of one of the latter's mintages. The same applies to the SECVRITAS P.R. and HILAR. TEMPOR. issues of Didius Julianus and his daughter. SECVRITAS AVG.,[12] SECVRITAS PVBLICA[13] and HILARITAS[14] had all appeared during the last phase of the same series of Antoninus (A.D. 140–4). Even Pertinax was not pro-Antonine in so comprehensive a manner as his successor Didius Julianus, for the latter included Commodus as well as Antoninus and Aurelius among the predecessors whom he held in honour.[15] It was,

---

1 M. & S. IV, p. 8. 8 f., p. 10. 20 and 27, p. 12. 35.
2 Ibid. p. 15. 4.
3 Ibid. p. 16. 10, p. 18. 20 and 21.
4 Ibid. p. 34. 69a, etc.: there are many variants.
5 *BMC. Imp.* IV, p. 34. 221, p. 202. 1258.
6 Ibid. p. lxxxi; cf. Strack, III, pp. 75 f.
7 *BMC. Imp.* IV, p. lvi.
8 Cf. Piganiol, *Histoire de Rome*, p. 395, etc. Similarly the Augustan *ara Opis Augustae* was linked to an *ara Cereris Matris*; cf. Gagé, *RGDA*. p. 177; Grether, *American Journal of Philology*, 1946, p. 226. For *Ops*,

see Vogt, *Gnomon*, 1940, p. 380; Weinstock, *JRS.* 1946, p. 109 n. 48; Lugli, ibid. p. 3 (possible temple); Mattingly, *Harvard Theological Review*, 1937, p. 104; id. *Numismatic Review*, loc. cit. p. 105.
9 Cf. Miller, *CAH.* XII, p. 1.
10 Cf. Piganiol, loc. cit.
11 Cf. Besnier, *Histoire Romaine*, IV, 1, p. 3.
12 *BMF. Imp.* IV, p. 209. 1311, etc.; cf. Strack, III, p. 128.
13 *BMC. Imp.* IV, p. 209. 1312, etc.
14 Ibid. p. 86. 606, etc.; cf. Strack, III, p. 109.
15 Piganiol, loc. cit. p. 396

incidentally, Commodus who had associated himself particularly closely with the type of *Hilaritas*, by being the only emperor, as far as is known at present, to show that divinity on medallions.[1]

Pescennius Niger introduced or revived a number of unfamiliar features on his coinage, but the theme which he stresses most frequently is ROMA AETERNA. This appears in many forms. The same type, like those of Pertinax and Didius Julianus just described, had formed part of the important series issued by Antoninus Pius half a century earlier.[2] Niger's epithet was *aurea saecla volens*; Antoninus Pius is recorded as one of the emperors whom he most admired;[3] he also adopted the title *iustus*. These are all reasons why he should have adhered to the prevailing custom of recalling the rule of Antoninus. Strack[4] attributes the type of Antoninus to as early a date as A.D. 140, and to the alleged completion at that time of the temple of Roma *Aeterna* and Venus *Felix* (p. 127). If he is right, Niger's issues are scarcely half-centenary issues. But there is no need to assume so early a date, and it is in any case unnecessary to suppose that the government of Niger knew in which part of the period A.D. 140–4 any of these indefinitely dated issues of Antoninus had been made.[5]

The choice of the great series of A.D. 140–4 for revival is particularly appropriate. That period had proved to be the beginning of a great epoch of peace. Moreover, it had been heralded by much talk of just such a new golden *saeculum* as actually followed, and this idea had pervaded the coinage of Antoninus during those years. The importance of the period A.D. 140–4 is further outlined by its great series of medallions.

Septimius Severus followed the example of all his immediate rivals and predecessors by commemorating the half-centenary of the same

---

1 Cf. Toynbee, p. 201. For the type, see Mattingly, *Proceedings of the Cambridge Philological Society*, 1927, pp. 3 ff.

2 *BMC. Imp.* IV, p. 205. 1279, etc. For the origins of the Roma cult, see Altheim, *History of Roman Religion*, p. 527 n. 7 (bibliography); Hommel, *Die Antike*, 1942; Hannestad, *Classica et Mediaevalia*, 1944, pp. 194 ff.; Toynbee, *NC.* 1936, pp. 325 ff. on *BMC. Imp.* III, pp. xlviii, cxxxvii f.; Picard, *Revue archéologique*, 1947, p. 103,

Delos; also an awaited publication on an inscription of Cibyra.

3 Spartian, *SHA. Vita Nigri*, 12.

4 III, p. 69 (tentatively).

5 If Niger's mint-master intended his coinage to commemorate the half-centenary, but judged the date of the prototype wrongly, then his issues with ROMAE AETERNAE may be described as 'pseudo-anniversary' (p. 128 n. 2); but there is no need to suppose this.

great coinages and medallions issued by Antoninus Pius in A.D. 140–4. Those issues had, towards the end of the four-year period in question, included the type APOLLINI AVGVSTO[1] (a type also reproduced on contemporary medallions).[2] It was just 50 years later that Severus issued pieces with the same inscription:[3] it had not appeared, as far as is known, on any issues of the period between the two coinages in question. Apollo is one of the many deities whose official character gained new aspects during the second century. The types of Antoninus and Severus deserve study in connection with the APOLLINI PALATINO of Commodus (p. 110) and APOLLINI SANCTO of Pescennius Niger.[4] The former legend was repeated by Severus on a medallion[5] (in the case of Commodus it has been shown to refer to Augustus, with whom the cult had so special a connection).

A little later than the Apollo issues, Geta, in c. A.D. 200–2, provides the inscription LAETITIA PVBL.[6] Laetitia had likewise made its début on the Roman coinage of Antoninus Pius. It had appeared on issues that were perhaps just half a century earlier than Geta's, in A.D. 150 and 151 (LAETITIA COS. IIII: Ceres and Proserpina[7]—though its first use by an empress [not necessarily a precise precedent, cf. p. 109] may perhaps slightly antedate this).[8] Severus paid great official attention to the Antonines,[9] whose descendant he claimed to be[10]—thus, according to Frank,[11] establishing a legal claim to their former properties. He even deified Commodus[12] (already honoured

---

1 BMC. Imp. IV, p. 30. 186, etc.; cf. pp. lv f.; and Strack, III, p. 85, cf. n. 246.
2 Toynbee, p. 137; Gnecchi, II, p. 9. 4.
3 M. & S. IV, 1, p. 96. 40, p. 135. 345, p. 184. 682, p. 186. 699, cf. pp. 66, 80; cf. Bellinger, Dura, VI, pp. 128 f., for mintage.
4 M. & S: IV, 1, p. 22. 2; for the god, p. 20. For sanctus, see Kerényi, La Religione Antica (Storia delle Religioni, XIV, 1940), p. 74; de Sanctis, Rivista di Filologia, 1940, pp. 201 f.
5 Gnecchi, II, p. 73. 3.
6 M. & S. IV, 1, p. 315. 10; and Gnecchi, II, p. 73. 3. The type had also appeared for Julia Domna. See M. & S. IV, 1, pp. 71, 77; Babelon, Rn. 1945, p. 150; cf. Blanchet, ibid. p. l, for LAETITIA TEMPORVM (galley) of the decennalia in A.D. 202. Possibly LAETITIA PVBL. also is attributable to the decennalia.
7 BMC. Imp. IV, p. 102. 714, p. 105. 724; cf. Strack, III, p. 115.

8 Strack, III, p. 112.
9 Thus Severus and his immediate predecessors would clearly not have agreed with Kornemann's remarkable description of Antoninus, Aurelius and Commodus as die drei kleinen Antonine (Römische Geschichte, II, p. 206 n.).
10 Cf. Strong, JRS. 1939, p. 154; Guey, Bulletin de la Société Toulousaine d'Études Classiques, 1939; id. Mélanges d'Archéologie et d'Histoire, 1940; Hoey, YCS. 1940, p. 186 n. 884; etc. The portraits of Severus were also consciously Antonine; cf. Rodenwaldt, CAH. XII, p. 545.
11 Economic Survey of Ancient Rome, V, p. 80; Last, JRS. 1940, p. 201.
12 Cf. Piganiol, loc. cit. p. 397; Miller, CAH. XII, p. 16.

by Didius Julianus); he also repeated an anniversary coinage of
Aurelius (p. 119), who had admitted him to the senate.[1] In his
numismatic commemoration of Antoninus Pius, Severus is following
the example of Pertinax, whom he greatly honoured.[2] 'Spartian'
quotes a rumour that Severus gave his sons the name Antoninus in
honour of Pius rather than of Aurelius.[3]

Severus struck a more unusual note by stressing his descent,
through the Antonines, from the first of the line of so-called 'good'
emperors, namely Nerva.[4] The centenaries of Nerva's accession,
reign and death occurred in A.D. 196–8, and the same dates witnessed
the mintage of three types reminiscent of that *princeps*. The legends
on these coins of Severus are FORTVNAE REDVCI (A.D. 195–6),[5]
PROVIDENTIA AVG. (A.D. 196–7),[6] and CONCORDIA[E] MILITVM (on
coins[7] and medallions[8]—of Geta—A.D. 197–8). The issues of Nerva
had been inscribed FORTVNA AVGVST.[9] and FORTVNA P.R. (from
A.D. 96),[10] PROVIDENTIA SENATVS (A.D. 97)[11] and CONCORDIA EXERCI-
TVVM (A.D. 96–7).[12] Should we regard these resemblances as due to
mere chance? The fact that the personifications in question are not
particularly unusual ones might lead to this conclusion. But it is
rendered unlikely by the keen interest of the Romans, and of their
mint, in centenaries; also by Severus's independently attested claim
of descent from Nerva, whose centenaries conveniently occurred
during his reign and whose half-centenary may already have been
commemorated by Antoninus Pius (Appendix II).[13]

A supporter of Nerva was likely to be a supporter of Trajan.[14]
Severus probably selected the anniversary of Trajan's *dies imperii*
for the celebration of his own eastern victories (refs. on p. 2

---

1 Piganiol, loc. cit. p. 396.

2 Besides deifying Pertinax, Severus in-
stituted (but later apparently abolished)
celebrations for the same emperor's *dies
imperii*, cf. Hoey, loc. cit. p. 50 n. 109.

3 *SHA. Vita Getae*, 2. 2.

4 Cf. Miller, *CAH*. XII, p. 13; Ensslin, ibid.
p. 355; Hoey, loc. cit. p. 186 n. 885.

5 M. & S. IV, 1, p. 187. 703 a: the legend
continues for several years. Cf. FORTVNAE
AVGG., A.D. 196–7 (ibid. p. 100. 77).

6 Ibid. p. 102. 92 a, cf. p. 67.

7 Ibid. p. 104. 108.

8 Gnecchi, II, p. 78. 3.

9 *BMC. Imp.* III, p. 2. 10, etc.

10 Ibid. p. 2. 12, etc.

11 Ibid. p. 21 (Paris), etc. The contrast in
phraseology between the Providence types
of Nerva and Severus is characteristic of
their respective times.

12 *BMC. Imp.* III, p. 1. 4, etc.; cf. Syme,
JRS. 1930, p. 64.

13 Nerva, in his turn, provided links with
the founders of the Principate: his aunt
was descended from Tiberius (cf. Longden,
CAH. XI, p. 189), and he was the last *princeps*
to be buried in the mausoleum of Augustus
(ibid. n. 5; cf. Groag, *Jahreshefte des öster-
reichischen archäologischen Instituts*, 1924,
Beibl. pp. 425 f.).

14 This remains true in spite of differences
in policy (*BMC. Imp.* III, p. lxix).

n. 1).[1] Trajan was to remain a favourite, for example under Severus Alexander, Gordian III and Trajanus Decius, and in the fourth century (p. 150). An *aureus* issued by Severus between *c.* 202 and *c.* 210[2] shows a view of the *Circus Maximus* which Trajan had introduced to the coinage just a century earlier, in *c.* A.D. 103–11.[3] Trajan had expended large sums on the *Circus* in *c.* 103, and Severus restored that building in *c.* 203 (p. 5).[4] This restoration was in accordance with his general preference of the *plebs* to the senate, a tendency which—though his policy was usually in favour of the provinces[5]—led him to revive the Italian *alimenta*.[6] To that occasion should probably be attributed issues with the legend INDVLGENTIA AVGG. IN ITALIAM,[7] which fall within the same general period. Now the series of Trajan, to which reference has been made, had included the famous issues inscribed ALIM(*enta*) ITAL(*iae*).[8] The centenary of those issues was a particularly apt occasion for the revival of the *alimenta* by Severus, since that organisation, developed by Trajan, had probably originated with the ostensible earlier ancestor of Severus, namely Nerva.[9]

But Severus did not merely revive the coin-types of the imperial heyday. He also repeated the practice of that period (and of Julius Caesar, Tiberius and Claudius) by commemorating the anniversaries of the great Republican temples. In this category there seem to be at least five issues: (1) FIDES PVBLICA (A.D. 196–8);[10] (2) SALVTI AVG[G]. (A.D. 197–8);[11] (3) CASTOR (Geta, *c.* A.D. 200–2);[12] (4) AESCULAPIUS (A.D. 207);[13] (5) IOVI VICTORI, on a large silver medallion of the same year.[14]

To take the last of these issues first, we must bear in mind the extreme rarity of silver medallions hitherto and at this period. This

1 Hadrian may already perhaps have commemorated Trajan's *tricennium* by an Alexandrian 'Nome' coinage: see Appendix II.
2 M. & S. IV, I. p. 124. 260.
3 *BMC. Imp.* III, p. 180. 853 (S.P.Q.R. OPTIMO PRINCIPI).
4 M. & S. loc. cit. attribute the coins conjecturally to *c.* A.D. 207.
5 Caracalla was to appoint officials *ad corrigendum statum Italiae*; cf. Ensslin, *CAH.* XII, p. 391.
6 Cf. Miller, *CAH.* XII, pp. 24 f. Recent articles on *Italia* are those of Klingner, *Die Antike*, XVII, 2. 1941; Rauhut, *Würzburger Jahrbücher*, I, 1946, p. 133.

7 M. & S. IV, I, p. 125. 268; cf. RESTITVTOR VRBIS; ibid. p. 113. 167 ff. (A.D. 200–1), p. 127. 288 ff. (A.D. 202–10).
8 *BMC. Imp.* III, p. 82. 378 (COS. V.P.P.S.P. Q.R. OPTIMO PRINC., ALIM. ITAL.), etc.
9 Cf. Longden, loc. cit. p. 192. Or had Domitian really been the originator?—as Asbach, *Römisches Kaisertum und Verfassung*, pp. 188 ff.; cf. tentatively Syme, *JRS.* 1930, p. 63 n. 3, *pace* Longden, loc. cit. n. 2.
10 M. & S. IV, I, p. 213. 8; cf. p. 75.
11 Ibid. p. 105. 119, p. 192. 747.
12 Ibid. p. 3, 15. 6, p. 330. 111, p. 331. 116.
13 Ibid. p. 196. 775.
14 Toynbee, pp. 45, 148 (10-*denarius* piece).

one was (as far as we know) the largest yet to have been struck. Only four earlier emperors are known to have issued silver medallions, and in the case of two of these, Domitian and Hadrian, anniversary occasions have been suggested (pp. 94 f., 101).[1] The clue to the medallion of Severus lies in its reverse type of Jupiter in a quadriga, throwing a thunderbolt at two giants. Jupiter *Victor*, who comes immediately after the Capitoline Triad in the Arval Acts,[2] was already not an unknown type on the coinage of Severus,[3] but here is an exceptional rendering of the theme in an exceptional medium. It is probably connected with the half-millenary of the temple of that deity (founded by Q. Fabius Maximus in 295 B.C.),[4] an anniversary which had occurred in the previous year. (There is nothing strange about a centenary coinage occurring a year after the date on which it fell precisely due [p. 11].) Just 50 years later (again apparently a year late) Valerian was to commemorate the next half-centenary of the temple on his coinage. The type of Severus gained added point from the British victories, probably under the titular command of Caracalla, which are attributable to the years A.D. 206 and 207.[5]

This type of anniversary is common to all the five issues which have been summarised. The issue of Severus with FIDES PVBLICA (a legend which had not appeared on the coinage since Hadrian) coincided with the 450th anniversary of the earlier of the two dates (*c.* 254 and *c.* 250 B.C.) assigned to the dedication of the *Aedes Fidei Publicae* by A. Atilius Calatinus.[6] *Salus* is a more frequent type; but she seems not to have previously figured on the Roman series of Severus,[7] so the revival of issues in her honour in A.D. 197–8 may well refer to the half-millenary of the traditional date, 303 or 302 B.C., of her temple's dedication by C. Junius Bubulcus.[8]

As regards CASTOR, it was customary for young princes to be equated with the Dioscuri.[9] But Castor (though he had appeared on

1 The others celebrate an accession (Trajan) and a marriage (Verus): Gnecchi, I, pp. 44 f.; Toynbee, p. 128; *BMC. Imp.* IV, p. cxlv, cf. p. 856.

2 Cf. Fink, *YCS.* 1940, p. 57; Henzen, *Acta Fratrum Arvalium*, pp. xciv, cxli.

3 E.g. M. & S. IV, I, p. 118.

4 Livy, X, 29.14; cf. Thulin, *PW.* X, I. 1133.

5 Cf. Miller, *CAH.* XII, p. 38 and n. 5.

6 Otto, *PW.* VI, 2. 2281; cf. Platner and Ashby, *Topographical Dictionary of Ancient Rome*, p. 209.

7 Her appearances on the coins of Antonine emperors (not empresses) are also somewhat abnormal, often being very rare; further study is needed here, in connection with evidence regarding *auguria salutis* (pp. 71 f.).

8 Cf. Platner and Ashby, loc. cit. p. 462; Beloch, *Römische Geschichte*, p. 411.

9 Cf. *FITA.* pp. 145, 219, etc. for origins. For Severus as *propagator imperii*, see Instinsky, *Klio*, 1941, pp. 212 ff.

a medallion of Commodus)[1] had never before been mentioned on the coinage: and 499 B.C., one of the legendary dates for the temple of the twin deities, was just 700 years before Geta's issue (seven being a number of special importance [p. 2 n. 3]). A coin of Julius Caesar had apparently commemorated the quadringenary (another special landmark) of the same temple (p. 15). His moneyer, unlike Geta's, seems to have calculated from the other traditional date 496, and not from 499 B.C.; but the disparity is not surprising or significant (cf. p. 12).[2]

Aesculapius has been met with before in this book, on coins and medallions of Antoninus Pius for Marcus Aurelius, celebrating the 450th anniversary of the arrival of that deity (p. 106). During the intervening period—just 50 years—there has been only one coin in honour of this formerly popular divinity.[3] The issue of Severus may therefore perhaps be considered, in conjunction with the SALVTI AVG[G]. pieces, as a second Severan example of a half-millenary issue. The topical *raison d'être* of Aesculapius, and probably of the *Salus* group also, was no doubt the health of Severus, which was giving him trouble.[4] Babelon has shown that the god bears the attributes of Eschmoun of Carthage.[5] We are by now accustomed to ancient deities, on the celebration of their anniversaries, displaying the signs of recent and current exotic developments in official religion (pp. 108 f.).

The reference to Carthaginian Aesculapius is only one of several allusions to Carthage and Africa on the anniversary issues of Septimius Severus. Attention has often been given to his type of *Dea Caelestis* riding on a lion, with the legend INDVLGENTIA AVGG. IN CARTH. This appears on coins[6] and medallions (Caracalla),[7] some of the former being dated to A.D. 203 and 204. *Dea Caelestis* probably figures as a general symbol of Carthage.[8] For the topical

1 Gnecchi, II, p. 62. 96 f.; *BMC. Imp.* IV, p. clxxxi.
2 It may not be necessary on this account to classify one of the two issues as 'pseudo-anniversary' (p. 128 n. 2), since both traditional dates received acceptance (p. 15 n. 6).
3 Of Clodius Albinus (M. & S. IV, 1, p. 44.2). Aesculapius was especially popular on medallions (Toynbee, pp. 138, 160; Gnecchi, II, p. 9. 1 ff., p. 19. 86; *BMC. Imp.* IV, p. xcv, etc.), but in this medium too no examples are known between Antoninus and Severus.

A recent work on the god in general (not seen by the present writer) is that of E. J. & L. Edelstein, *Asclepius*.
4 Cf. M. & S. IV, 1, p. 70.
5 *Mélanges Numismatiques*, IV, p. 123, cf. pp. 121 f.
6 M. & S. IV, 1, p. 116. 193 (TR.P. XII), p. 125. 266, p. 194. 759 (TR.P. XI), p. 195. 763 (TR.P. XII), etc.; cf. Babelon, loc. cit. pp. 114 ff.
7 Gnecchi, III, p. 39. 7.
8 Nock, *CAH.* XII, p. 416.

significance of such a type referring to that city we may compare Ulpian's statement that Severus gave the *ius Italicum* to Carthage as well as to Utica and Lepcis Magna.[1] Blanchet[2] has suggested that the type may specially allude to the construction of the Zaghouan aqueduct at Carthage. At all events some favour was granted to that city, and this no doubt occurred on the occasion of a visit to Africa by Severus in *c*. A.D. 203–4.[3] The imperial beneficence, and these coins, are considered to be connected with the Secular Games celebrated in A.D. 204.[4]

This issue is clearly parallel to the pieces inscribed INDVLGENTIA AVGG. IN ITALIAM (p. 117). Those have been attributed to a centenary occasion, and a similar motive seems to have contributed to the issue recording the favour to Carthage. Carthage had been refounded as a Roman colony by the triumvir Lepidus in accordance with a plan of Julius Caesar's.[5] Now the Caesarian plan for another African colony—Hippo Diarrhytus—may have dated from 46 B.C. (pp. 78 f. n. 7). If we postulate the same date for Caesar's plan for Carthage—and there is plausibility in attributing such a plan to the centenary of Carthage's destruction (p. 4)[6]—we find that the issue of Severus recording the favour to that city coincides with the quarter-millenary of the foundation plan. But these pieces with INDVLGENTIA AVGG. IN CARTH. also occur just half a century after the *aes* issues of Antoninus Pius with INDVLGENTIA AVG.[7] The word *Indulgentia* occurs but rarely on coinage; and other pieces also of Septimius Severus have commemorated anniversaries of Antoninus Pius.

The mintages of Severus make further references to Africa. Almost immediately after the beginning of his reign, in A.D. 194 and 195, he issued the famous *sestertii*[8] and medallions[9] with DIS AVSPICIB(*us*), etc. These show Hercules and Bacchus, the gods of Lepcis[10] Magna, where Septimius Severus was born;[11] he gave them

1 Cf. Babelon, loc. cit. pp. 126 f. At this time (unlike the earliest days of the principate, cf. *FITA*. pp. 315 ff.) such a privilege always conveyed remission of taxes.
2 *Rn*. 1937, p. 334.
3 Hasebroek, *Untersuchungen zur Geschichte des Kaisers Septimius Severus*, pp. 132 ff.; Miller, *CAH*. XII, p. 20 n. 3; Besnier, *Histoire Romaine*, IV, I, p. 27 n. 143.
4 Nock, loc. cit. p. 416; for the Games, cf. M. & S. IV, I, p. 69; Besnier, loc. cit. p. 35; Babelon, *Rn*. 1945, p. 150.

5 Cf. *FITA*. pp. 227, 231 f., 302.
6 On that event, see Adcock, *The Cambridge Historical Journal*, 1946, pp. 117 ff.
7 *BMC. Imp*. IV, p. 320. 1920 (A.D. 152–3), p. 324. 1939 (A.D. 153–4), etc.
8 M. & S. IV, I, p. 94. 25, p. 95. 31, p. 181. 661, p. 182. 666, p. 183. 669.
9 Toynbee, p. 210; Gnecchi, II, p. 73. 4.
10 For spelling, see Ward-Perkins, *JRS*. 1948, p. 58 n. 3.
11 Spartian, *SHA. Vita Severi*, I, 2.

temples at Rome.[1] Now similar representations of these two deities, in purely Semitic guise,[2] had occurred on the coinage of that city under Augustus; and the present writer has elsewhere endeavoured to show that Augustus had promoted Lepcis Magna to the status of *civitas libera*, in *c.* 7 B.C.[3] Acceptance of that view will make the coins and medallions of Severus into another anniversary issue, this time commemorating the bicentenary of the *liberatio* of Lepcis Magna.[4] There are many precedents for the celebration of local anniversaries by local coinage—including a quarter-centenary issue for Lepcis Magna itself under Tiberius.[5] But here Severus innovates (as far as our knowledge extends at present) by celebrating the double centenary of his home town on an *official* issue.[6] He was apparently to repeat the practice ten years later for the quarter-millenary of the plan to colonise the capital of its province (p. 120). The practice of celebrating important local anniversaries on the official coinage was to be repeated by Gallienus (pp. 136 f.).

Thus the custom that is the theme of this book attained an interesting and varied efflorescence under Septimius Severus. His recognisable anniversary commemorations show a wider scope than those of any other emperor. They include references to the early Republic, to Caesarian and Augustan city foundations,[7] and to the reigning emperor's 'ancestors' Nerva and Trajan. To these examples should be added the allusions to Antoninus Pius (which had become customary in the months preceding Severus's accession), and the revival of an anniversary coinage of Aurelius.[8] This multiplicity of anniversary coinages is relevant to the deep interest of the Severi in religion. Septimius Severus was not the first to import non-

1 Cf. Besnier, loc. cit. p. 44.
2 Cf. Dieudonné, *Rn.* 1936, p. 185.
3 *FITA.* p. 341.
4 For the new buildings there at this period, see Miller, loc. cit. p. 21; Ward Perkins, *JRS.* 1948, pp. 59 ff.
5 *FITA.* loc. cit.
6 At about the same date Clodius Albinus shows a type relating to his own city of origin, Hadrumetum (M. & S. IV, 1, p. 45. 10, cf. pp. 41 f.; also on medallions, Gnecchi, II, p. 73. 4). Severus has the same legend SAECVLO FRVGIFERO (M. & S. IV, 1, p. 180. 655), but without the distinctive type.
7 As regards Augustus, a gold *quinarius* of A.D. 208 may conceivably commemorate the

quarter-millenary of 43 B.C. (see Appendix I). The opening of the official mint for tetradrachms at Tyre in A.D. 208–12 (*BMC. Phoenicia*, p. 304. 36 f., p. 305. 42 f.; cf. Bellinger, *The Syrian Tetradrachms of Caracalla and Macrinus, Numismatic Studies*, III, 1940, p. 5) might be thought to celebrate the same anniversary. But doubt is cast on this interpretation—or rather an alternative or supplementary one is provided—by the explicitly decennalian character (for Caracalla) of colonial issues of Berytus bearing the same date (*BMC. Phoenicia*, p. 70. 122 ff.).
8 Mention may also be made of the deification issue for Commodus, which perhaps coincided with the *quinquennium* of his death.

Roman attributes of deities into the coinage: anniversary issues of the second century have already provided examples of this practice (pp. 108 f.). But by promoting the cults of his home country to imperial status Severus created a precedent for similar, and more startling, action by his Syrian grand-nephew Elagabalus.

The anniversary coinages of Severus as usual provide a traditional Roman accompaniment, or corrective, to the religious innovations of the times. In this period the comparison and contrast of the two themes is striking. The age of Severus was a revolutionary one,[1] and yet the coinages refer to events from all the chief epochs of Rome's past. It was an age of violent religious development,[2] yet the coins stress the anniversaries of the most antique temples; alongside the new exotic practices, the old official cults were still in favour.[3]

Severus's commemoration of whole series of Republican temple anniversaries reminds us that he was, in his way, a student of Republican history; for he was reported to express admiration for the crueller measures of Marius and Sulla.[4] Those measures had been far removed in character from the nobility retrospectively attributed to events of the earlier Republic. But, by another paradox, the policy of Severus was equally different from that of the man whom he imitated by commemorating these temples, Antoninus Pius.[5] Just as different from Severus was Tiberius, who had first developed the potentialities of the anniversary coinages, of which Severus became (as far as can be seen) the most comprehensive exponent. Neither emperor had harmonious relations with the senate, but how divergent were their attitudes to that body! Yet Tiberius and Severus shared a deep interest in matters of religion, and to Romans that meant a corresponding interest in the past history of Rome. That is why their two reigns witnessed two climactic periods in the history of the anniversary coinages. Incidentally, Caracalla was an avowed admirer of Tiberius (p. 123), and therefore presumably himself saw, or endeavoured to create, resemblances between the latter's régime and that of the Severi.

---

1 Cf. Piganiol, *Histoire de Rome*, p. 407, etc.
2 Ibid. p. 403.
3 Cf. Besnier, loc. cit. p. 129.

4 Ibid. p. 398. Pescennius Niger, too, was reported to be an admirer of Marius; cf. Spartian, *SHA. Vita Nigri*, 12. 1.
5 Piganiol, loc. cit. p. 400.

(ii) *The later Severi*

One of the anniversary coinages attributable to the sole reign of Caracalla shows a type of the emperor sacrificing before a round temple of Vesta, with three Vestals, two men and two children. The issue begins in A.D. 214,[1] continuing into the next year.[2] Except for the coinage of empresses (which obeys rules of its own, p. 109), the last appearance of a round temple of Vesta had been on Vespasian's coinage of A.D. 73 (p. 91).[3] That issue had commemorated the centenary of the *restituta respublica* of Augustus; it had also taken place just half a century after the mintage of Tiberius which, introducing the type to the coinage, had celebrated the *decennium* of the consecration of Augustus (p. 34). An issue of Nero with identical type had signalised the fiftieth anniversary of the same event (p. 80). Caracalla's coins were presumably struck because A.D. 214 was the bicentenary year of the very same occasion. This type will next occur (except for Etruscilla whose types, like those of other empresses, are usually outside the main stream) under Postumus in A.D. 264—precisely half a century after Caracalla's issues, and a quarter of a *millennium* after the death of Augustus (p. 135). It was not likely that this type of celebration would be ignored by Caracalla, who carried to extremes the religious interests of his parents.[4] He was an admirer of Tiberius,[5] who had inaugurated the type: this admiration was a rarer phenomenon now that Tacitus had done his worst than it had been during the first century (p. 97 and n. 4).

The same anniversary celebration in A.D. 214 seems to have occasioned the issue, in the name of Julia Domna, not only of coins,[6] but also of a great silver medallion,[7] as well as a bimetallic 'pseudo-medallion'[8] and a small *aes* medallion.[9] All these have the same type as the issues of Caracalla described above (VESTA [MATER]). The

1 M. & S. IV, 1, p. 247. 249.
2 Ibid. p. 251. 271.
3 For evidence, see Brown, *Numismatic Notes and Monographs*, XC, 1940, pp. 40 ff. (Caracalla on p. 44). Brown considers this temple to be that of Vesta *in Foro*, but earlier ones to represent Vesta *in Palatio*: but this is doubtful.
4 Cf. Dio 78. 16. 1; Besnier, loc. cit. p. 64; Miller, loc. cit. p. 44.

5 Cf. Besnier, loc. cit. p. 57.
6 M. & S. IV, 1, p. 274. 392, p. 313. 607.
7 Ibid. p. 171. 587A; Toynbee, p. 148 n. 10, p. 158; cf. Gnecchi, I, p. 45 (10-*denarius* piece).
8 Toynbee, p. 27 and n. 44; Gnecchi, III, p. 92. 10 (Milan) (IVLIA AVGVSTA).
9 Gnecchi, III, p. 39. 9 (Berlin). VESTA only; and IVLIA PIA FELIX AVG.

obverse of the silver medallion shows the legend IVLIA AVGVSTA, and her half-length diademed bust with *cornucopiae* and statue of *Concordia*, who herself holds *cornucopiae* and *patera*. Silver medallions had hitherto been, and were still, exceptionally infrequent. It was only a very few years earlier that the type of the *Tres Monetae* had passed from bronze to silver medallions,[1] inaugurating for the first time an extensive non-anniversary series in that genre.[2] Previously (though, as usual, no formal *argumentum a silentio* is advisable) only three known silver medallions, two of Trajan and one of Lucius Verus, had celebrated topical events (p. 108 n. 1). All others recorded—those of Domitian (p. 94), Hadrian (p. 101) and Severus (p. 117)—had apparently been inspired by anniversary occasions, as, also, were the gold medallions of the same periods (p. 110). The type of Julia Domna gained added significance from the fact that the shrine of Vesta *in Foro* had been restored by her and her husband.[3]

This bicentenary occasion also witnessed, not wholly by chance, a revival at Alexandria and a major monetary reform at Rome. The former consisted of the issue, in A.D. 213–14 and 214–15, of bronze pieces of a large denomination which had previously been in abeyance for many years. The new output, which was in the names of Caracalla and Julia Domna, was remarkable for its variety and evidently medallic character.[4] Such Alexandrian revivals and innovations were frequently timed to take place on anniversary occasions (p. 41 n. 5). The same applies to reforms of the coinage at Rome (ibid.): and the greatest monetary innovation for a century, the introduction of the *antoninianus* by Caracalla, occurred in this

---

1 M. & S. IV, 1, p. 229 (Caracalla, A.D. 210, AEQVITATI PVBLICAE). For *Aequitas* see Kenner, *NZ.* 1886, pp. 7 ff.; *BMC. Imp.* III, pp. xxxv f.; ibid. IV, Index s.v.

2 For the type, see Toynbee, pp. 148 f., cf. p. 149 n. 25; and for its origins *BMC. Imp.* IV, pp. clxxi n. 1, cxlv.

3 Cf. Rodenwaldt, *CAH.* XII, p. 551.

It might be objected that the legend IVLIA AVGVSTA on the silver and bimetallic medallions requires attribution to a date before A.D. 211. But (1) there is no positive evidence for the inauguration of the IVLIA PIA FELIX AVG. titulature until c. 215 (M. & S. IV, 1, p. 63; cf. Pink, *NZ.* 1934, p. 7; Alföldi, *Röm. Mitt.* 1935, p. 90 n. For the titles of Julia Domna, see Instinsky, *Klio*, 1941,

pp. 200 ff.). (2) Even if that titulature was inaugurated before c. A.D. 215, the style IVLIA AVGVSTA is likely to have persisted simultaneously: there are other medallions of apparently late date which bear it (e.g. Gnecchi, II, pp. 76 f.), and these seem to fill the gaps due to the absence of any known large aes medallion with IVLIA PIA FELIX AVG. (3) The portraits on the silver and bimetallic pieces, far from supplying evidence for the earlier date, tend to support the later attribution. The bust of the silver piece in particular, however, is of so exceptional a character that no chronological deductions can be based on it.

4 Milne, *Catalogue of Alexandrian Coins in the Ashmolean Museum*, p. xxiii.

same year 214.[1] Apparently, then, Caracalla did not yield to his predecessors in his observation of a great Augustan anniversary. We may wonder whether the opening of the official mints for tetradrachms at about two dozen Syrian[2] and one Cypriot city,[3] at some date between A.D. 213 and 217, may not have signalised the same bicentenary.[4]

The next piece to be considered[5] seems to provide yet another commemoration of an Augustan anniversary. This is the great gold medallion of Severus Alexander dated to A.D. 230.[6] On its reverse, with inscription P.M. TR. P. VIII. COS. III. P.P., is the emperor seated, holding 'Victory' and long sceptre; he is crowned by another figure of 'Victory', with palm, and before him stands *Virtus* (?), with a shield inscribed VOT. X. resting on a column. On the obverse is another of the complicated, nearly half-length, busts that we have met with under Julia Domna (p. 124). Now A.D. 230 was the quarter-millenary year of the recovery of the standards from the Parthians by Augustus. May the gold medallion not have been intended to commemorate that anniversary? The Augustan event had received unparalleled publicity (p. 65), and continued to be commemorated until at least the fourth century of our era.[7] Tiberius had celebrated its half-centenary on Eastern tetradrachms, and Titus and Hadrian signalised similarly its 100th and 150th anniversaries respectively. The relevance of the present gold medallion to the East (its fine style may perhaps be Egyptian)[8] is suggested by the discovery of the only known specimen at Tarsus[9] (it is apparently the only gold medallion ever found in Cilicia).[10] There was special topical significance in such a commemoration in A.D. 230. It was in that year that news reached Rome of Ardashir's invasion of Mesopotamia, and that elaborate preparations were begun for the subsequent

1 M. & S. IV, 1, p. 246. 245, cf. p. 85 (A.D. 214). The main issue occurred in A.D. 215: not apparently the earliest one, as Mattingly, *Roman Coins*, p. 125. The fact that the reform was of a primarily inflationary character (cf. Miller, *CAH.* XII, p. 45; Oertel, ibid. pp. 262, 267) does not make it any the less likely that the new denomination should have been given publicity and a commemorative character.

2 Bellinger, *The Syrian Tetradrachms of Caracalla and Macrinus, Numismatic Studies*, III, 1940, pp. 36 ff.   3 Ibid. p. 104.

4 Ibid. p. 6 tends to prefer *c.* A.D. 215.

5 Except for a silver *quinarius* of Elagabalus in A.D. 221, which may well commemorate a further Augustan occasion, namely the tercentenary of *Aegyptus capta*: see Appendix I.

6 Toynbee, pp. 5, 24 n. 23, 147, 155 (8-*aureus* piece). Also bronze medallions, ibid. p. 81 n. 62; Gnecchi, II, pl. 99. 5, III, p. 45. 20.

7 Cf. Anderson, *CAH.* x. p. 263.

8 Seltman, *Approach to Greek Art*, p. 115.

9 Longpérier, *Rn.* 1868, p. 322.

10 Toynbee, p. 63.

campaign.[1] The successes of Augustus in 20 B.C. provided a comparison all the more obvious, since they had taken place just two and a half centuries previously.[2] Severus Alexander's régime in no way fell behind those of his predecessors both in celebrating *divi* in general[3] and particularly in recalling Augustus—especially in the sphere of civil cult,[4] to which such anniversary occasions belonged.[5]

Gold medallions had hitherto been, and were still, no less rare than those of silver. The only true gold medallions before Severus Alexander—as far as our present knowledge extends—had been those of Augustus, Domitian and Commodus.[6] All of those seem to have commemorated anniversary occasions. This gold medallion of Alexander is, admittedly, not the first gold medallion of his reign, for it appears that a 4-*aureus* (?) piece was struck on his accession;[7] there is also (or was until the Paris theft) another of Severus Alexander and Julia Mamaea.[8] As far as is known at present, the former of these—despite the obvious appropriateness of accessions for such commemoration—was the first gold medallion ever issued for an occasion which apparently had no anniversary significance; moreover, apart from such isolated exceptions, the custom of restricting gold medallic issues to anniversaries (a phenomenon exactly paralleled in silver medallions) was to continue until the time of Gallienus.[9] Indeed, the only known Roman gold medallion of an emperor between Severus Alexander and Gallienus[10] was a 5- (or possibly 6-) *aureus* piece issued by Philip on the millenary of Rome.[11]

On issues of A.D. 228 Severus Alexander introduces a new theme to the anniversary issues, namely commemoration of another *divus*,

1 Cf. Ensslin, *CAH*. xii, p. 69.
2 Cf. also the emperor's name 'Alexander': for the cult under the Severi see Brühl, *Mélanges d'Archéologie et d'Histoire*, 1930, pp. 214 ff. (for Caracalla, Miller, *CAH*. xii, pp. 44, 47 f.). Cf. Seltman, loc. cit.
3 Hoey, *YCS*. 1940, p. 185 n. 881; for their importance at this time, see Nock, *Harvard Theological Review*, 1930, p. 258.
4 Hoey, loc. cit. p. 174 n. 805.
5 Fink, *YCS*. 1940, p. 159, believes Severus Alexander to have been unlikely to recall Augustan tendencies. But there was a general practice, among emperors, of paying tribute to Augustus.
6 This statement excludes Gnecchi's *aurei*

eccedenti—2 *aurei* (*biniones*), 1½, 1⅞ (Mattingly, *NC*. 1946, p. 75, of Gallus), etc. Toynbee, pp. 24 f., etc., classes these as medallions, but Pink, *NZ*. 1936, p. 22, seems to consider them as coins. (For their commencement see ibid. p. 11, but also ibid. 1935, pp. 27, 30.)
7 Toynbee, p. 24 n. 24.
8 Ibid. pp. 5, 24 n. 24, 147 n. 5, 148 n. 12; Gnecchi, i, p. 5.
9 Cf. Toynbee, pp. 22, 147.
10 Other than a *binio* or 1½-*aureus* piece of Gordian III (Toynbee, pp. 106, 147). Barbaric *aurei* must be disregarded (ibid. p. 31 n. 30).
11 Ibid. pp. 5, 147; Gnecchi, i, pp. 5 f.

Hadrian. A bronze medallion of Alexander[1] represents a temple identified as that of Venus and Rome. Gagé,[2] considering that Hadrian's great temple of Venus and Rome had been founded in A.D. 128, notes that this was just a century earlier; and—almost alone in this attention to anniversaries—he adds *cette coincidence nous paraît mériter réflexion* (cf. p. 9). Mattingly[3] and Strack[4] both now prefer rather later dates for the temple (*c.* A.D. 136–7 and *c.* 140 respectively); but Dr Toynbee[5] reconciles the various views by suggesting that, as—apparently—in the case of numerous imperial Altars (pp. 12 f., n. 6), the earliest date (*c.* A.D. 128) may have been that of foundation or consecration, and one of the later dates that of dedication or completion. The temple of Venus and Rome had played a large part in the 'new age' of Hadrian. Its centenary was likely to be an important occasion, especially as it occurred in the third century, in which Severus Alexander, like other emperors, included among his coin-types ROMAE AETERNAE[6] as well as SAECVLI FELICITAS[7], etc.

It cannot, however, be proved that Severus Alexander intended any complimentary reference to Hadrian the emperor. It is true that the latter's bust appears on coinage of Bithynium at this date;[8] but Hadrian's *dies imperii* seems to have been omitted from the *Feriale Duranum*,[9] though certain other Hadrianic allusions were to continue as late as Constantine,[10] the *Fasti* of 'Philocalus',[11] and (including reference to Eternal Rome) the contorniates.[12] Severus Alexander was an admirer of Hadrian's adoptive father Trajan;[13] and the government of Severus Alexander desired a return to the Antonine period, though matters probably did not move very far

1 Gnecchi, II, p. 81. 11 (P.M. TR.P. VIII. COS. II. P.P.), p. 82. 25 (ROMAE AETERNAE), etc.; Toynbee, p. 103.
2 *Transactions of the International Numismatic Congress of* 1936, p. 183 n. 1.
3 *BMC. Imp.* III, p. cxlv.
4 II, pp. 174 f.
5 P. 103.
6 M. & S. IV, 2, p. 84. 25, etc.
7 Ibid. p. 97. 325 (Orbiana), p. 99. 348 (Julia Mamaea).
8 *BMC. Bithynia*, p. 120. 16.
9 Cf. Fink, *YCS.* 1940, pp. 77 n. 241, 82 n. 262; Snyder, ibid. p. 152 n. 688. There was also an artistic reaction against Hadrian, Rodenwaldt, *CAH.* XII, p. 553.

10 Cf. Toynbee, *JRS.* 1941, p. 193.
11 Mommsen, *CIL.* I², p. 310; Wissowa, *Religion und Kultus der Römer²*, pp. 459, 460 n. 3; Hoey, *YCS.* 1940, p. 181 n. 855; cf. p. 183 n. 870. But the reference is to the adoption of Antoninus Pius, and so probably intended to honour him rather than Hadrian.
12 Alföldi, *Die Kontorniaten*, p. 114; cf. p. 97 (VRBS ROMA AETERNA and HETERNA [sic]). Also Antoninus, ibid. p. 101.
13 Hoey, loc. cit. p. 186. Rostovtzeff, *Social and Economic History of the Roman Empire*, p. 606 n. 43 (=*Storia Economica e Sociale dell' Impero Romano*, p. 489 n. 43) links his land-policy with that of Trajan and Hadrian.

in this direction.[1] At all events it would probably be an exaggeration to discern any reference to Hadrian personally in Severus Alexander's medallions and coins with ROMAE AETERNAE.[2] Rather do they suggest that, by reflecting in his publicity the happier days of the second century, he was imitating his great-uncle Septimius Severus. Alexander stressed his connection with Severus, as well as with Caracalla.[3]

1 Cf. Piganiol, *Histoire de Rome*, p. 405 (cf. p. 410); Hoey, loc. cit. p. 34 n. 77; Besnier, *Histoire Romaine*, IV, 1, p. 88 and n. 216. See also Scullard, *JRS.* 1944, p. 145; for Lampridius (*SHA.*), Alföldi, *Archaeologiai Ertesitö*, 1940, pp. 195 ff.; Seston, *Revue des études anciennes*, 1943, p. 164.

2 Mention should be made here of another Hadrianic allusion on the issues of Severus Alexander, namely the ROMVLO CONDITORI type which appears on his coins (M. & S. IV, 2, p. 77. 85, p. 109. 481) of the same year A.D. 228, and possibly also on contemporary medallions (Gnecchi, III, p. 18. 84, pl. 145. 7; but this looks doubtful). This type had not appeared since the Antonines; its introducer had been Hadrian, whose issues with this type are as follows: (1) rare and semi-medallic 'border-line' *aes* with obverse HADRIANVS AVGVSTVS (*BMC. Imp.* III, p. 443, cf. p. 442; Toynbee, pp. 33, 208; Gnecchi, III, p. 18. 84, p. 19. 85). (2) *aurei* with obverse HADRIANVS AVGVSTVS P.P. (*BMC. Imp.* III, p. 306. 528). (3) *denarii* with obverse HADRIANVS AVG. COS. III. P.P. (ibid. p. 329. 709). The obverse HADRIANVS AVGVSTVS is normally of *c.* A.D. 124–8, HADRIANVS AVGVSTVS P.P. is of *c.* A.D. 128–32 (*BMC. Imp.* III, p. cxvi), and HADRIANVS AVG. COS. III. P.P. is of *c.* 134/5–8 (ibid. p. cxviii). But curiously enough there are very strong reasons for believing that all these issues with ROMVLO CONDITORI, like one or two other equally anomalous types, occurred more or less simultaneously in *c.* 137. The portrait of the *aes* is clearly of Hadrian's last period (cf. ibid. p. clxviii), and for the stylistic characteristics of the *aurei* see Mattingly, ibid. pp. cxvii, cxli. All these pieces (if not posthumous: cf. Toynbee, *NC.* 1936, p. 330) were probably issued in connection with the completion of the temple of Venus and Rome in A.D. *c.* 136–7 (?), and

with Hadrian's pretensions to be the refounder of Rome.

But the mint-master of Severus Alexander (in this no more inaccurate a numismatist than a predecessor under Trajan, *BMC. Imp.* III, p. xci) is very likely to have thought that Hadrian's semi-medallic *aes* issue (and *denarii*) with ROMVLO CONDITORI were contemporary with nearly all the other issues with the same obverse legend, i.e. of *c.* A.D. 125–8; or, if he did not think it, there was reason to assume or pretend it, A.D. 128 being tentatively considered the *foundation-year* of the temple of Venus and Rome. If either of these conclusions is correct, the type was presumably revived by Severus Alexander to commemorate the alleged centenary of this event. If so, the issues of Severus Alexander may be described as a 'pseudo-anniversary' coinage; and so may others, not yet certainly identifiable, which may likewise celebrate centenaries, etc., on dates which, by any computation known to us, are inaccurate. Cf. (if Mattingly is right) an issue of Vespasian commemorating a *past* anniversary, that is an anniversary which had coincided with the accession-year of his 'model', Galba (p. 87 n. 3).

The issues of Severus Alexander may be connected with his building achievements (cf. Lambrechts, *CAH.* XII, p. 238; Ensslin, ibid. p. 66; Ramsay, *L'Antiquité Classique*, 1935, pp. 419 ff.). Emperors continued to be hailed as second Romuli until much later (cf. Alföldi, *Röm. Mitt.* 1935, p. 100 n. 1). For the origins of the Romulus cult, see (lately) Abaev in the Marr memorial volume (in Russian), Dumézil, *Naissance de Rome, Jupiter-Mars-Quirinus*, etc.

3 Hoey, *YCS.* 1940, p. 186 nn. 887 f.; Miller, *CAH.* XII, p. 58; M. & S. IV, 2, p. 128. 717 ff. and n. (DIVO ANTONINO MAGNO).

(iii) *The Gordians and Valerian*

Our next anniversary issue constitutes another and a more orthodox example of reversion to the Antonine period. This is provided by the coins of Gordian I in A.D. 238 showing a type that appears to be *Pax*.[1] The reign of that emperor was so fleeting that all his issues must be described as accession coinages. Now no previous *princeps* had included *Pax* on his accession issues since Antoninus Pius, whose initial mintages had stressed the type greatly.[2] This reminiscence on the accession pieces of Gordian I is likely to have been deliberate. In the first place his policy was pro-senatorial,[3] and thus naturally recalled the days of Antoninus Pius in contrast to the intervening epoch of the military monarchy. Secondly, the wife of Gordian I was the granddaughter of Antoninus Pius.[4] Thirdly, the common belief that Gordian I was a descendant of Trajan[5] implied a further relationship with Trajan's adoptive grandson Antoninus. Fourthly, Gordian I wrote a eulogy of the last-named emperor and an epic with him as hero.[6] Fifthly, the accession of Gordian I coincided with the centenary of the accession of his peaceful and pro-senatorial 'ancestor'. Carausius was to benefit from a precisely similar coincidence just 50 years later (p. 144).

Gordian III followed the same policy as his grandfather Gordian I,[7] and there is a numismatic suggestion of this in a coin, apparently of his principate, honouring their ancestor Trajan.[8] Again, one of Gordian III's commonest types owed its introduction to the coinage to his great-great-grandfather Antoninus Pius.[9] This is the type of Jupiter *Stator* (IOVI STATORI,[10] IOVIS STATOR[11]). This is something of an innovation (or an archaism), for the type is not recorded under Aurelius, Commodus or the earlier Severi and had only figured on a single *denarius* of Severus Alexander.[12] The date of its introduction by Antoninus lay between A.D. 140 and 144. Mattingly[13]

1 M. & S. IV, 2, p. 160.
2 *BMC. Imp.* IV, p. 169: Paris (actually the second, not first, issue of A.D. 138 after his accession), etc. *Pax* is also a very rare type on medallions: Toynbee, p. 200.
3 Cf. Ensslin, *CAH.* XII, p. 77.
4 *SHA. Vitae Gord. trium*, 2; cf. Besnier, loc. cit. p. 145 n. 23.
5 Cf. Besnier, loc. cit.; Miller, *CAH.* XII, p. 77. Also of the Gracchi, ibid.

6 *SHA.* loc. cit. 7; cf. Rand, *CAH.* XII, p. 598.
7 Cf. Ensslin, loc. cit. pp. 81 f., 84, etc.
8 *BMC. Imp.* III, pp. 98 n., 487, 131 (VIA TRAIANA).
9 *BMC. Imp.* IV, p. 32. 210, p. 200. 1247.
10 Cohen, V, p. 32. 108 ff.
11 Ibid. pp. 113 ff.
12 M. & S. IV, 2, p. 86. 202.
13 Ibid. p. lvi.

has plausibly attributed its issue to the heavy fighting that preceded the British victory of A.D. 143, Jupiter *Stator* being the god who averts panic and defeat. Now it was exactly 100 years later, in A.D. 241–3, that the armies of Gordian III, under Timesitheus, were likewise converting a grim position into victory, first against the Carpi and then against the Persians.[1] It is to these years that Mattingly ascribes his issues with Jupiter *Stator*.[2] By reviving, on an anniversary, a type from the great series issued by Antoninus in A.D. 140–4, Gordian III—in this as in other things resembling Severus Alexander—is imitating Septimius Severus. The Gordiani consciously maintained continuity with that emperor, and one of them deified Severus Alexander[3] who had stressed his relationship with Septimius Severus.[4]

Both Antoninus Pius and Septimius Severus had been moved by their religious interests to signalise on the coinage the great Republican anniversaries. A similar purpose is ascribable to certain issues of their imitator Gordian III, namely his *aes* pieces with LIBERTAS AVG. S.C. (*c.* A.D. 240–4).[5] This type is absent from the coins of the immediate predecessors and successors of Gordian III[6] (it does not seem to appear on any medallions at all until a later date).[7] Now the coins of Gordian III, though not exactly dateable, occur just about two centuries after the introduction of the type to the imperial coinage by Claudius in the year of his accession (p. 74). The issue of Claudius has been attributed to the 550th anniversary (fifth *saeculum* according to one reckoning) of the foundation of the Republic, and the coinage of Gordian III may likewise be ascribed to its three-quarter millenary.

But the type of Claudius had also possessed a topical reference owing to the character of his public policy, and the same may well

1   Cf. Ensslin, loc. cit. p. 87.
2   *NC.* 1939, p. 48. See also below, pp. 132 f.
3   Cf. Miller, loc. cit. Cf. in A.D. 248 Iotapianus, *Alexandri tumens stirpe* (Aur. Victor 29. 2), probably referring to Severus Alexander (Momigliano, *JRS.* 1945, p. 131) rather than Alexander the Great (as Altheim, *Soldatenkaiser*, p. 241 n. 2). On Iotapianus, see also Bersanetti, *Laureae Aquincenses*, II (*Dissertationes Pannonicae*, II, 11. 1941), p. 267, Rostovtzeff, *Berytus*, 1943, p. 31.
4   Possibly another Antonine centenary is provided by Gordian III's coinage at *colonia*

Iconium (*BMC. Lycaonia*, etc. p. 5. 8 ff.), the only known previous issue of the colony having been made under Antoninus Pius (ibid. 6 f.)—perhaps very early in his reign (for it might commemorate the foundation of the *colonia* by Hadrian, ibid. pp. xxiv, 4, not recorded on any known coin of the latter).
5   Cohen, v, p. 36. 153 f.
6   Apparently only Gallienus, Magnentius and Decentius; Toynbee, p. 201.
7   Cohen, v, p. 193. 77 (Decius) is a misreading for VBERTAS.

be true of Gordian III. The capable administration of Timesitheus,[1] in its little known publicity programme, may have drawn upon the theme of the Republic as well as on the Antonines. 509–8 B.C. was traditionally the date at which were founded, not only the Republic, but also the temple of Jupiter *Capitolinus*: anniversaries of the latter event had received numismatic commemoration both from Commodus (p. 111) and from Antoninus Pius (p. 105)—the last-named being, as we have seen, the forerunner of at least two other issues of Gordian III. Incidentally, LIBERTAS had also been a type of Antoninus Pius at the same date as his issues commemorating the Capitoline temple.[2]

The issue of Gordian III that has just been described provides the last identifiable reference, by an emperor reigning at Rome, to the foundation of the Republic. It is fitting that this antiquarian distinction should belong to an emperor who was alleged to be descended from the Gracchi (p. 129 n. 5).

Even more marked, however, was the interest of Gordian III's Arabian successor, Philip, in the remote past of Rome: for the whole of Roman history has nothing to equal the attention, numismatic and otherwise, that was devoted to the Millenary Games of A.D. 248. Equally striking are the issues of the next emperor, Trajanus Decius —here recalling the even remoter reminiscences of Trajan whose name he bore (cf. p. 150 and n. 4)—in honour of the *divi*.[3] Coins issued for such purposes (unless coinciding with an anniversary, as does not seem to be the case here) are beyond the scope of this book; but they need to be borne in mind as a phenomenon closely parallel in aim to other sorts of retrospective issue.

Less than ten years later we seem to find a recrudescence of a further traditionalist category of coinage, namely of the anniversary

---

1 Cf. Ensslin, loc. cit. pp. 85 ff., and (somewhat differently) Rostovtzeff, *Social and Economic History of the Roman Empire*, p. 615 n. 26 = *Storia Economica e Sociale dell' Impero Romano*, pp. 527 f. n. 26, who considers that Timesitheus probably followed the policy of Maximinus.

2 *BMC. Imp.* IV, p. 177. 1141, p. 181. 1150, p. 183, etc. Mention has not been made of this under Antoninus Pius, since his use of the type was by no means an isolated one and thus hard to link conclusively with an anniversary.

3 Cf. Mattingly and Salisbury, *NC.* 1924, pp. 210 ff.; Mattingly, ibid. 1939, p. 26 n. 7. Id. *Numismatika* (Zagreb), 1936, p. 12, attributes them to Milan, against Laffranchi, *R. it.* 1908, pp. 199 ff. ('Viminacium'), and Alföldi ('Rome': quoted by Mattingly, *NC.* 1939, loc. cit.); cf. Elmer, *NZ.* 1937, p. 99. There is also a colonial series, attributed to Patrae by Muensterberg, *Blätter für Münzfreunde*, 1923, pp. 361 ff., and to Philippopolis by Mattingly, *Roman Coins*, p. 207. I have not seen M. & S. IV, 3.

genre with which this book is concerned; and this and other resuscitations of the great past are the more arresting since we have now reached a period when pagan sources and monuments are diminishing.[1] The coinage of Valerian shows almost simultaneous types of IOVI VICTORI (Gallienus)[2] and IOVI STATORI.[3] The commencements of these two series are ascribed by Webb to *c.* A.D. 256 and *c.* 255–6 respectively:[4] Ritterling[5] and Alföldi[6] prefer *c.* A.D. 257–8 for the former. Now A.D. 256 was the 550th year after the vowing of the temple of Jupiter *Stator* by M. Atilius Regulus (294 B.C.),[7] and also the 550th year of the vowing of the temple of Jupiter *Victor* by Q. Fabius Maximus (295 B.C.) (p. 118)—550 years representing, according to one reckoning, exactly five *saecula*.

According to the chronology of Ritterling and Alföldi, the issues under Valerian with Jupiter *Victor* occur just half a century after a remarkable silver medallion of Septimius Severus (p. 117). That medallion seems to have celebrated the half-millenary of the vowing of the temple of Jupiter *Victor*; Valerian is apparently commemorating (perhaps, like Severus, a few months late) the 550th anniversary (fifth *saeculum* of one hundred and ten years) of the same occasion. Jupiter *Victor* appears still to have been a particularly important deity in the third century.[8]

The second of the divinities whose appearance under Valerian has been mentioned, Jupiter *Stator*, has already occurred on an anniversary coinage of Gordian III (p. 129). It was in A.D. 256 that the Goths launched their second great naval expedition which resulted in the temporary overrunning of most of Bithynia.[9] Mention has been made of the appropriateness of Jupiter *Stator* to times of military crisis: his anniversaries continued to be honoured

---

1   Cf. Piganiol, *Histoire de Rome*, p. 434. In discussing the issues of Valerian and Gallienus here, no attempt will be made to deal with the numerous difficult questions connected with mint-attributions. A few modern sources on this subject will be quoted in connection with individual coins: add Elmer, *Bonner Jahrbücher*, 1939 (Cologne); Mattingly, *NC*.1936, p. 99; Laffranchi, *Transactions of the International Congress of 1936*, pp. 198 ff. (Milan); and, more recently, on the Eastern mints, Olmstead, *Classical Philology*, 1942, pp. 419 f.; Rostovtzeff, *Berytus*, 1943, pp. 47, 52 f. n. 67; Bellinger, ibid. pp. 61 ff., id. *Dura*, VI, p. 138.

2   M. & S. V, I, p. I. 39. 7 (GALLIENVS CVM EXER. SVO). Elmer, *Bonner Jahrbücher*, 1941, p. 18, believes that the punctuation was intentionally 10. VI VICTORI. For Jupiter *Victor* and *Victoria Aeterna* see d'Ors Pérez-Peix, *Emerita*, 1943, p. 330 n. 1.

3   Ibid. p. 46. 95, cf. Alföldi, *Berytus*, 1938, p. 49.

4   Though he ascribes variants to A.D. 257 and 258–9 (ibid. p. 70).

5   *PW*. XII, 1341.

6   *NC*. 1929, p. 258 n. 46; *CAH*, XII, p. 182.

7   Livy, X, 29. 14; cf. Thulin, *PW*. X, I. 1133.

8   Fink, *YCS*. 1940, p. 58; cf. p. 57.

9   Cf. Alföldi, *CAH*. XII, pp. 148, 170.

as late as the fourth-century *Fasti* of 'Philocalus'.[1] These Republican references of Valerian may be linked with the general traditionalism of his policy, and, one may add, with the probability that he claimed descent from an ancient Republican *gens*.[2]

It is under Valerian, too, that we find the legend RELIGIO AVGG.,[3] providing the first numismatic mention of *religio* since Marcus Aurelius (p. 107). The latter *princeps* was, incidentally, a fashionable object of comparison to certain emperors of the mid-third century, and it is he to whom one of Valerian's immediate predecessors, probably Philip, is compared in the Εἰς Βασιλέα.[4] Now the coin of Aurelius with RELIG. AVG. has been shown to coincide with the bicentenary of the *respublica restituta* of Augustus (p. 108). Valerian's issue with RELIGIO AVGG. is attributed by Webb[5] to *c*. A.D. 258, and by Alföldi[6] to *c*. 259—the year of another great centenary. It was in A.D. 259 that occurred the 300th anniversary of Julius Caesar's deification (42 B.C.).[7] The *Feriale Duranum* seems to tell of honours paid to anniversaries of that occasion during the third century,[8] and the birthday of Julius was even to be included among the few ancient anniversaries recorded by the fifth-century *Fasti* of Silvius.[9] These are facts which must be borne in mind in contrast to the marked emphasis of official records[10] and official coinage[11]—including anniversary issues—on Augustus rather than Julius.[12] The latter was by no means forgotten: for example, his colonies continued to honour him long after his death[13] (one such city seems to celebrate its tercentenary numismatically in this reign)[14] and his cult is likely to have been of special importance to the army.[15]

1 *CIL*. I², p. 256.
2 Cf. Babelon, *Mélanges Numismatiques*, III, pp. 179 ff.; Toynbee, p. 163 n. 171.
3 M. & S. v, 1, p. 47. 114 (Diana).
4 Besnier, *Histoire Romaine*, IV, I, p. 201; Piganiol, *Histoire de Rome*, p. 430; *CAH*. XII, p. 735.   5 M. & S. v, 1, loc. cit.
6 *ZfN*. 1938, p. 194.
7 Cf. Piganiol, loc. cit. p. 209; Préchac, *Revue d'Histoire et de Philosophie*, 1934, p. 306, etc.
8 Cf. Snyder, *YCS*. 1940, p. 146.
9 *CIL*. I², p. 269; Gagé, *RGDA*. p. 174.
10 E.g. omitted in calendar and *Natales* of 'Philocalus': *CIL*. I², pp. 268 ff., 255, cf. Snyder, loc. cit. p. 147. For the Arvals cf. Hoey, *YCS*. 1940, p. 184, Gagé, *Revue historique*, 1936, p. 282.

11 E.g. omitted on most 'restoration' series: cf. Mattingly and Salisbury, *NC*. 1924, p. 236 (Decius). Trajan is an exception (p. 100).
12 It is, however, possible that Valerian's only known gold *quinarius* may commemorate the tercentenary of Julius Caesar's death (of which Trajan had celebrated the sesquicentenary); but, alternatively, it might signalise the tercentenary of 43 B.C. See App. I.
13 Cf. *FITA*. p. 318.
14 Grose, *Catalogue of the McClean Collection*, 7666, of Parium: PARIO CON[D]IT. For the foundation in *c*. 42–41 B.C. see *FITA*. pp. 247 f.
15 Cf. Hoey, loc. cit. p. 185.

Such a reference by Valerian in *c.* A.D. 258–9 may be connected with his campaign against the Christians and in favour of the traditional religion. That campaign had started in the previous year,[1] and in that very year the ancient faith is described as *Romana religio*.[2] In the observances thus described, a large part was played by the cult of the *divi*. For this cult, which had seemed rather 'advanced' to traditionalists of Julio-Claudian date, had ended by becoming a symbol of patriotic and conservative thought.[3]

1   Cf. Alföldi, *CAH.* xii, p. 205.

2   *Acta Cypriani* 1 ff. = *Corpus Scriptorum Ecclesiasticorum Latinorum*, 3, cx ff., cf. Alföldi, *Röm. Mitt.* 1935, p. 77. Cf. *religiosissimus Augustus* (id. 25 *Jahre Römisch-Germanische Kommission*, 1930, pp. 42 ff.), apparently dating from Caracalla.

3   Cf. Alföldi, *CAH.* xii, p. 194.

CHAPTER VII

FROM POSTUMUS TO VALENTINIAN I

(i) *Gallienus, the Gallic Emperors, and Claudius II*

Emphasis on the *divi* continues on issues of Postumus and Gallienus. These apparently commemorate the quarter-millenary year of the death of Augustus, which fell in A.D. 263–4. The Postumus issue is dated to A.D. 263 and its type is Vesta's temple.[1] Apart from certain non-anniversary issues of imperial ladies,[2] this type has hitherto never(?) appeared except on the *decennium* (p. 34), half-centenary (p. 81), and bicentenary (p. 123) of the death of Augustus; and on the fiftieth anniversary of the introduction of the type on the above-mentioned *decennium* (p. 91). The revival of the type by Postumus on so historic an occasion is in keeping with his aspirations to world-rule,[3] which were illustrated by the legend RESTITVTOR ORBIS[4] and encouraged by his victory over the Germans in the very year 264.[5] Representations of the temple of Vesta had particular significance in the latter half of the third century, when her cult gained a new lease of life.[6]

But Postumus was obliged to confine these ambitions within the Gallic Empire.[7] The emperor at Rome was Gallienus, whose unusual coin-types during his sole reign include a portrait of Augustus, labelled DEO AVGVSTO, on very rare *aurei* and *aes* medallions.[8] This legend invites attribution to the same quarter-millenary in A.D. 264. Such a date is not inconsistent with Alföldi's ascription of these pieces to an early period after the opening of the Siscia

1 M. & S. v, 2, p. 337. 9, Brown, *Numismatic Notes and Monographs*, XC, 1940, p. 46. For the coinage of Postumus see also Mayreder, *Deutsche Münzblätter*, 1934, pp. 97 ff., Elmer, *Bonner Jahrbücher*, 1941, pp. 28, 40 ff.
2 But an alleged medallion of Etruscilla (Gnecchi, II, p. 101. 2) is probably false.
3 Cf. Ensslin, *CAH*. XII, p. 374, for the intention of s.c. on his coinage.
4 M. & S. v, 2, p. 363. 324; cf. Alföldi, loc. cit. p. 187. On the character of his policy, see also Lambrechts, *JRS*. 1939, p. 238. Rostovtzeff, *Social and Economic History of*

the *Roman Empire*, p. 614 n. 8 = *Storia Economica e Sociale dell' Impero Romano*, p. 517 n. 8, points out that the Hercules of Postumus is not German (as von Domaszewski), but Roman; cf. Andreotti, *Studi Ciaceri*, pp. 1 ff.   5 Alföldi, loc. cit.
6 Cf. Nock, *Harvard Theological Review*, 1930, pp. 251 ff.; id. *CAH*. XII, p. 414.
7 For gold and billon *quinarii* see Appendix I (? tercentenary of *ovatio*).
8 M. & S. v, 1, p. 131. 9 and p. 133. 28; Alföldi, *ZfN*. 1928, p. 199; Toynbee, p. 118 (Padua), cf. pp. 73 ff.

mint[1] (and *decennalia* of Gallienus[2]) in A.D. 262. (Attribution of these rare issues to A.D. 264 recalls that it was on 1 Jan. of the same year [p. 1 n. 3], no doubt partly to celebrate the same quarter-millenary occasion, that Gallienus issued an unusual group of *aes* medallions inscribed GALLIENVM AVG. SENATVS.[3])

Gallienus adopted Augustus as his model,[4] and may have deliberately resuscitated in new forms the 'Golden Age' mysticism of the first *princeps*.[5] The use of DEO rather than DIVO differentiates the cult of Augustus from that of the many other deified emperors for whom coins had been posthumously issued by Trajanus Decius, etc.:[6] though, very soon after A.D. 14, a Spanish colony had already labelled its coins DEO AVGVSTO.[7] The anniversaries of that year were still remembered for many years after Gallienus (p. 155).

That emperor himself appears to have commemorated the quarter-millenary occasion of A.D. 264 not only at Siscia but at Alexandria, where he issued (in his year 12) the last but one—after a long gap—of all the bronze issues of that mint, and one of medallic appearance at that.[8] To the same anniversary seems to be owed the fact that the same year witnessed a marked artistic revival and reform in the Alexandrian coinage.[9]

Probably almost contemporary was an issue of very rare Siscian *antoniniani* with the reverse type SISCIA AVG.[10] The empire was passing through a phase of Illyrian hegemony[11] which had found expression on the coinage as early as Trajanus Decius (A.D. 249–51).[12]

1 *Numizmatikai Közlöny*, 1927–8, p. 16.

2 For these, see especially von Domaszewski,*Rheinisches Museum*,1902,pp. 510 ff.; Piganiol, loc. cit. p. 425; Miller, *CAH*. xii, p. 19; Alföldi, *Röm. Mitt.* 1935, pp. 90 f. n. 2, id. *Berytus*, 1938, pp. 50 f.

3 Toynbee, p. 34, Gnecchi iii, p. 55. 67. For earlier New Year issues of Gallienus, cf. Alföldi, *JRS*. 1940, p. 9, etc.

4 Alföldi, *CAH*. xii, pp. 189, 230; id. *ZfN*. 1928, pp. 197 ff. Cf. above, p. 126 n. 5.

5 Id. *NC*. 1929, p. 265; Mattingly, *Classical Review*, 1934, pp. 164 ff., doubted by Syme, *Classical Quarterly*, 1937, p. 39; cf. Piganiol, loc. cit. p. 431, etc.

6 Alföldi, *CAH*. xii, p. 194; id. *ZfN*. 1928, loc. cit. For *deus* in general, see Bailey, *Roman Religion*, p. 12; Warde Fowler, *The Religious Experience of the Roman People*, p. 137 n. 3, etc. For a third-century differentiation between *di* and *divi* (by Dio), see

Pippidi, *Revue historique du Sud-Est Européen*, 1942=*Autour de Tibère*, p. 136 n. 2.

7 *APT*. Chapter II, section v; cf. *CMG*.

8 Milne, *Catalogue of Alexandrian Coins in the Ashmolean Museum*, pp. xvii, xxiv; medallic in character, as was its only known successor, see below, p. 139. On the chronology of Alexandria under Gallienus, see Laffranchi, *Aegyptus*, 1937, pp. 25 ff.; cf. Alföldi, *Berytus*, 1938, pp. 68 ff.; id. *JRS*. 1940, p. 7 n. 20.

9 Milne, loc. cit. p. xli. For the frequent coincidences of Alexandrian monetary innovations with anniversary occasions, see above, p. 41 n. 5.

10 M. & S. v, 1, p. 182. 582, Alföldi, *Numizmatikai Közlöny*, 1927–8, pp. 21 ff., cf. pp. 14 ff.

11 Alföldi, *25 Jahre Römisch-Germanische Kommission*, 1930, pp. 11 ff.

12 Mattingly, *NC*. 1939, pp. 55 f.

Siscia, especially, was a great military centre.[1] It had first become urbanised (perhaps colonised) under Tiberius[2]—very probably at the same time as Emona, in A.D. 14–15.[3] The coinage of Gallienus probably celebrated the quarter-millenary of this decisive point in Siscia's history,[4] thus constituting another honorific reference to an event of the reign of Tiberius (p. 97). Septimius Severus had already introduced the innovation of commemorating city-anniversaries on official rather than, as hitherto, on local issues (p. 121);[5] it would be characteristic of the two periods that, whereas Severus selects Africa, Gallienus should single out Pannonia for this rare honour.

Soon after the death of Gallienus, two of the Gallic successors of Postumus again invoked the past through the medium of anniversary coinages. In the first place, this must have been one of the purposes of the legionary coinage of Victorinus.[6] That emperor reigned from A.D. 268 or 269[7] until about A.D. 270, a period including the third centenary of the original legionary series of M. Antonius (p. 86). The first and second revivals of that series had likewise coincided with the centenary (Clodius Macer, p. 86) and bicentenary (Aurelius and Verus, p. 107) respectively of the same issues of the triumvir. It is possible that Macer's issue had been motivated by some political affinity with Antony; but this does not apply to the coins of Aurelius and Verus, and we may similarly assume that Victorinus is merely commemorating the occasion on which this numismatic honour had first been paid to the army.[8] Victorinus was of course also alluding to his own military power. But the essentially historical character of

---

1 On the establishment of a 'medallion mint' at Siscia, see Horvat, *Numismatika* (Zagreb), 1933, p. 22; Toynbee, p. 50 n. 43.

2 Cf. Ciaceri, *Tiberio Successore di Augusto*, p. 221.

3 Chilver, *JRS*. 1939, p. 269; Alföldi jun., *Archaeologiai Értesitö*, 1943, p. 84; cf. *APT*. Appendix V.

4 Alföldi, *Numizmatikai Közlöny*, 1927–8, p. 22, attributes it to *c*. A.D. 262, but the present view requires ascription to 263 or 264.

5 For the Severi as originators of the policy of Gallienus cf. Piganiol, loc. cit. p. 425; Hoey,

YCS. 1940, p. 206 n. 1028. For artistic analogies with Severus Alexander cf. Mathew, *JRS*. 1943, p. 66.

6 M. & S. v, 2, pp. 328 f.; Oman, *NC*. 1924, pp. 54 ff.

7 A.D. 268 according to Mattingly, *Transactions of the International Numismatic Congress of* 1936, p. 215; id. *CAH*. XII, p. 305. Alföldi, ibid. p. 191, and *JRS*. 1940, p. 7, prefers A.D. 269.

8 On the other hand a gold *quinarius* of Victorinus (A.D. 270) may well celebrate the tercentenary of Actium and *Aegyptus capta*: see Appendix I.

his mintage is further indicated by the inclusion in the series of many legions not under his command.[1]

The second of the successors of Postumus who appears to issue an anniversary coinage is Tetricus senior. Among his *antoniniani* is a rare one inscribed TVTELA (mint-mark ×); a female figure stands with *patera* and spear.[2] This is a legend of great rarity in the Roman series; and its début under Vespasian (actually believed to represent the only previous appearance of the legend) occurred (in A.D. 70–1, p. 89) exactly two centuries before the probable date of the accession of Tetricus in Gaul.[3] The mint-master of Tetricus can scarcely have failed to be conscious of this only forerunner. Must he then not, also, have appreciated that the latter issue had celebrated the centenary of 31–30 B.C.? It seems that the government of Tetricus itself intended to commemorate the tercentenary of the same great occasions.

The special reference of Vespasian's *dupondii* had been to the *tutela plebis* of Augustus, effected by the *tribunicia potestas* as adjusted for this purpose in 30 B.C. (p. 90). It is not impossible that Tetricus's moneyers appreciated this. For, in spite of the total obsoleteness of this conception, the *tribunicia potestas* was still regularly mentioned on the coinage of the third century: the Gallic emperors claimed it, and the coinage of Tetricus himself records his possession of the power.[4] Moreover, the policy of Gallienus, however Augustan, had strongly supported the *plebs*; and, in this as in other respects, it was very likely that the emperors in Gaul should imitate those at Rome.[5] But, whether this meaning can be read into the *Tutela* of Tetricus or not, it was rather national defence that constituted its primary significance. This aspect of *Tutela* had been stressed even by the Augustan poets, and, on the single recurrence of the type hereafter, under Carausius, it will be the dominant theme (p. 147). The *Tutela* of Tetricus carries a spear: the Gallic empire, though under Tetricus conciliatory to Rome, prided itself on successful defence of the frontiers. Probably therefore these coins were issued for the anniversary of Actium or *Aegyptus capta*. These occasions have already

---

1 Cf. Oman, loc. cit. p. 56. On legions and their titles see now Bersanetti, *Athenaeum*, 1943, pp. 79 ff.
2 M. & S. v, 2, p. 411. 137, cf. p. 400, Nock, *JRS.* 1947, p. 105 n. 30.
3 Cf. Elmer, *Bonner Jahrbücher*, 1941, p. 81,

Mattingly, *CAH.* xii, p. 306 n. 3, p. 307 and n. 1; Robertson, *NC.* 1945, p. 153 prefers A.D. 271.
4 E.g. M. & S. v, 2, p. 402. 1 ff., p. 406. 46, p. 416. 204 f.
5 Cf. Alföldi, *CAH.* xii. p. 187.

inspired several anniversary coinages since those of Vespasian (e.g. Titus [p. 92] and Hadrian [p. 102]).[1] But, as has been suggested, the undertone of the type may have been *tutela plebis*. Very little is known of the government of Tetricus except what the coins tell us;[2] but the present issue reinforces the probability that his régime was of a primarily Roman character.[3]

When Tetricus was issuing these coins, apparently in honour of the tercentenary of Actium or *Aegyptus capta*, Claudius Gothicus had already commemorated one of the same occasions on the last of all the large bronze issues of the official mint of Alexandria.[4] This is a very rare and evidently medallic issue. The three immediately preceding large bronze issues of the same mint—under Severus Alexander,[5] Philip[6] and Gallienus (p. 136)—had possessed precisely the same medallic and commemorative character. That of Gallienus had celebrated an anniversary of Augustus: the issue of Claudius Gothicus is dated to A.D. 268–9 (year 2), and it was in 269 that the tercentenary of Actium began. There is also one, and only one, large Roman medallion of Claudius Gothicus known to bear a date; and the date is likewise 269.[7] It may be conjectured that this too was issued for the third centenary of Actium.

(ii) *Aurelian and Carausius*

Perhaps reference to anniversaries may enable a little progress to be made in our knowledge of Aurelian. The coins that inspire this claim are the well-known bronze ones with GENIVS P.R., laureate or radiate head of *Genius* to right, crowned by turret (the second earliest example known of this *motif*),[8] and INT. VRB. S.C. (or plain S.C.) in oak-wreath.[9] Stylistic considerations reinforce Mattingly's[10] reiteration that this issue may have been made, not under Gallienus,[11]

1 Certain third-century inscriptions may likewise refer to *Aegyptus capta*, though this is uncertain; Snyder, *YCS.* 1940, p. 282.
2 Cf. Mattingly, *CAH.* XII. p. 306.
3 Ibid.; also p. 301.
4 Milne, *Catalogue of Alexandrian Coins in the Ashmolean Museum*, pp. xvii, xxiv. Possibly other late issues may still come to light.
5 Ibid. pp. xvii, xxiii: year 10, i.e. decennial.
6 Ibid.: years 5 and 6, i.e. millenary.
7 Gnecchi, II, p. 113. 7 (bimetallic): P.M. TR.P. II. COS. P.P. (Hercules). Gnecchi

wrongly gives the inscription as P.M. TR.P. COS. II. P.P. For coins with P.M. TR.P. II. COS. P.P. cf. M. & S. v, I, p. 212. 10, etc.
8 Cf. Momigliano, *JRS.* 1940, p. 215.
9 M. & S. v, I, p. 361. For the turret, see Toynbee, p. 36 n. 85.
10 *NC.* 1944, p. 123; ibid. 1946, p. 75; cf. M. & S. v, I, p. 35.
11 As Alföldi, *ZfN.* 1928, p. 192 and n. 5, *Röm. Mitt.* 1934, pp. 90 f.; *CAH.* XII, p. 189; and tentatively Toynbee, p. 36. Cf. Haines, *NC.* 1946, p. 32.

but under Aurelian: it was the latter and not the former who introduced the official cult of *Genius Populi Romani*.[1] Moreover the carefully rounded module and the fabric of these pieces recall the rare *aes* of Aurelian[2] rather than the misshapen *sestertii* and 'second brass' of Gallienus. Nor does there seem to be any need to detect the posthumous features of Gallienus.[3] Even if Gallienus was deified by Claudius Gothicus,[4] the whole policy of Aurelian (who was a party to the former's murder)[5] ran rather on the contrary lines followed by Decius[6] and Valerian.[7] INT. VRB. means *intrat urbem*[8] (or *introitus urbis*), and does not refer in any way to the interregnum between Aurelian and Tacitus.[9] Now it was in A.D. 274[10] (rather than A.D. 273)[11] that Aurelian entered the city after his resounding victories; and it was in accordance with an established custom for such occasions[12] that his entry was commemorated by medallions and coins inscribed ADVENTVS AVG.[13] (though a precedent is created by the issue of the medallions in gold).[14] The present *aes* issue was well suited to complete the series.

But these same pieces with ADVENTVS AVG. possessed another distinction: they seem to have comprised the earliest issue of the monetary reform of Aurelian,[15] which has so strongly attracted the

1 Cf. Mattingly, *NC*. 1944, loc. cit. On the *Genius p. R.* see Blanchet, *Comptes-Rendus des Séances de l'Académie des Inscriptions et Belles Lettres*, 1943, pp. 333 ff.; Magi, *I Rilievi Flavi del Palazzo della Cancelleria*, pp. 76 f.; Cahn, *RS*. 1944, p. 43.
2 M. & S. v, i, pp. 274 f.
3 As e.g. Mattingly, loc. cit., *NC*. 1946, p. 75. 'Adjustment' of the features of historical figures according to recent models (*FITA*. pp. 463 ff.) still occurs; and the fact that Gallienus had been dead a few years (very few) does not make it necessary to assume that portrait styles inaugurated during his reign were already out of date.
4 Cf. Ensslin, *CAH*. xii, p. 372; see also Barbieri, *Studi italiani di Filologia Classica*, 1934, p. 329; Piganiol, *Histoire de Rome*, p. 431; Alföldi, *CAH*. xii, pp. 224 f.
5 Cf. Alföldi, loc. cit. p. 190. Aurelian deified Claudius Gothicus, cf. coins attributable to the former's reign; Blanchet, *Rn*. 1940, p. 8 (he may have dated his tribunician power from 268, Mattingly, *CAH*. xii, p. 298). Other such coins appear to be as late as Probus (p. 99 n. 2).

6 Mattingly, *CAH*. xii, p. 309; Mathew, *JRS*. 1943, pp. 65 f. The present writer has not seen Manni, *Aurelianus* (Diss.): Berlin, 1939.
7 Mattingly, loc. cit.
8 Cf. Mattingly, *NC*. 1944, p. 123.
9 As M. & S. v, i, pp. 35, 361.
10 Cf. Mattingly, *CAH*. xii, pp. 306 n. 3, 307.
11 As, for example, Platner and Ashby, *Topographical Dictionary of Ancient Rome*, p. 491; le Gentilhomme, *Rn*. 1943, p. 21.
12 Cf. Toynbee, pp. 103 ff., 106 ff. For early official *adventus* coins, see Laffranchi, *Atti e Memorie dell' Istituto Italiano di Numismatica*, 1921, pp. 55 ff.; for local ones in honour of governors, see Ramsay, *Social Basis of Roman Power in Asia Minor*, p. 49. For Flavian *adventus*, see Toynbee, *JRS*. 1946, pp. 180 f.
13 M. & S. v, i, pp. 266, 270; Gnecchi, ii, p. 113. 1.
14 Toynbee, p. 108; Gnecchi, i, pl. iii, 9 ff.
15 Cf. le Gentilhomme, loc. cit.

interest of numismatists.[1] The year 274 witnessed another important occasion also, namely the tercentenary of the *respublica restituta* of Augustus in 27 B.C. There are reasons for believing that the GENIVS P.R. issue was partly intended to signalise this anniversary. Indeed, this applies to the whole of Aurelian's reform of the coinage. Tiberius had selected the half-centenary of the same occasion for his monetary reforms, just as many other emperors chose other anniversaries for their own reforms and innovations (p. 41 n. 5). Augustus was far from forgotten in the third century (pp. 126, 136), and it was not unnatural that Aurelian should wish to compare his successes with those of the first *princeps*. This, surely, is one of the implications of the legend RESTITVT(*or*) SAECVLI,[2] which—recalling the connection of *Genius P.R.* with the *aureum saeculum*[3]—makes its début on Roman coinage at precisely this time[4] (we may compare the apparently anniversary significance of the somewhat later inscriptions ROMANORVM RENOVATIO [p. 148] and FEL. TEMP. REPARATIO [p. 153]). This too, probably, is the interpretation of the wreath on the reverse of the INT. VRB. issues: like others labelled 'laurel-wreath'[5] it is likely to be an oak-wreath, such as had been presented to Augustus in 27 B.C. and may be represented on coins commemorating the centenary of that occasion (p. 91 n. 1). Aurelian was a keen supporter of the traditional divinities,[6] among whom Augustus now figured so prominently.

The problem of the exact definition of these issues suggests another early imperial analogy also. They have sometimes been called coins and sometimes medallions:[7] their module and only moderate degree of rarity suggest the former alternative, and their unusual types the latter. Dr Toynbee's description of them as 'gift *sestertii* or *dupondii*'[8] recalls similar anniversary issues of the first century (pp. 60, 78). Since then customs had changed, for it had become usual to distribute larger medallions than in the earlier

1 See (most recently) Mattingly, *CAH.* XII, p. 307; Haines, *NC.* 1941, pp. 40 ff.; also Giesecke, *Frankfurter Münzzeitung, NF.* XLI, 1933, pp. 65, 99; Pridik, *Numismatik* (Munich), XXXIV, 1933, p. 160, etc.
2 M. & S. V, 1, p. 270. 52, p. 290. 235.
3 Cf. Manni, *Rendiconti delle Sessioni della Reale Accademia di Scienze dell' Istituto di Bologna,* IV, 2, 1939.
4 Cf. Ensslin, *CAH.* XII, p. 358; Alföldi,

Röm. Mitt. 1935, p. 99; Besnier, *Histoire Romaine,* IV, 1, p. 241 n. 121; Homo, *Essai sur le Règne de l' Empereur Aurélien,* p. 126 n. 1.
5 Cf. Schulz, *Die Rechtstitel und Regierungsprogramme auf römischen Kaisermünzen,* pp. 12, 9 n. 19, etc.; cf. above, pp. 21 n. 7, 42 n. 4.
6 Cf. Besnier, loc. cit. p. 261.
7 The former according to Mattingly, *NC.* 1944, p. 23, *pace* Toynbee, p. 36.
8 Cf. Besnier, loc. cit. p. 261.

days. But the more modest early imperial module may perhaps have been revived on this tercentenary: the archaistic 's.c. in wreath' conveys just such an impression (cf. p. 97). One hundred years earlier, M. Aurelius had celebrated the bicentenary of the same occasion, by his pieces inscribed RELIG. AVG. (p. 108). Those had been monetary and not medallic; like them, Aurelian's issue bears the letters s.c. But so, in most cases, had those of the first-century distribution pieces that were struck at Rome (p. 78). On the pieces of that earlier period, this symbol had indicated a direct or indirect connection with a *senatusconsultum auctoritate Augusti*, which had often been primarily intended to authorise a simultaneous large issue or group of issues. Circumstances had changed very greatly; but even under Aurelian the letters are likely to have had some at least formal significance. They had never appeared under his predecessor Claudius Gothicus, but Aurelian is known to have charged the senate with certain tasks.[1] Probably that body, after consultation with the imperial bureaux, organised this *aes* issue to signalise the great events of A.D. 274. None of the other *aes* of Aurelian (some of it rare and perhaps again semi-medallic) bears the same mark[2]—which, curiously, was to recur for the last time exactly two centuries later, at the accession of Leo II and Zeno.[3]

In view of the anniversary occasion, those who saw this head of the *Genius Populi Romani* would perhaps associate it not only with the ruling emperor, who in the guise of the *Genius* entered the city,[4] but also with Divus Augustus, on the tercentenary of whose régime it was issued. But they would also think of two important religious developments which occurred in Rome very shortly after Aurelian's return in this same year 274. First, Aurelian, in addition to inaugurating the cult of *Genius Populi Romani*, founded the temple of his

1 E.g. *SHA. Aurelian*, 21. 9 (rebuilding of walls); cf. Homo, loc. cit. pp. 221 f.; Ensslin, *CAH*. XII, p. 374.
2 It was to recur under Florian (M. & S. V, I, p. 355. 51 ff., cf. Mattingly, *CAH*. XII, p. 311, Ensslin, loc. cit.) though not under the equally constitutional Tacitus or Probus; (but on the so-called senatorial 'restoration' of the former, see Bersanetti, *Rivista indogreco-italica*, 1935, pp. 131 ff. etc.); it then appears again (somewhat strangely, in view of Carus' disregard of the senate in his election: Aurelius Victor, *Caes.* XXXVII. 7; cf. Ensslin,

CAH. XII, pp. 369 f.) on *aes* medallions of Carinus and Numerian (Gnecchi, II, Pl. 161. 10 and 9: P.M. TRI. P. COS. P.P. S.C.). For these emperors see now Wuilleumier, *Revue des études anciennes*, 1945, pp. 116 ff.
3 Sabatier, *Monnaies Byzantines*, I², pp. 140 f.—the largest *aes* pieces since Arcadius. For Leo II, see Bansa, *Numismatica*, 1942, pp. 8 ff. For s.c. in fifth-century Constantinople, see Ensslin, *CAH*. XII, p. 370.
4 For this aspect see Alföldi, *Röm. Mitt.* 1934, p. 91.

chosen deity Sol[1] (an occasion celebrated by the issue, at Milan (?), of 'medallic coins' inscribed SOL DOMINVS IMP. ROMANI,[2] and, at Rome, of medallions with SOLI INVICTO).[3] The radiate crown of the *Genius* on our INT. VRB. coins shows close kinship with Sol.[4] Secondly, it is on coins of identical date that Aurelian is described as DEVS.[5] He was the first emperor whose moneyers (even if they did so unofficially)[6] took this step on his official issues (though Gallienus had described Augustus similarly [p. 136]). This development too is connected with sun-worship.[7]

The whole essence of such anniversary coinages was their composite character, in which historical and topical allusions were blended. The recipients of Aurelian's pieces would see on them, in addition to the specific allusions to the *Genius Populi Romani* and to the *introitus urbis*, references to the tercentenary of the régime introduced by Augustus (whose features and *corona civica* seem to appear), as well as to the cults of Sol and of Aurelian himself. We have travelled a long way from the spirit of the types of Tiberius, but the anniversary issues have retained their same composite nature.

We must now pass to the following decade,[8] and to the North-western corner of the empire, where Carausius established his short-lived but apparently not unenlightened administration. The large variety of his types includes a few that appear to have an anniversary character. The keynote of his publicity is PAX AVG[VSTI],[9] which begins at once and recurs again and again: an early *aureus* bears the unparalleled inscription PAX CARAVSI AVG.[10] *Pax*, though a rare type

---

1 Cf. Mattingly, *CAH.* XII, p. 309; Piganiol, *Histoire de Rome*, p. 442. On the cult see Altheim, *Die Soldatenkaiser*, pp. 278 ff., id. *Die Welt als Geschichte*, 1939, pp. 290 ff., Nilsson, *Archiv für Religionswissenschaft*, 1933, pp. 141 ff., Baynes, *Proceedings of the British Academy*, 1929, pp. 57 f., 96 ff., Audin, *Les Fêtes Solaires*, L'Orange, *Symbolae Osloenses*, 1935, pp. 86 ff.
2 Toynbee, pp. 33 f.; Gnecchi, III, p. 64. 6 ff.
3 Gnecchi, II, p. 113. 2 f.
4 Beurlier, *Essai sur le Culte rendu aux Empereurs Romains*, pp. 48 ff., Alföldi, *Röm. Mitt.* 1935, pp. 142 f., Piganiol, loc. cit. pp. 331, 452, etc.
5 M. & S. v, 1, pp. 258 f. etc.; cf. Beurlier,

loc. cit. p. 251, Besnier, loc. cit. p. 262, Ensslin, *S.B. München, ph.-h. Abt.,* VI, 1943, p. 42. For Aurelian's increased autocracy see Piganiol, loc. cit. p. 441.
6 As Kubitschek, *NZ.* 1915, pp. 170 ff.; Hoey, *YCS.* 1940, p. 179.
7 Cf. Besnier, loc. cit.
8 As regards this decade in Rome, there is a slight possibility that a billon *quinarius* of Probus dated to A.D. 281 commemorates the tercentenary of the Eastern settlement of 20 B.C.: see Appendix I.
9 M. & S. v, 2, pp. 440, 471 ff., 504 f., 535 ff., 538. 937: PAX AVGVSTI.
10 Ibid. p. 463. 5. This type of formula was found under Otho (VICTORIA OTHONIS, *BMC. Imp.* I, p. 367. 21—breaking away

on accession issues, had figured on those of Antoninus Pius in A.D. 138, and was deliberately repeated just 100 years later on the brief mintages of Gordian I (p. 129). The exceptional emphasis by Carausius on this type from the beginning may well be related to the fact that the probable first year of his reign, A.D. 287,[1] was also the 150th year since the accession of Antoninus Pius. It seems as though Carausius should join the ranks of those emperors who looked back with special attention at the Antonine period, and, in particular, at the early years of the reign of Antoninus (cf. pp. 113 ff., 167 f.).

This impression is confirmed by the type of a very rare *aureus* which, though a specimen was found near Chester, belongs to the class attributed to Gesoriacum or Rotomagus.[2] This has on its reverse OPES IVI (*sic*) AVG., and a figure of *Ops* standing with grapes and *cornucopiae*.[3] Of the only two known previous appearances of *Ops*, the first had again occurred during the early years of Antoninus (*c.* 143–4) just 150 years before the last year of Carausius;[4] whereas the second manifestation of the same deity had been in the reign of Pertinax (p. 113), exactly 50 years after the issue of Antoninus, and a century before the same Carausian occasions. The explanation of the letters IVI is surely to be found in the fact that, under Pertinax, *Ops* had been described as *divina*: OPES IVI AVG. probably represents OPS [D]IVI[na] AVG[usti].[5] The emblem of the grapes recalls the agricultural *Ops* of Pertinax rather than the *Ops Consiva* of Antoninus, and we may have here a deliberate reminiscence of the former's agricultural interests; but in any case Carausius and his moneyers presumably intended to allude to the début of *Ops* under Antoninus.[6]

from the stereotyped Augustan VICTORIA AVGVSTI). Mattingly allots the form VICTORIA GALBAE AVG. to Vespasian (ibid. p. 353. 244)—but see p. 87 n. 3.
1 Cf. Mattingly, *CAH*. xii, p. 331. Alternatively late A.D. 286, ibid.
2 For Gesoriacum, see Mattingly, ibid. p. 333; id. *Antiquity*, 1945, p. 123. For Rotomagus, see Webb, M. & S. v, 2, pp. 431, 433, 435. Or Rutupiae?
3 Sutherland, *NC*. 1944, p. 19. 175 (Oxford =Trau 3483); cf. Sotheby sale 10/xi/1881 (Neligan Coll.), lot 165. Not in M. & S. v, 2.
4 Mattingly, *CAH*. xii, p. 332.
5 A possible doubt is raised by comparison with TVTELA DIVI AVG., on which see below,

p. 146. But *Ops divi Augusti* seems a less likely rendering.
6 Antoninus remained a stock favourite as late as *SHA*.: e.g. Lampridius, *SHA. Vita Sev. Alex.* 10. 1; Spartian, ibid. *Vita Nigri* 12. 1; Trebellius Pollio, ibid. *Vita Claud. Goth.* 2. 3. The more recent publications on the date of *SHA*. include those of Baynes, *CAH*. xii, pp. 710 ff., 730 cf. p. 783; Piganiol, loc. cit. pp. 302 f., 411 (bibliography); Hartke, *Geschichte und Politik im spätantiken Rom, Klio Beih. NF.* 1940, xxxii; Alföldi, *Archaeologiai Ertesitö*, 1940, pp. 195 ff.; Seston, *Revue des études anciennes*, 1943, p. 164; Mattingly, *Harvard Theological Review*, 1946, pp. 213 ff. But however early

The first year or two of Carausius, in which the *Pax* issues started, apparently also witnessed a monetary reform which, though short-lived, must have been very important at its time, namely his revival of the silver *denarius*.[1] Reforms and revivals of this kind were frequently, indeed usually, timed to accompany anniversary occasions (p. 41 n. 5). In the present case the reform may have been a gesture by Carausius on the occasion of his accession; but it may have been motivated, alternatively or in addition, by the sesquicentenary of the accession of Antoninus Pius.

Carausius also looks back as far as Augustus. The message of the inscription ROMA ET AV. on his *antoniniani*, with Rome standing by an altar,[2] is unambiguous. This type clearly recalls the similar legend on the famous Lugdunum issues of the first *princeps*, which had signalised the establishment of the Altar of Lyons. This altar may well have been consecrated in 12 B.C. and dedicated in 10 B.C. (p. 13 n.). The tercentenary of both occasions fell within the reign of Carausius, and the present issues seem to commemorate one or the other of them. The fabric of the coins is semi-barbarous, and their mint uncertain.[3] They could certainly not have been issued at Lugdunum,[4] which was never controlled by Carausius. Nor are they classed with the series attributed to the Gallic mint of Gesoriacum or Rotomagus. But their significance is unmistakably Gallic, and they allude to the ambitions of Carausius in Gaul.[5] The specific reference to Lugdunum may perhaps be connected with that city's discontent with Roman rule, which had apparently led it, a few years earlier, to support the usurper Proculus against Probus.[6]

At a much earlier date the emperor Claudius I had been another reviver of the *Rom. et Aug.* type (p. 74). Claudius was born in Lugdunum in 10 B.C. and had coined with this type in A.D. 41, on the fiftieth birthdays of himself and the Altar. He is pointedly

---

or late *SHA.* are, it must be borne in mind that speeches attributed to the emperors who are the subjects of these biographies *might* conceivably be genuine, i.e. may date from the times of those emperors rather than merely from the times of *SHA.*

1 Cf. Mattingly, loc. cit.; id. *Antiquity*, 1945, p. 124; id. *Roman Coins*, p. 128; M. & S. v, 2, pp. 436 f. There had not been good *denarii* for over a century: Carausius anticipated Diocletian (on whose silver coinage, see especially Pink, *NZ.* 1930, pp. 9 ff.).

2 M. & S. v, 2, p. 540. 973.
3 Ibid. n. 2.
4 According to Elmer, *NZ.* 1934, p. 109, even Postumus had not coined at Lugdunum, though his immediate successors may have.
5 M. & S. v, 2, p. 444.
6 Mattingly, *CAH.* XII, p. 316, cf. n. 5; Bersanetti, *Laureae Aquincenses*, II (*Dissertationes Pannonicae*, II, 11), 1941, p. 266 n. 15; etc.

recalled to mind by another *antoninianus* of Carausius, reading
CONSTANT. AVG. (?)[1] It was Claudius who had inaugurated the
legend *Constantiae Augusti*[2] in the same year A.D. 41 (p. 49 n. 6);
and it had never been repeated. Carausius is clearly celebrating the
quarter-millenary of Claudius' issue. Claudius had always taken
much interest in Gallic affairs, and was Britain's conqueror; but the
intention of Carausius may also have been to honour the memory of
the house of Germanicus, still remembered and ever popular in Gaul.

This honour to Claudius and perhaps Germanicus was timed to
coincide with an Augustan anniversary, namely that of the consecration or dedication of the Altar of Lyons. Another Augustan
event seems to have prompted the issue by Carausius of a further
series of *antoniniani*. These are inscribed TVTELA,[3] TVTELA P[?*ublica*],[4]
TVTELA AVG.,[5] and TVTELA DIVI AVG.[6] All the pieces in question were
issued at the Gallic mint considered to be Gesoriacum or Rotomagus.[7] Even without the last of the four inscriptions there would
be reason to expect a reference to Augustus: for the only two
previous appearances of *Tutela*, under Vespasian and Tetricus
senior, had commemorated the centenary and tercentenary respectively of Augustan rule (pp. 89, 138). TVTELA DIVI AVG[*usti*]
perhaps refers to the protection of Augustus himself over the empire[8]
and over those named *Augusti* after him, of whom Carausius
considered himself to be one. Such an allusion ascribes great posthumous repute to Augustus: we may compare the recent *aurei* of
Gallienus with DEO AVGVSTO (p. 136), and an even later Augustan
allusion under Constantius II (p. 152).

The present issues seem to have been struck at a Gallic mint only,
and a specifically Gallic occasion is perhaps to be sought. One
mintage of Carausius has seemed to commemorate the tercentenary
of the Altar of Lyons (p. 145), and the same might possibly apply

1   M. & S. v, 2, p. 483. 215 (nude male figure
standing r., head l., holding sceptre). It is of
the 'c.' mint formerly attributed to Camu-
lodunum (ibid. pp. 431 f.), or Corinium,
but to Clausentum by Mattingly, loc. cit.
p. 333; cf. *Antiquity*, 1945, p. 121 (but ibid.
n. 3, he doubts Stukeley's reading CLA.).
2   *BMC. Imp.* I, p. 154. 1, p. 180. 109,
p. 184. 140.
3   M. & S. v, 2, p. 521. 682 ff. ('female
figure with *patera*, wreath or flower, and
cornucopiae or sceptre').

4   Ibid. p. 522. 692 ff. (ditto 'with flower
and *cornucopiae*').
5   Ibid. p. 521. 682 ff., p. 522. 690 (ditto
'with anchor and broken shaft').
6   Ibid. p. 522. 691 (ditto 'with *patera* and
cornucopiae').
7   Ibid. p. 445 (RSR.). See p. 144 n. 2.
8   The interpretation of OPES IVI AVG. as
Ops Divina Augusti (p. 144 and n. 5) suggests
an alternative explanation of *Tutela Divina
Augusti*: but even if the latter is right the
anniversary interpretation is unaffected.

to the present issue; but the *Tutela* legend does not seem particularly relevant. However, the reign of Carausius (A.D. 286/7–93) witnessed other Augustan anniversaries also. One of these was the 350th year after the birth of Augustus (63 B.C.). This was an occasion still remembered in later centuries (p. 68 n. 6). Moreover, Tiberius and Caligula, in commemorating its centenary, had selected Gaul for their medallic issues (p. 68). This suggests a special Gallic connection, which is probably to be found in the fact that the great reorganisation of Gaul by Augustus (signalised by major numismatic developments)[1] was completed in his fiftieth year (an occasion for celebration as Claudius has shown). Tiberius and Caligula had apparently celebrated simultaneously the centenary of his birth and the half-centenary of his Gallic reorganisation; and it is appropriate that Carausius should likewise combine in one issue anniversary celebrations of the same events. He compares his own 'protection' of Gaul (TVTELA AVG.) with the protection accorded to it—as well as to himself—by Augustus (TVTELA DIVI AVG.), and embodied in the latter's reorganisation of that country just three centuries earlier.

In the case of Tetricus (p. 138), *Tutela* may well have lost the original Flavian allusion to the *tutela plebis* through the *tribunicia potestas*. The same is likely to be true of Carausius, especially as no relevant anniversary connected with the tribunician power of Augustus occurred during his reign. But the significance of types is often composite and, even if defence represents the overtone of this series,[2] there may be an undertone of *tutela plebis*: this may be the intention of the peaceful attributes often carried by the figure on the coins, and by the variant TVTELA P[*?ublica*]. In any case the repetition of a type of Tetricus is characteristic of Carausius's imitation of the Gallic emperors.[3]

The coinage of Carausius pays marked attention to the past, and we can see why Carausius imitates Aurelian's RESTITVTOR SAECVLI[4] (p. 141). Like so many of his predecessors, Carausius may also have celebrated at least one anniversary dating, not only from the Principate, but from the earliest days of Rome. He issued many coins

1 Cf. *CSNM.*
2 Cf. M. & S. v, 2, loc. cit.
3 Ibid. pp. 443 f. For the popularity of the coins of the Tetrici in Britain, see Mattingly, *Bulletin of the Board of Celtic Studies*, 1938, p. 168.

4 M. & S. v, 2, pp. 496 f., 384 ff., 540. 971 ff. (emperor and Victory). Probus may be the emperor whom he is actually imitating; cf. Evans, *NC.* 1905, p. 33.

with the unprecedented inscription ROMANO(*rum*) RENOVA(*tio*),[1] etc., showing the wolf with Romulus and Remus. The same type is quoted by Stukeley[2] on a coin, which has now disappeared but need not be rejected, reading P.M. OR. (*sic*) PTI. (*sic*) COS. IIII. This blundered issue, and the *Romanorum renovatio* issues too, should perhaps be ascribed to A.D. 290, the probable year of the fourth consulship of Carausius.[3] This was also the date of issues with SAECVLARES AVG.:[4] Carausius apparently celebrated some sort of secular ceremony in that year.[5] The calculation of *Saecula* is notoriously variable, but it seems not unlikely that Carausius selected A.D. 290 on the pretext that it was in that year that the eighth centenary of the Roman Republic occurred. This was a great occasion, of which the immediately preceding half-centenary had received numismatic record from Gordian III (p. 131). It was also a peculiarly suitable occasion for *saeculares* and for the unusual legend *Romanorum renovatio*: a similar type, *Fel. temp. reparatio*, was later inaugurated on another occasion, namely the eleventh centenary of Rome (p. 153).

If this interpretation is right, Carausius provides the last of our examples of anniversary coinage recalling the Republic, though interest in the early history of Rome was to remain unabated. But whether this is so or not, the varied coinage of Carausius, in marked contrast to the stereotyped contemporary issues of Diocletian and his colleagues, exhibits a vigorous recrudescence of anniversary themes, comprising several periods of Roman history and even mobilising the Gallophile emperor Claudius as a prototype.

---

1 M. & S. V, 2, p. 496. 382, p. 508. 534, p. 512. 571 ff., p. 540. 974 ff.; cf. Seston, *Dioclétien et la Tétrarchie*, I, p. 83 n. 5.

2 *Medallic History of Carausius* (1757), p. 253; cf. M. & S. V, 2, loc. cit. pp. 432, 447, 483 n., p. 548. 1091. This is the coin alleged by Stukeley to bear the mint mark CLA. (p. 146 n. 1). M. & S. V, 2, p. 447, conjectures that it may be a more or less barbarous imitation of another emperor; but surely the COS. IIII. is better considered as applying to Carausius.

3 M. & S. V, 2, pp. 447, 451. Mattingly, *Antiquity*, 1945, p. 121 calls the *Renovatio* issues 'an early programme type', issued

at the C. and RSR. mints only (p. 146 nn. 1, 7).

4 M. & S. V, 2, p. 497. 391 ff.; cf. p. 451 (lion: *cippus*); Seston, loc. cit. p. 98.

5 SAECVLARES AVG. (broken column) also occurs under Diocletian (ibid. p. 228. 78) and Maximian (AVGG. ibid. p. 268. 415); but since the latter is inscribed *M*(*ultis*) XX, it seems that Carausius was the first to use the type. However, no celebration of the true *ludi saeculares* is known after Philip's: Pighi, *Pubblicazioni dell' Università Cattolica del Sacro Cuore* (ser. V, sc.-fil.) vol. XXXV, 1941; cf. Bernini, *Athenaeum*, 1943, p. 148; Seston, *Dioclétien et la Tétrarchie*, I, p. 98.

(iii) *The House of Constantine*

The next issues to which attention has to be called present certain features in common with Trajanic mintages. These are the *aes* coins issued by Constantine the Great[1] inscribed S.P.Q.R. OPTIMO PRINCIPI.[2] They are attributed to the period immediately following the battle of the Milvian Bridge, that is to say to late A.D. 312 or early 313.[3] The reminiscence of Trajan in this legend is indisputable. Though other emperors had repeated the inscription during the intervening period,[4] it was essentially with Trajan that it was associated, and it was at this very time (312) that Constantine began to construct the Arch bearing his name, which incorporates Trajanic reminiscences.[5] A.D. 312 or 313 was the bicentenary of the dedication of Trajan's greatest monuments, the *Forum Trajanum* and the *Basilica Vlpia*.[6] The moneyers of the present issue of Constantine the Great may well have been aware of this anniversary. For, apart from his favours to the Circus (pp. 5, 117) and his military successes, Trajan owed much of his posthumous reputation to his building

1 A number of Constantine's monetary innovations may—but equally may not— have been thought of by him in connection with great contemporary anniversaries. Thus in A.D. 309, the 350th anniversary of Caesar's deification, Constantine is said by Maurice to have first issued the *solidus* (*Numismatique Constantinienne*, I, pp. xli, xlvii, lxix); but 312 is the more probable date (Mattingly, *Roman Coins*, p. 223). Likewise Maurice (ibid. p. xcviii) attributes a series of consecrationary issues (Claudius Gothicus, Constantius I and Maximian) to A.D. 314, the tercentenary of the death of Augustus (just one *saeculum* of 110 years after the secular games of Septimius Severus, cf. Ginzel, II, p. 203); but this too is controversial (cf. Mattingly, loc. cit. p. 299). A.D. 324 witnessed the 350th anniversary of the *respublica restituta* of Augustus, and it is unquestionable that this year witnessed important monetary developments (ibid. pp. 219, 223, etc.; cf. Maurice, loc. cit. pp. x, xliv, cxxxii, etc.); but there is no evidence to link these with the anniversary rather than with the contemporary victories of Constantine.

2 Maurice, loc. cit. pp. 204, 287, 401, etc.; cf. Pearce, *Numismatic Review*, I, 4 (March 1944), p. 9; Brett, *NC*. 1933, Pl. 26, no. 8;

Alföldi, *Corvina* (*Rassegna italo-ungherese*), VII. 2, 1943, pp. 535, 537. They include portraits of Maximinus II and Licinius I as well as of Constantine. Schoenebeck, *Beiträge zur Religionspolitik des Maxentius und Constantin*, *Klio, Beih. NF*. 1939, XXX, p. 97, prefers A.D. 313.

3 Cf. Maurice, loc. cit. We are, however, faced by the difficult counter-consideration that the usurper L. Domitius Alexander also used the type (ibid. p. 361; Carthage; cf. Kubitschek, *Mitteilungen der numismatischen Gesellschaft in Wien*, 1929, pp. 1 ff.): he was suppressed before A.D. 312 (cf. Mattingly, *CAH*. XII, p. 350; Schoenebeck, loc. cit. p. 15). Was Alexander coining for the anniversary in 311? Either Constantine borrowed the type from Alexander—a curious but not impossible happening—or *vice versa*, in which case at least a few examples of Constantine's type slightly preceded the main output of c. A.D. 312–13. This difficulty is pointed out by Schoenebeck, loc. cit. pp. 102, 128.

4 E.g. Gallienus: M. & S. v, I, p. 165. 393, etc.

5 Cf. Toynbee, *JRS*. 1941, pp. 190, 193.

6 Longden, *CAH*. XI, pp. 206 f. (A.D. 112); *BMC. Imp*. III, pp. lxxxi, ciii (A.D. 113).

achievements.[1] This reputation had long been an outstanding one,[2] and was maintained even in the Middle Ages.[3] Septimius Severus had commemorated Trajan's centenaries and celebrated his own victories on the day of the latter's *dies imperii* (p. 6 n. 1). Another admirer of the same emperor had been Severus Alexander (p. 127); and it was from the same motive that Decius had adopted the name *Trajanus*[4] and that Gallienus had issued coinage with this same Trajanic legend.[5] Moreover, a later series, that of the contorniates, will confirm the evidence of the Arch of Constantine, Eutropius,[6] the *Historia Augusta*,[7] and Julian's *Caesars*[8] to the effect that Trajan lost nothing in popular estimation even in the last years of the fourth century and later (p. 158).

In those years the empire had become Christian; and Constantine's coinage with S.P.Q.R. OPTIMO PRINCIPI occurs almost immediately after the battle from which that emperor is said to have himself dated the beginnings of his conversion.[9] But Constantine's attribution of significance to that occasion could have developed in his mind some time after that battle.[10] (Many even consider the whole story of the vision to be an invention of later date.)[11] For our present purpose, however, this may not be an important question, since even a fully Christian emperor could pay honours to his pagan predecessors. Indeed, SOL INVICTVS, too, continued in favour for

1 Cf. Toynbee, p. 118. Constantius II admired the *Forum* of Trajan more than any other Roman building: Ammianus, XVI, 10. 15; cf. Moss, *The Birth of the Middle Ages*, p. 13.

2 A discordant note is struck by the *Oracula Sibyllina*, XII, 126, where Domitian is preferred; cf. Syme, *JRS*. 1930, p. 63; Longden, *CAH*. XII, p. 200 n. 2; and on the *Oracula* (but especially XIII), Rostovtzeff, *Berytus*, 1943, p. 18 n. 1.

3 Cf. Marchetti Longhi, *Quaderni Augustei*, VII, 1939, p. 11.

4 See Besnier, *Histoire Romaine*, IV, 1, p. 157; Mattingly and Salisbury, *NC*. 1924, p. 236 n. 40; Pink, *NZ*. 1936, p. 11; Alföldi, *CAH*. XII, p. 166, cf. n. 1. See also p. 129 above.

5 M. & S. V, 1, p. 189, may itself celebrate the sesquicentenary of the *Forum Trajanum* and the *Basilica Ulpia*, if, as Alföldi (*Berytus*, 1937, p. 53, ibid. 1938, pp. 48 f.) believes, it was issued in c. 262; but it is not included in the present study among Gallienus's

anniversary issues because the same legend had already appeared several years earlier (M. & S. V, 1, p. 71. 37).

6 VIII, 5; cf. Henderson, *Five Roman Emperors*, p. 179.

7 E.g. Spartian, *Vita Nigri*, 12. 1; Lampridius, *Vita Sev. Alex.* 10. 1; Trebellius Pollio, *Vita Claud. Gothici*, 1.

8 317 *b*, etc.

9 Cf. Besnier, *Histoire Romaine*, IV, 1, p. 349, etc.

10 Piganiol, *L'Empereur Constantin*, p. 50, disbelieves in the vision of A.D. 312; cf. Besnier, loc. cit. p. 355 n. 86. See also recently Brasseur, *Latomus*, 1946, pp. 35 ff.; Alföldi, *Olasz Szemle*, VI, 1942, ibid. 1943; id. *Corvina* (*Rassegna italo-ungherese*) VI, 11, 1943, pp. 529 ff. Ensslin, *Klio*, 1939, pp. 357 f., gives references.

11 Grégoire, *Byzantion*, 1938, pp. 561 ff.; Lambrechts, *JRS*. 1939, p. 239; Mattingly, *CAH*. XII, p. 350, against Baynes, ibid. pp. 684 ff. etc.

some time;[1] and, after the Milvian Bridge, the statue of Constantine himself was dedicated in a traditionally divine pose.[2] This was on the occasion of his triumphal entry to Rome (as *liberator*);[3] our last anniversary coinage of Rome, Aurelian's, had commemorated an *introitus urbis* (p. 140), and so may Constantine's. The same Constantinian occasion prompted the rare and perhaps semi-medallic small *folles* with RESTITVTOR ROMAE, issued at Ostia by Constantine with the portrait of Maximinus II:[4] so this too may be not unconnected with the Trajanic bicentenary.

Indeed the *adventus* motif is the most characteristic feature of the anniversary coinages of this epoch. It seems to recur under Constantius II also. It is to the latter's visit to Rome in A.D. 357 that Alföldi[5] attributes the remarkable homogeneous (and clearly contemporaneous) series of silver medallions (4-*argenteus*) of five or six mints with AVGVSTVS (diademed head to right)—CAESAR (in oak-wreath); and CAESAR (bare head to right)—XX (in oak-wreath).[6] The ascriptions of these heads to Constantine I[7] or II,[8] and Constantine II[9] or Constantius Gallus,[10] respectively, are less convincing than Alföldi's attribution to Constantius II and Julian:[11] XX seems to allude to the 20th anniversary of the conferment on Constantius II of the title of Augustus, which had taken place in 337.

The frequent connection of such medallions with an *adventus Augusti* has been pointed out by Laffranchi (p. 140 n. 12). By this time ADVENTVS medallions had become a well-established institution.

1 Cf. Alföldi, *JRS*. 1937, p. 259; Sydenham, *Proceedings of the Royal Numismatic Society*, 1937–8, pp. 9 f.; Schoenebeck, loc. cit. pp. 24 ff.; cf. Baynes, *Constantine the Great and the Christian Church* (*Proceedings of the British Academy*, 1929), pp. 96 ff., etc.
2 Cf. Besnier, loc. cit. p. 360 and n. 110, etc.
3 Cf. Alföldi, *Olasz Szemle*, 1943, VII, pp. 971 ff.; *Die Kontorniaten*, p. 53 n. 32.
4 Maurice, *Numismatique Constantinienne*, I, p. 287; cf. Gnecchi, *R. it.* 1896, p. 59; Monti-Laffranchi, *Bollettino numismatico di Milano*, 1905. For the denomination, see Kubitschek, *Festschrift Poland* (*Philologische Wochenschrift*, 1932), p. 177; cf. Mattingly, *Roman Coins*, pp. 217 ff. etc.
5 *Die Kontorniaten*, p. 52 n. 26, cf. n. 5: the visit lasted from 28 April to 29 May.

6 Gnecchi, I, p. 64. 1 ff., p. 72. 6 ff., Pl. 31. 5 ff., Pl. 33. 15 f.; Mattingly, *Roman Coins*, p. 223 n. 3; Alföldi, loc. cit.; Toynbee, pp. 83 n. 83, 168 f., 175 f., 178. These are probably distinct in purpose from the smaller silver 'border-line' pieces of the Constantinian period, on which see Toynbee, pp. 38 f.; cf. Pink, *NZ*. 1930, pp. 9 ff.
7 Lafaurie, *Bulletin de la Société française de numismatique*, 1948, pp. 3 ff. (references).
8 E.g. Toynbee, pp. 169, 175, 178.
9 Lafaurie, loc. cit.
10 E.g. Toynbee, pp. 83 n. 83, 176, 178.
11 Loc. cit. p. 52; cf. Gnecchi (AVGVSTVS). This may be described as the occasion of his *vicennalia*, though in so doing it must be borne in mind that his *vota* were instead calculated from his assumption of the title Caesar in A.D. 324 (Alföldi, loc. cit.).

Constantius II himself issued a number of other medallions specifically referring to his visit to Rome in A.D. 357.[1] He ostensibly came as *liberator*,[2] in just the same way as had Magnentius a few years earlier[3] and Constantine the Great in A.D. 312 (p. 151). In A.D. 312 Constantine had issued an anniversary coinage, just as had Aurelian for his equally notable *introitus urbis*. The same is true of the silver medallions of Constantius II. Attention has been called to the allusions of their legends (and, to some extent, of their portraits) to Augustus himself. These allusions bear witness to a deliberate comparison of Constantius to that *princeps*[4]—probable enough in the light of the invocation that new emperors should be *melior Augusto, felicior Trajano*.[5]

According to one calculation, the medallions were issued in the 400th year of the 'accession' of Augustus.[6] For it was in 43 B.C. that Augustus obtained his *imperium*, which came to be viewed by subsequent generations as the very foundation of the Principate. The celebration of its bicentenary by Antoninus Pius must have been enhanced by this consideration (p. 106); and Augustus himself had posthumously contributed to this view by suppressing from his *Res Gestae* all mention of other conferments of *imperium* or the title of *imperator* (p. 84). Anniversaries involving important multiples of four were likely to enjoy a somewhat special significance (p. 2 n. 3). But in any case such emphasis on 43 B.C. was particularly persistent during the later Principate. Victor and Eusebius consider the Principate to have begun in that year (p. 84); likewise the Chronographer of A.D. 354 ('Philocalus') seems to allude to the first salutation of Augustus as *imperator*, which occurred in the same year.[7]

It was therefore naturally considered significant, and can easily have influenced the issues of medallions, that the visit of Constantius to Rome coincided with the quadringenary year of the *imperium* of the first *princeps*. Thus, too, the oak-wreath on the

---

1 Cf. Toynbee, p. 109.
2 Alföldi, loc. cit. p. 53 n. 33; cf. Themistius, *Orationes* 3 and 4, and Straub, *Vom Herrscherideal der Spätantike*, p. 177.
3 E.g. types of Magnentius and Decentius, *Libertas* associated with *Victoria*: Toynbee, p. 186. For the coinage of Magnentius, see especially Laffranchi, *Atti e memorie dell' Istituto Italiano di Numismatica*, 1930.
4 *Eine Augusteische Erneuerung*: Alföldi,

Die Kontorniaten, p. 52 n. 26, cf. p. 53 and n. 31.
5 Eutropius, VIII. 5.
6 The same year witnessed the end of the first *saeculum* of 110 years following the millennium of Rome; cf. Ginzel, II, p. 203.
7 Cf. Snyder, *YCS.* 1940, p. 231 n. 13. A third great occasion of 43 B.C. was the first consulate of Augustus: cf. above, p. 84 n. 8.

reverse refers to the *corona civica* of which the imperial use had been inaugurated by Augustus. That Constantius II, like so many of his predecessors, was 'anniversary-minded' is independently suggested by the apparently deliberate coincidence of the FEL. TEMP. REPARATIO type with the eleventh centenary of Rome[1] (cf. p. 148). Alföldi,[2] unlike other historians, holds the view that the visit of that emperor to Rome was part of a plan to conciliate the pagan traditionalists. Be that as it may, any emperor, however Christian, might easily have wished to be compared to Augustus or Trajan. Pagan customs, and an interest in earlier times, survived during the reign of Constantius II and, indeed, throughout the whole of this period.[3]

(iv) *Jovian and Valentinian I: the contorniates*

The same considerations are illustrated by the types of the contorniates, which began their strange career at Rome[4] in the second half of the fourth century. We shall not deal here with the question whether these medallic pieces, evidently connected with the *ludi*,[5] were 'Spielsteine'[6] or something else. Alföldi[7] rightly calls many of them

1 *NC.* 1933, pp. 182 ff.; id. *Antiquity*, 1943, p. 164; cf. Pearce, ibid. 1941, p. 90 and pp. 90 f. n. 1. For the *Fel. Temp. Reparatio* type, see also Strauss, *Rn.* 1945, p. 9.
2 *Die Kontorniaten*, p. 51; *Olasz Szemle*, 1943, VII, pp. 971 ff. For pro-Christian gestures on the same occasion, id. *Dissertationes Pannon.*, II. 7, 1937, pp. 33 f.; Baynes, *Cambridge Medieval History*, I, p. 67.
3 E.g. (1) the SABINAE medallions imitated from Antoninus Pius (Toynbee, pp. 121, 185 n. 6; id. *Archaeological Journal*, 1942, p. 47; Alföldi, *Die Kontorniaten*, p. 12; Lambrechts, *Latomus*, 1946, p. 328; id. *L'Antiquité Classique*, 1947); (2) the continued glorification of *divi*; (3) the acceptance of godlike honours by living emperors, cf. Setton, *The Christian Attitude towards the Emperor in the Fourth Century*, pp. 52, 83; Kaniuth, *Breslauer Historische Forschungen*, XVIII, 1941, Schneider, *Göttingische Gelehrte Anz.* 1942, pp. 217 ff.; (4) the persistence of conquest types of grim and brutal character, cf. Toynbee, p. 182; (5) and of Sol *Invictus*, e.g. under Vetranio (A.D. 350), Alföldi, *Pisciculi: Festschrift Dölger, Antike und Christentum, Ergänzungsband*, I, 1939, p. 7, pl. I. 1, cf. Rostovtzeff, *JRS.* 1942, p. 142; (6) and of *Victoria*: Mattingly, *Roman Coins*,

p. 251; Wytzer, *Der Streit um den Altar der Victoria* (1936); Malunowicz, *De Ara Victoriae in Curia Romana quomodo certatum sit* (Diss., Vilna), 1937; Ensslin, *Klio*, 1939, pp. 439 ff.; Baynes, *JRS.* 1946, p. 175, etc.; (7) and of Serapis and Isis, Alföldi, *Dissertationes Pannonicae*, loc. cit. *passim*. Cf. also Toynbee, pp. 119, 193, 210 f., Alföldi, *Die Kontorniaten*, p. 59, for the interest in the past. Even a much later emperor, Heraclius I, was hailed as a second Scipio; cf. Moss, *The Birth of the Middle Ages*, p. 141 (for the reputation of the Scipios in the later Roman empire, cf. *SHA.* Spartian, *Vita Nigri*, 12. 1, Trebellius Pollio, *Vita Claud. Gothici*, 1). For *pontifex maximus* in Christian times, cf. Schoenebeck, loc. cit. p. 67 n. 4 (sources).
4 All appear to be Roman except perhaps a few of Theodosius I and Arcadius: Toynbee, *JRS.* 1945, p. 116.
5 Cf. Robert, *Études sur les Médailles Contorniates* (1882).
6 Mattingly, loc. cit. pp. 222 f. n. 1; cf. first Froehner, *Annuaire de la Société française de Numismatique*, 1894, pp. 83 ff.; but see Alföldi, *Die Kontorniaten*, p. 17 (who gives references on pp. 4 ff.).
7 Loc. cit. pp. 37 ff.

New Year gifts; but Dr Toynbee[1] points out that, as the year contained many other *ludi* (to which vast importance was attributed at this
time), the contorniates are unlikely to have been restricted to those
celebrating the New Year. An attempt will here be made to demonstrate that the occasions which a number of the most important
contorniates celebrated were early imperial anniversaries.

Let us first take the small and rare group with reverse of winged
'Victory' to left, carrying shield inscribed s.p.q.r., with s.c. in field.
The obverses of this group are of DIVVS AVGVSTVS (bare head to
right),[2] Nero[3] and Trajan.[4] In the light of earlier anniversary issues
we cannot fail to be struck by the evidently simultaneous appearance
of Divus Augustus and Nero on contorniates with this same reverse.
For the type had been inaugurated by Tiberius for the former, and
had been imitated by the latter (pp. 34, 81). The connection between
the prototype and its Neronian revival is closer still. The 'Victory'
type of Divus Augustus had commemorated the *decennium* of his
death, and the repetition of the type by Nero had marked the half-
centenary of the same occasion.

Now Nero, as patron of the Games,[5] is—despite his low repute
among fourth-century intellectuals like Julian[6]—a common type on
the contorniates. He also appears in this capacity in fourth-century
art[7] (as indeed does Christ too).[8] Augustus, on the other hand,
occurs very rarely on contorniates.[9] His anniversaries, however,
continued to be honoured in the fourth century (p. 152); we have
seen that the first 'Victory' issues both of Divus Augustus and of
Nero had been of an anniversary character; and there is a fitting
anniversary occasion for the significant recurrence of the type on
contorniates with the portraits of both these emperors. This is the year
A.D. 363–4, in which coincided the tercentenary of Nero's 'Victory'

1 Loc. cit. pp. 117 ff. For her theory of
the contorniates, ibid. p. 120. But see also
id. *JRS*. 1946, p. 236. Cf. above, p. 1 and
n. 3.
2 Alföldi, loc. cit. pp. 16, 90, Pl. VII. 1.
3 Ibid. p. 16, Pl. VII. 2, 3.
4 Ibid. pp. 16, 91, Pl. IX. 7, 8. *BMC. Imp.*
III, p. xcvi, speaks of the Trajanic original
as an imitation of Nero, and compares their
love of the Circus; but Trajan may rather
have been imitating Tiberius or Titus (*BMC.
Imp.* II, p. lxxvii; for attention by Trajan
to the memory of Titus, cf. *CIL.* VI, 946;

Syme, *JRS.* 1930, p. 56 n. 4), though it is not
necessary to assume this.
5 Alföldi, loc. cit. pp. 60 ff.; Toynbee,
JRS. 1945, p. 118, *NC.* 1948, p. 141.
6 E.g. *Caesars*, 310c.
7 E.g. Babelon, *Catalogue des Camées
Antiques et Modernes du Cabinet des Médailles*,
no. 228, pl. 32; cf. Alföldi, *Röm. Mitt.*
1935, p. 34 n. 1; id. *Die Kontorniaten*, p. 61.
8 E.g. Wilpert, *I Sarcofagi Cristiani*, I,
pl. 82 and fig. 108; cf. Alföldi, *Röm. Mitt.*
1935, loc. cit.
9 Alföldi, *Die Kontorniaten*, p. 16.

issue and reintroduction of the *aes* coinage (p. 80), and the 350th anniversary of that favourite occasion for such commemorative issues, the death of Augustus (p. 163)—of which, moreover, Nero's reform and issues had celebrated the half-centenary.

This is an appropriate occasion for the issue of these contorniates, but it remains to show that internal evidence will permit such an attribution. In his chronological arrangement, Alföldi interprets only three sets of contorniates as preceding the 'Victory' issues. These three are the following: (1) small pieces with the head of Alexander the Great,[1] (2) larger pieces with a variant head,[2] (3) perhaps a Nero '*sestertius*' with Roma seated (ROMA S.C.).[3] He attributes (1) to *c.* 356, (2) and (3) to successive New Years, and the 'Victory' issues and other pieces to about 359 or 360.[4] But (*a*) the initial Alexander issue may have been made rather later than A.D. 356;[5] (*b*) contorniates need not be connected with New Years (p. 154); and (*c*) there may (especially at the beginning) have been gaps longer than a single year between successive issues.

Thus there is no internal obstacle in the way of ascribing the 'Victory' contorniates to *c.* 364 (from which, in any case, they cannot have been far removed in date). As Alföldi[6] points out, issue (3) above, the Nero contorniate with ROMA S.C., does not need to precede the 'Victory' type, but may have been issued simultaneously with it. This seems particularly probable since its type, like 'Victory', probably registered its tercentenary year in A.D. 363–4.[7] The same applies to DECVRSIO[8] and ANNONA AVGVSTI CERES[9] types, of which the début on contorniates (coupled with the heads of Trajan) seems to coincide with that of ROMA.[10] The prototypes had all formed part of Nero's memorable reform (p. 80). This had produced the greatest masterpieces of Roman numismatic art; and, Nero being a special favourite of the issuers of contorniates, it was not impossible for the latter to recognise and to commemorate the

1 Ibid. p. 14; cf. Grenier, *Revue des études anciennes*, 1944, p. 373.
2 Alföldi, *Die Kontorniaten*, loc. cit.
3 Ibid. p. 15, Pl. X. 11.
4 Ibid. pp. 12 ff., 15.
5 Toynbee, loc. cit. pp. 116, 121 (the visit of Constantius II to Rome); cf. Piganiol, *Histoire Romaine*, IV, 2, p. 98; id. *Journal des Savants*, 1945, p. 22.

6 Loc. cit. p. 91 ('ungefähr gleichzeitig').
7 It was issued in *c.* A.D. 64, near the beginning of the reform: *BMC. Imp.* I, p. clxxv; Sydenham, *The Coinage of Nero*, p. 87. The uninscribed type occurred a few years earlier (ibid.).
8 Alföldi, loc. cit. p. 116, Pl. XIII. 3.
9 Ibid. p. 116, Pl. X. 6–8.
10 Ibid. pp. 15, 91, etc.

tercentenary of this monetary landmark, especially as it coincided with a great Augustan anniversary (cf. also pp. 8 f., 41 and n. 5, 161 f.).

If so, the earliest of the contorniates with heads of emperors were issued together on the 350th anniversary of the death of Augustus, and on the tercentenary of the *aes* reform of Nero which had commemorated the half-centenary of that occasion. This suggestion has a certain historical plausibility. The tercentenary year in question was A.D. 363–4. The first occasion within that period that comes to mind is that of the *adventus* of the new emperor Valentinian I to Italy (Milan) in October A.D. 364. The examples of Aurelian, Constantine and Constantius II have shown that imperial arrivals were often signalised by anniversary issues, and it was at a date very close to Valentinian's *introitus* (in September) that the tercentenary actually fell. Moreover, the recently published 'pattern' coin of Valentinian I, struck at his birthplace Sirmium, with PERPETVITAS IMPERII [1] may well combine a reference to this tercentenary with the topical allusion to his parting from Valens in that city in August of the same year.[2]

But it is doubtful whether the imperial contorniates were launched so late in the year. Contorniates were connected with *ludi* (p. 153), and the annual occasion on which the death of Augustus was most forcefully recalled to the attention of the Roman people was provided, at this period, by the *ludi Palatini*. These Games had been established by Livia in honour of her dead husband, and Claudius had selected them for her consecration (p. 70). The Palatine *ludi* were specifically included in the narrowing list of pagan anniversaries in the works both of the fourth-century 'Philocalus' and the fifth-century Polemius Silvius.[3] Such an occasion was appropriate for the tercentenary contorniates. The *ludi Palatini*, however, were celebrated as early as 17 January. Possibly the *ludi Palatini* of January A.D. 365, the first after the accession of Valentinian I and Valens,[4] were the relevant ones. But those games fell outside the tercentenary year; and the contorniates, which are at this date exclusively pagan in emphasis,[5] harmonise badly with the pronounced Christian character

1 Pearce, *NC.* 1938, p. 127.
2 Cf. E. Stein, *Geschichte des Spätrömischen Reiches*, p. 266 n. 6 (bibliography). For the military character of the Sirmium mint, see Mattingly, *Roman Coins*, p. 258.
3 Cf. Gagé, *RGDA.* p. 166.
4 Cf. Stein, loc. cit. p. 265 and n. 6.
5 Cf. Serafini, *Scritti in onore de B. Nogara*,

p. 437. There is no known exception until Majorian, Alföldi, loc. cit. p. 22, Toynbee, p. 236 n. 34. Alföldi rightly links them with the traditional circus-favouring elements in society, loc. cit. pp. 57 ff.; cf. earlier in *Dissertationes Pannonicae*, II, 7, 1937, pp. 39 n. 59, 41 n. 79.

of Valentinian's accession-type PERPETVITAS IMPERII.[1] The January of the previous year, 364, fell within the tercentenary year, and—no less than the following January—was important as the first New Year after an accession; for it was the first (and, as it turned out, the only one) within the principate of the predecessor of Valentinian and Valens, namely Jovian.

Perhaps, then, the 'imperial' contorniates were inaugurated in connection with the *Ludi Palatini* of January A.D. 364, which signalised the accession of Jovian in the previous June.[2] Jovian, though he had initiated anti-pagan measures in the summer of A.D. 363, cancelled them a few months later with an edict of toleration.[3] He even deified the pagan Julian,[4] to whom, in writing to Jovian, Athanasius attributed godlike epithets.[5] Celebration of Jovian's edict of toleration may have been one of the *raisons d'être* of the pagan contorniates with the heads of Nero and other pagan emperors. However, there is no reason to suppose that the issue of these contorniates represents a conflict with imperial policy. Even the pious Constantius II could issue pagan types (p. 153); and this absence of conflict is particularly likely in the case of a tolerant emperor like Jovian, especially as his *volte-face* must have raised the spirits of the traditionalist elements who, officially or semi-officially or unofficially,[6] were responsible for these issues.[7]

But even if it is unlikely that Valentinian started this series, it was apparently allowed by that usually tolerant emperor to continue.[8]

1 Cf. Pearce, *NC.* 1938, p. 127. Emperor stands with shield inscribed with swastika-shaped cross; above, hand from heaven.
2 Stein, loc. cit. p. 262.
3 Ibid. p. 265 (n. 4, references); Piganiol, *Histoire Romaine,* IV, 2, pp. 147 f.
4 De Rossi, *Inscriptiones Christianae Urbis Romae,* I, p. 164; cf. Setton, *The Christian Attitude towards the Emperor,* p. 59 n. 8.
5 *Petitiones ad Iovianum Imperatorem*; Migne, *Patrologiae Graecae Cursus Completus,* 26. 820B, 821C; cf. Setton, loc. cit. p. 83. There are also (later) posthumous contorniates in Julian's honour (Alföldi, loc. cit. p. 19), perhaps recalling his own short-lived revival of large *aes* issues (Elmer, *NZ.* 1937, pp. 30 ff.), which were subsequently associated by Christians with his pagan policy (ibid. p. 42).
6 May be unofficial, according to Toynbee, loc. cit. p. 116, *pace* Alföldi, *Die Kontorniaten,* pp. 12 f. To the present writer it

seems likely that the Roman senate could have had a hand in the issues; perhaps that is partly why there is so much emphasis on the types of the old 'senatorial' *aes.* For the senate at this period, see Alföldi, *Revue d'Histoire Comparée, NS.* III, 1946, *Extract,* p. 17.
7 Alföldi, *Dissertationes Pannonicae,* II, 7, 1937, p. 50, refers to coins celebrating Jovian's consulship in 364, and this may have played a part in the issue of the contorniates too.
8 For the tolerance of Valentinian, see Lindsay, *Cambridge Medieval History,* I, p. 97; Gwatkin, ibid. p. 137; Stein, loc. cit. p. 268; Alföldi, loc. cit. pp. 34 f.; id. *Revue d'Histoire Comparée, NS.* III, 1946, *Extract,* p. 23. But see also Andreotti, *Nuova Rivista Storica,* 1931, pp. 456 ff. Jovian was made *divus.* On Valentinian in general see now Nagl, *PW.* VII A, 2158 ff.

For a large bulk of contorniates must be attributed to his principate.[1] Those of them which have 'imperial' types may in many cases resemble their forerunners in having been issued on anniversary occasions. This particularly applies to the earliest of the numerous contorniates commemorating Trajan. Alföldi links these in date (as in type) with the earliest of Divus Augustus and Nero (cf. p. 155), and they may well have been issued in the time of Jovian. But there is no reason why a year or two should not have elapsed between the issues, and attribution of the Trajan pieces to Jovian is somewhat unpropitious. For, while A.D. 364 was the quarter-millenary of Trajan's annexation of Armenia and Mesopotamia,[2] this was an anniversary best forgotten under an emperor like Jovian, whose policy was to cut Julian's losses and make peace. On the other hand it became clear very shortly after the accession of Valentinian I and Valens that the peace was a failure;[3] and the consequent reaction may well have inspired a reminiscence of Trajan, whose achievements (as well, no doubt, as his love for the Circus) still enjoyed high repute at this period (cf. p. 150). Alternatively, the earliest contorniates in Trajan's honour may have commemorated the quarter-millenary of his death and consecration, which fell in 367.[4]

Other contorniates which are attributable to the 60's of the fourth century, or thereabouts, include the earliest of those in honour of Agrippina senior,[5] Galba[6] and Vespasian.[7] The last-named pieces may perhaps coincide with the tercentenary of Vespasian's accession (A.D. 369), especially as the Flavian origin of the Colosseum was likely to be known in Games-loving circles; the reputation of Vespasian and Titus seems to have been high in the later empire.[8]

---

1 Alföldi, *Die Kontorniaten*, p. 17, etc.
2 Cf. Longden, *CAH*. xi, pp. 243 f.
3 Cf. Stein, loc. cit. p. 288; Baynes, *Cambridge Medieval History*, i, p. 225.
4 Mention should be made of Trajan's COLONIA DEDVCTA contorniate (Alföldi, *Die Kontorniaten*, p. 115; cf. p. 94, Pl. x. 2; Toynbee, loc. cit. p. 120), which is possibly intended to celebrate the quarter-millenary of a foundation or of Trajan's colonies in general. On these, see especially Rostovtzeff, *Social and Economic History of the Roman Empire*, p. 587 n. 6=*Storia Economica e Sociale dell' Impero Romano*, p. 413 n. 6.
5 Alföldi, loc. cit. pp. 18, 61, 100, Pl. XXIII. 2 ff.; Toynbee, loc. cit.

6 Loc. cit. pp. 93, 115, Pl. XLVIII. 1 ff.
7 Ibid. p. 18, Pl. xv. 1 ff. It does not seem necessary to follow Alföldi in supposing that the Vespasian issue is slightly earlier than the one for Galba; they could well be contemporary, just as Vespasian might have struck posthumous coins for Galba simultaneously with those bearing his own portrait (Mattingly's theory: p. 87 n. 3).
8 E.g. references in *SHA*.: Spartian, *Vita Nigri*, 12. 1; Lampridius, *Vita Sev. Alex.* 10. 1. For earlier commemoration (by Nerva and Trajan) cf. *ILS*. 5819; *CIL*. VI. 946; Syme, *JRS*. 1930, p. 56 n. 4. For Vespasian's birthday, cf. 'Philocalus' (*CIL*. I². pp. 255, 276) and Silvius (ibid. p. 277).

An anniversary occasion for the contorniates of Galba is less likely since, unlike Vespasian, he is omitted from the fourth-century *Natales Augusti* attached to the *Fasti* of 'Philocalus'. The *raison d'être* for these pieces is rather their type LIBERTAS PVBLICA,[1] already selected for 'restoration' by Trajan.[2] Equally, the contorniates of Agrippina senior may owe their origin to their reverse type of a *carpentum* (closely connected with *ludi*). But an anniversary of her husband Germanicus remained in vogue at least until the *Feriale Duranum*;[3] so it may well have persisted until the following century.[4] Attribution of the contorniates to the years 364–9, probable for internal and comparative reasons, would place them just 350 years after the last and greatest *lustrum* of the life of Germanicus.

The contorniate in honour of Vespasian is the last of the issues which will here be attributed to anniversaries. Subsequent 'imperial' contorniates,[5] like later coins (p. 142 and n. 3) and monetary reforms (pp. 41 f. n. 5), may have commemorated other anniversaries, and so may have other contorniates with non-imperial references.[6]

1 For *libertas* in the 280s (Saturninus), see Mathew, *JRS*. 1943, p. 66 n. 4.
2 *BMC. Imp.* III, pp. xcii, 143. 701.
3 Snyder, *YCS*. 1940, pp. 136 ff.
4 Or perhaps she was confused with Agrippina junior (as Nero's mother).
5 E.g. the last known contorniates, those of Majorian (Alföldi, loc. cit. pp. 22, 100, 176; Toynbee, p. 236 and n. 34) and Anthemius (Alföldi, loc. cit. pp. 22, 104, 176), may possibly have commemorated, respectively, the half-millenaries of the first *imperium* of Augustus (A.D. 457–8) and of Actium and *Aegyptus capta* (A.D. 469–71). Both Majorian and Anthemius were traditionalists (cf.

Barker, *Cambridge Medieval History*, I, p. 397; on the former, see Solari, *Studi Ciaceri*, pp. 286 f.). The present writer hopes to deal elsewhere with the nomenclature of the later emperors. Majorian and Nepos were among the few *Iulii*.
6 This may conceivably apply to some of the contorniates commemorating Republican and Augustan writers (Alföldi, *Die Kontorniaten*, p. 89—Accius, Horace, Terence, Sallust). We know from the *Fasti* of Silvius that birthdays of Virgil and Cicero at least were still celebrated as late as the fifth century (*CIL.* I², pp. 257, 275).

CHAPTER VIII

SUMMARY OF THE ANNIVERSARY ISSUES

(i) *Recapitulation*

It would perhaps be useful here to give a brief summary of the different occasions of which it has been suggested, in the foregoing pages, that the anniversaries are commemorated by official coins and medallions.[1] Leaving aside the **foundation of the city, ascribed to 753 B.C.,**[2] of which the anniversaries are outside the scope of this book, these occasions can be approximately divided into three groups: I. Republican, II. Augustan, and III. post-Augustan.

I

The traditional year of the expulsion of the kings, 510–508 B.C., seems to have been celebrated by the antiquarian Claudius on its 550th anniversary (which coincided with the year of his accession), again about two centuries afterwards by Gordian III—who traced his ancestry back to Republican days,—and just 50 years later again by Carausius (*Romanorum Renovatio*). The foundation of the **temple of the Capitoline Triad ascribed to 509–508 B.C.** was apparently signalised by the traditionalist Antoninus Pius (midway between Claudius and Gordian III); and then by Commodus on its seventh centenary. As regards the fifth century B.C., M. Cordius Rufus, under Caesar the dictator, seems to indicate the quadringenary of the vowing of the **temple of the Dioscuri (traditionally c. 499 or 496 B.C.)**; whereas Geta, under Septimius Severus, seems to allude to its seventh centenary (seven being a figure of special importance [p. 2 n. 3]).

This custom of celebrating supposed anniversaries of Republican temples is one of the commonest manifestations of such coinage (cf. pp. 1, 3). At least four foundations of the fourth century B.C. seem to have been selected for this purpose. The **temple of Mars ('388 B.C.')** appears to have its half-millenary celebrated by *aurei* of Trajan.

---

1 Similar issues by mints of Roman and peregrine cities are not here included.

2 And other dates: cf. Piganiol, *Histoire de Rome*, p. 55, Ginzel, II, p. 193.

Two other emperors, Tiberius (from A.D. 34) and Commodus (A.D. 184–5), commemorate respectively the 400th and 550th anniversaries (the latter figure representing five *saecula* of 110 years [p. 2 n. 7]) of the **temple of** *Concordia* (traditionally 367 B.C.). It should be added (pp. 3 f.) that the second temples of Mars (138 B.C.) and Concord (218 B.C.) coincide with the quarter-millenary and sesquicentenary respectively of the first temples of those deities. The tercentenary of another religious foundation of the fourth century B.C., the **temple of Juno Moneta (345–4 B.C.)**, seems to have been recalled by the coinage of T. Carisius (*c.* 45 B.C.) and L. Flaminius Chilo (*c.* 44 B.C.); and issues of Septimius Severus (A.D. 197–8) may be associated with the half-millenary of the **temple of Salus (c. 303–2 B.C.)**.

The same emperor, and others before and after him, commemorate the temples of the third century B.C. Septimius Severus apparently refers to the 450th anniversary of the **temple of** *Fides Publica* (c. 254 B.C.) and to the half-millenary of the **temple of Jupiter** *Victor* (295 B.C.). The next half-centenary of the latter deity, bringing the figure to five 110-year *saecula*, is signalised by Valerian, who adds a reference to the **temple of Jupiter** *Stator* (294 B.C.). The 450th and 500th years of **Aesculapius'** Roman cult (293 B.C.) are noted by Antoninus and Severus. Claudius and Antoninus referred to the third and fourth centenaries respectively of the **temple of Janus (260 B.C.)**, while the latter also alludes to the 350th anniversaries of **temples of** *Honos* (208 B.C.) (rededication) **and** *Iuventas* (207 B.C.). Hadrian's coins with TELLVS STABIL. recalled the 400th anniversary of the **temple of** *Tellus* (?268 B.C.). M. Mettius notes the 150th year of the temple of **Juno** *Sospita* (194 B.C.). The coins of Claudius which referred to the temple of Janus alluded to the bicentenary of the first known *augurium salutis* (160 B.C.). Pertinax celebrates the 300th anniversary of the restoration of the **temple of** *Mens Bona* (?107 B.C.). When we pass on to the next century, the half-centenary of the **consulship of A. Postumius Albinus (99 B.C.)** seems to be celebrated by his son, Dec. Albinus Bruti f.

From now on for some years it seems to have been coins and coin-types, rather than events, which were selected (as their religious character readily enabled them to be [pp. 7 ff.]) for anniversary commemoration—just as Trajan later chose many for 'restoration'.

The representation of Venus by **L. and C. Memies (Memmii)** (c. 87 B.C.) seems to be recalled on its half-centenary by Octavian; so do the Neptune and Mercury types of **L. Rubrius Dossennus** (c. 86 B.C.). The introduction of the curule chair to the coinage by **P. Furius Crassipes** at about the same time (c. 87–5 B.C.) may receive a centenary reference from Tiberius. The same applies to the double *cornucopiae* type inaugurated by **Sulla's** *aurei* of c. 81 B.C., and to the *caduceus*, eagle and bolt of **M. Plaetorius Cestianus** (c. 69–8 B.C.). The coins of the last-named moneyer received more than their share of anniversary commemoration if, as has been tentatively suggested, the half-centenaries of his new type of *Fortuna* had already been signalised by the moneyer of Augustus, Q. Rustius. Another, M. Durmius, seems to refer to the *Hercules Musarum* of **Q. Pomponius (c. 67 B.C.).**

The death of **Julius Caesar (44 B.C.)** was signalised, on its sesquicentenary, by issues of Trajan;[1] while the tercentenary of his **deification (42 B.C.)** seems to have been commemorated by the emperor Gallienus. Further to the period of the triumvirate, the first Roman **legionary coinages,** *denarii* **of M. Antonius** (c. 33–2 B.C.), received, remarkably enough, no less than three successive centenary celebrations: these were provided by Nero and L. Clodius Macer on their 100th, by M. Aurelius and L. Verus on their 200th, and by the Gallic emperor Victorinus on their 300th anniversary.

II

The events of the life and principate of Augustus dominated the anniversary coinages of later epochs. These refer to a wide variety of occasions connected with him (in addition to city-foundations). For the present purpose these occasions can be divided into four categories: (*a*) the birth and death of Augustus; (*b*) his *respublica restituta* in 27 B.C. and the further events timed to coincide with its *decennia* and quarter-centenaries; (*c*) the other great events in his life; and (*d*) the lives and deaths of his collaborators.

These will now be briefly reviewed in turn. To take (*a*), references to the **birth of Augustus (63 B.C.)** appear to occur on the semi-

1 A gold *quinarius* of Nero probably commemorates the centenary of the death of Julius Caesar; and another of Valerian might conceivably signalise the tercentenary of the same occasion (or of 43 B.C.); see Appendix I.

medallic issues of Tiberius and Caligula on the Rhine(?) commemorating the centenary of that event in A.D. 37; and probably on the coins of Carausius, 250 years later, reading TVTELA DIVI AVG. But anniversaries of the **death and consecration of Augustus** (A.D. 14) received more attention than those of his birth. The decennial and vicennial mintages of Tiberius alluded to that occasion even more than to the accession of Tiberius himself; and Nero provides an impressive celebration of its half-centenary. The practice continued. For, repeating Nero's Vesta type, Caracalla and Postumus issued coinages (and perhaps, in the former case, medallions) commemorating the bicentenary and quarter-millenary respectively of the death of the first *princeps*.[1] Contemporary with the issue of Postumus is an *aureus* of Gallienus with the same object. Just 100 years later, the 'imperial' contorniates seem to owe their inauguration to the tercentenary (probably in the reign of Jovian) of the same occasion, which also may have prompted the PERPETVITAS IMPERII type of Valentinian I.

Equally or even more popular in later times was the *respublica restituta* (27 B.C.) (category [*b*]), often described as the foundation of the Principate. Augustus himself paid great attention to the successive *lustra* of this occasion: for the *ludi saeculares* coincided with its *decennium*, whereas its 15th and its 25th anniversaries witnessed his assumption of the titles *pontifex maximus* and *pater patriae* respectively. Both these occasions were celebrated by important issues; and the same applies to the second, third and fourth *decennia*, and to the quarter-centenary, of the same great event of 27 B.C. In particular, the *vicennium* received more extensive commemoration than is customarily ascribed to it. But the recurrences of this motif were by no means limited to the time of Augustus himself. The coinage of the *decennium* of Tiberius owes much of its character to the coincidence of that occasion with the half-centenary of the 'restoration of the Republic'. Another great output of coinage celebrated its centenary in the reign of Vespasian, and—accompanied by innovations—its 150th anniversary under Hadrian. Its bicentenary apparently occasioned an issue of M. Aurelius; and, just 50 years later, a mintage of Severus Alexander seems to have had a similar purpose. Aurelian likewise made full use of the fact

---

1 For silver *quinarii* possibly celebrating its sesquicentenary, see Appendix I.

that he entered Rome, and accomplished important religious reforms, on the 300th anniversary of the *respublica restituta*.

The events timed to coincide with anniversaries of the new régime included the *aureum saeculum* (*ludi saeculares*) and the assumption of the high priesthood by Augustus. The two last-named occasions themselves were later apparently thought worthy of anniversary coinages. The half-centenary of the *aureum saeculum* (17 B.C.) received great numismatic honour from Tiberius, whose admirer Domitian paid equally scrupulous attention to its centenary. This process was repeated in the following century, when Hadrian's TELLVS STABIL. and 'Province' issues of *c.* A.D. 135 seem to show an allusion to the 150th anniversary of the era's first year (p. 11). Even more unmistakable are references by Commodus to the bicentenary of the same occasion. It is likewise Commodus who seems to recall the bicentenary of the **high priesthood of Augustus** (12 B.C.).

The *ludi saeculares* and assumption of the high priesthood by Augustus owe their anniversary issues to the fact that both events (like the *restituta respublica*) had some claim to be considered as the beginning of the Principate. To pass to our category (*c*), the same applies to a number of other Augustan occasions. First among these was the initial **conferment of *imperium* on Octavian (43 B.C.)** (though this is easily combined or confused, for anniversary purposes, with other events [p. 84 n. 8]). A monetary revival of Nero at Alexandria perhaps celebrated its centenary, while Antoninus Pius seems to have chosen the bicentenary of the same conferment of *imperium* to celebrate his restoration of the temples of Augustus and Livia.[1] Constantius II, 200 years later, signalises with medallic celebration the coincidence of his entry into Rome with the quadringenary of the same Augustan occurrence, no doubt in the belief that the Principate had really started in 43 B.C. Augustus himself seems to have issued coinage for the half-centenary of his **first** *ovatio* (40 B.C.).[2]

A further chronological landmark of particular importance is the period comprising the **battle of Actium (31 B.C.) and annexation**

---

1 Perhaps a gold *quinarius* of Septimius Severus celebrates the quarter-millenary of 43 B.C.; see Appendix I.

2 Trajan's 'Nome' coinage at Alexandria might commemorate the sesquicentenary of

that occasion (and Treaty of Brundusium): see Appendix II. Gold and billon *quinarii* of Postumus perhaps celebrated the tercentenaries of the same events; see Appendix I.

of Egypt (30 B.C.). Successive quarter-centenaries of one or both of these events were celebrated by Tiberius, Claudius, Vespasian, Domitian (all on eastern silver issues)[1] and Hadrian (by silver medallions).[2] Vespasian, too, added allusions from his Roman mint, as well as stressing the centenary of the imperial *ius auxilii* (30 B.C.) (TVTELA AVGVSTI);[3] and Tetricus recalled by a similar type the tercentenary of the same occasion.[4] Greatly emphasised also by the imperial governments was the **Parthian settlement (20 B.C.)** (*signa recepta*, etc.). This was the object of commemorations, at intervals of half a century, by Tiberius, Titus and Hadrian; moreover, the quarter-millenary of the same event seems to be recalled by a gold medallion of Severus Alexander.[5]

In addition to these major occasions in Augustan history, a number of lesser ones, mostly religious, continued to be remembered, mostly during the early empire. To take identifiable occasions in chronological order, the **western reorganisation of c. 14–13 B.C.** was achieved in the fiftieth year of the life of Augustus; and its memory may possibly have contributed not only to the mintages of Tiberius and Caligula on the Rhine (?), which were made on the centenary of Augustus's birth, but also to an issue of Carausius with TVTELA DIVI AVG., made 350 years after the same event. An *as* of Domitian may perhaps refer to the centenary of the *lectio* or *recognitio senatus* of 13 B.C. The isolated issue of Claudius at Lugdunum recalls the fact that his own birth, 50 years previously, had occurred in the year of the **dedication of the *Ara Romae et Augusti* (10 B.C.)**—an event which was also to be celebrated by Carausius on its tercentenary. As well as commemorating the Lugdunum altar, Claudius commemorates the half-centenary of the **altars of *Pax, Concordia, Salus* and *Janus* (10 B.C.)** (which had themselves been dedicated on an anniversary occasion); and two other Augustan *arae*, the **altars of *Concordia Augusta* (c. A.D. 10) and *Iustitia Augusta* (A.D. 13)**, receive celebration from Tiberius (who had been concerned in both) on their quarter-centenary and first *decennium* respectively.

---

1 And possibly their *vicennium* and *tricennium* by gold *quinarii*; see Appendix I.
2 Cf. also Hadrian's 'Nome' issues; see Appendix II.
3 It is just possible that a coin of Tiberius had honoured its half-centenary.

4 A silver *quinarius* of Elagabalus may have referred to the quarter-millenary; see Appendix I.
5 Its tercentenary may possibly have prompted an issue of billon *quinarii* by Probus; see Appendix I.

We now come to category (*d*), to find that anniversary attention is also paid to some of the helpers of Augustus.[1] It is possible that Tiberius, by coining in *c*. A.D. 29, intended to celebrate the quarter-centenary of his own **adoption in A.D. 4**. The **death of Nero Drusus (9 B.C.)** is commemorated on its half-centenary by extensive issues of Claudius (the son of that personage) and on its centenary by a silver medallion of Domitian, as well as, probably, by the inauguration of the Alexandrian 'Nome' coinage.[2] Domitian endeavoured to emulate the **victories of Nero Drusus**, and the first of these, in **15 B.C.**, contributed a centenary character to the great output of coinage in A.D. 85.

III

Nero, at Alexandria, commemorates the *tricennium* of the **death of Tiberius (A.D. 37)**. The half-centenary of the same event seems to be referred to by a semi-medallic *aes* issue of the latter's admirer Domitian; whose coinage also seems to echo, again on their fiftieth anniversaries, the new type of *Salus Augusta* (c. A.D. 31 [?]), the *caduceus*, and elephant *quadriga* (A.D. 34–7) (the last two allusions are combined with references to the centenary of the Augustan *aureum saeculum*). Vespasian recalls the *dupondii* of Tiberius with *Iustitia* (A.D. 23) on their half-centenary.

The relatives of Tiberius likewise receive a number of anniversary commemorations. The *decennium* of the **death of Drusus junior (A.D. 23)** is celebrated by Tiberius himself, in the East and possibly at Rome. His successor Caligula naturally stresses the **death of Germanicus (A.D. 19)**; whereas the quarter-centenary of the same event may have occasioned an issue by Claudius, just as its half-centenary had something to do with Vitellius' special use of the title *Germanicus* (p. 5, nn.). Germanicus had dedicated a **temple of Spes (A.D. 17)**, and the coinage of Claudius with this new type may have called attention to its quarter-centenary.

Several events connected with Claudius, in his turn, are celebrated by anniversary coinage. He himself commemorates his own

---

1　Certain colonies under Caligula (Patrae and Nemausus) seem to have stressed the coincidence of his accession year with the half-centenary of their own foundations in

14 B.C., the year of a much celebrated success of Agrippa: see *CSNM*.
2　See Appendix II.

fiftieth birthday (A.D. 41), coinciding with his accession year. Nero's decennial coinage honours the *decennium* of the **death and deification of Claudius** (A.D. 54), imitating in this respect the *Divus Augustus Pater* issues of Tiberius. Next, Gordian III, in celebrating the three-quarter-millenary of the Republic, follows the precedent of Claudius who had inaugurated the same type (*Libertas*) on the imperial coinage just two centuries earlier. Then Carausius repeats the *Rom. et Aug.* legend, which had last appeared 250 years earlier under Claudius; he also represents *Constant[iae] Aug.* just a quarter of a millennium after the inauguration of the type *Constantia* by that Gallic-born emperor. Titus strikes an unusual note in honouring the quarter-centenary of the **death of Britannicus,** his friend (A.D. 55). But **Nero** also has his share of praise, albeit much later. He plays a prominent part on the 'imperial' contorniates, issued for the first time by circus-loving Romans on the tercentenary of his **aes revival** (A.D. 64) (this tercentenary—occurring under Jovian or possibly Valentinian I—coincided with the 350th anniversary of the death of Augustus).

The centenaries of three **issues of Nerva** and two of **Trajan** (one of the **Circus Maximus** and the other referring to the *Alimenta*) are signalised by Septimius Severus, who claimed descent from each of them.[1] Constantine the Great refers to the bicentenary of the great **building achievements of Trajan** (A.D. 112–13). Hadrian's **temple of Venus and *Roma Aeterna*** appears to have received commemoration, on its centenary, by a coin and a medallion of Severus Alexander.

Particularly striking is a group of at least eight **issues of Antoninus Pius**—a second Augustus in this respect—of which the anniversaries are celebrated by a succession of later emperors. Most popular are the great series of A.D. 140–4. These receive detailed attention on their half-centenaries. The *Ops* type, inaugurated by Antoninus (*c.* A.D. 142–4), was repeated by Pertinax (A.D. 193) (and, perhaps for the centenary of Antoninus, by Carausius). *Securitas* and *Hilaritas*, again introduced to the coinage in the same years of Antoninus, were revived by Didius Julianus later in A.D. 193. It is also perhaps possible to see a similar significance in

---

1 The half-centenary of Nerva's death may already have been commemorated by the 'Nome' coinage of Antoninus Pius, and a similar issue of Hadrian may allude to the *tricennium* of the accession of Trajan; see Appendix II.

the repetition of **Roma Aeterna** by Pescennius Niger. Septimius Severus maintains the same practice by his revival (*c.* A.D. 194) of yet another type of A.D. 140–4 (again new under Antoninus), namely **Apollini Augusto**. The interest, for anniversary purposes, in the coinages of Antoninus Pius persisted for a further century and a half. Gordian III emphasises **Jupiter** *Stator* (A.D. 240–4) just 100 years after the first appearance of that deity under Antoninus. Gordian III is here following the example of his grandfather Gordian I. The latter, aware that his accession (A.D. 238) took place 100 years after that of Antoninus (A.D. 138)—the two occasions fell on the third and second centenaries of the birth of Augustus— imitated Antoninus's unusual accession type of *Pax*. But, before Gordian I, Septimius Severus had already shown that the years 140–4 were not the only part of the reign of Antoninus deemed suitable for anniversary purposes. The moneyers of Severus had reproduced, for Geta in *c.* A.D. 200–2, the type of *Laetitia* which Antoninus Pius had introduced some 50 years earlier (in *c.* A.D. 149–50). Likewise, in honouring (in *c.* A.D. 207) the half-millenary of the worship of **Aesculapius**, they had signalised the fiftieth anniversary of the first (?) appearance of that deity on the coinage in *c.* 156–7.

(ii) *Epilogue*

The identification of these issues in honour of 'anniversary years' has, it is hoped, helped to explain why certain coins and medallions bear the types that they do. Sometimes the anniversary motif is blended with, or only invoked because of, a topical occasion; sometimes too, as far as can be discovered, issues were made for anniversary occasions without combination with any topical *raison d'être*. The obscurities that encompass a great many types (and the occasions of a great many issues) are to some extent diminished if it is accepted that the types were often influenced, and the issues themselves sometimes prompted, by the commemoration of anniversary years. For example, this recognition makes a little more comprehensible some of the colourless, generalised, apparently inexplicable types which are met with so often at all epochs. Anniversary occasions likewise throw additional light on the 'Virtues' pr 'Blessings' which such 'colourless' types often present; for oeriodical recurrences of such types often seem to be connected with a jubilee occasion. The same applies to the portrayal of deities, and to certain special types such as *Tutela*.

Reference should again be made here to the distinction, insisted on by Pink and Elmer, between the main stream of Roman coinage on the one hand, and sporadic issues deviating therefrom on the other (p. 60). The latter often appear to commemorate 'anniversary years'. This is also the case with a number of special series, such as (*inter alia*) the gold and silver medallions, the Asian tetradrachms, the Caesarean drachms and didrachms of the early empire, and Alexandrian large bronze of the mid third century; and the Appendices will argue the same point in connection with Alexandrian 'Nome' coinage, and gold and silver *quinarii*. Such categories often scarcely had any existence at all apart from the anniversary theme. At a later date still, the same may well have been true of the contorniates with 'imperial' types. Again, it appears that a considerable number of monetary and stylistic reforms and revivals, of all periods, were timed to coincide with great anniversary occasions. Finally, in following up one of the themes of *From Imperium to Auctoritas*, it has been found that a considerable proportion of the coinage of Roman colonies and *municipia* (and, apparently, of peregrine cities also) was influenced, and indeed in many cases caused, by similar jubilee commemorations.

When these points have been made, there still remains a vast mass of monetary and medallic issues of the Roman Principate which cannot be attributed satisfactorily to any particular topical or anniversary occasion. Many of them may have had no such occasion, but it is highly probable also that many were prompted by occasions of both types, now unidentifiable. Thus the anniversary coinages singled out in this book may well form only a modest proportion of the issues really belonging to the anniversary category. Subsequent investigators will, it is hoped, fill up many of the gaps. Some of these gaps, however, may never be filled, owing to the fragmentary nature of our information and the inexplicitness of so many coin-types; for example, it is questionable whether it will be possible to date many Republican coinages closely enough for anniversary issues to be identified.

Viewed against this background, the present study is seen as a mere introductory sketch of the coins and medallions commemorating '.anniversary years'. It is the present writer's opinion that one day, for the Principate at least, a *Corpus* of such issues will be required by historians, to enable the policies underlying each principate to be accredited with this additional documentation. For these issues throw considerable light on contemporary imperial points of view, by showing (with greater force and variety than the more homogeneous 'restoration' series) what were the past events, personages and coins of which each successive *princeps* chose to perpetuate the anniversaries. This applies to many emperors who used their mintages for this sort of celebration; perhaps it applies most of all to Augustus, to the three Claudians, to Vespasian, Hadrian and Antoninus Pius, to Severus, and to certain of their successors in the later third century.

But each anniversary issue contributes evidence, not about one period only, but about two—not only the period in which it was struck, but also the earlier time of which it commemorates the anniversary. For about these earlier epochs too, these coinages and medallions provide us some information, admittedly at second-hand but none the less valuable: we discover from their types which of these epochs, and which of their great men, were most highly honoured—and for what reasons—at later periods of antiquity. For example, these issues add much to our knowledge of the veneration in which subsequent ages held the memory of Augustus, both in general and in respect of individual moments in his career. The anniversary coinages have also contributed to our knowledge of the posthumous honours awarded to Tiberius. Claudius and Nerva are among emperors in whose honour at least one or two of their successors—Nero and Carausius for the former, Septimius Severus for the latter—appear to have coined. Anniversary issues have also increased our knowledge of the reputations of Nero and Trajan in the later empire. It also becomes clear that the age of Antoninus Pius was celebrated in after times almost as vigorously as the 'golden age' of Augustus. Finally, there is fresh documentation for the keen interest of Romans of all periods in the great days of the Republic. The anniversary issues bear witness to this interest at many dates from Julius Caesar to Carausius.

These same issues also provide further evidence of the essentially Roman basis and background of the religious beliefs and events occurring throughout the centuries of the empire. In particular they show that this Romanism dominated all emperors alike, of whatever character or political views—'good' and 'bad', conservative and revolutionary, pagan and Christian. The Roman Republican, or Augustan, anniversary themes are as dear to Nero or Domitian as to Augustus or Vespasian; to innovators like Commodus or Septimius Severus as to traditionalists like the Gordians or Valerian; to the Christians of the fourth century as to the pagans of the third century. So these anniversary issues testify to the persistence and continuity of a vigorous public religion, and of a vigorous public interest therein. In this field the coins and medallions celebrating anniversaries greatly expand the information provided by *Fasti, Acta* and *Ferialia,* and by the somewhat fragmentary evidence of ancient authors. As the present writer has suggested elsewhere (in connection with one of the most complex anniversary types, issued under Claudius),[1] the identification of such issues 'means that the whole of this coinage takes on an infinitely more complex and more highly traditionalist appearance than has been believed; and the Romans are seen to be a people with an abnormally developed sense, not only of the past, but of its single ritualistic landmarks. These are the people, we recall, who cherished dates in *Fasti,* who attributed divinity to single momentary happenings, to a voice that spoke once and saved them, or to the Fortune of an individual day;[2] so it is not surprising that they outdo anything in our own experience in their elaborate and almost morbid attention to religious anniversaries.

'This was the mentality which made it out of the question that the mint-authorities...should limit themselves, in their choice of types, to thoughts of the present day; and indeed, they did nothing of the sort....An ingrained spiritual necessity made the Romans look far backwards, and they deliberately and meticulously recalled the great Republican occasions.[3]...So the institutions of Claudius were thought of by the government, and no doubt also by a large proportion of the educated classes at least, as linked with the remote past by an unbroken chain of continuity' (cf. p. 8).

This study may be concluded with the hope that its imperfect collection of material will before long be supplemented and superseded by a fundamental survey of these anniversary issues; and that this survey will take into further consideration the various ways in which these coinages may be of importance not only to Roman numismatics, but also to that study which provides the greatest justification for Roman numismatic research—the history of the State and of its religion.

---

1 *PR.* Cf. above, pp. 70 ff.
2 Cf. Altheim, *History of Roman Religion,* pp. 190 f., 386. See above, pp. 1 ff.

3 Cf., on the 'restoration' issues of Trajan, *BMC. Imp.* III, pp. lxxxvii, lxxxix f.

THE ANNIVERSARY CHARACTER OF GOLD AND SILVER *QUINARII*

Gold and silver (later billon) *quinarii* were issued by most emperors. But the issues were very often few and far between; and in the present Appendix an endeavour will be made to show that their 'timing' was frequently significant, and that the resumption of mintage after these long intervals often coincided with an anniversary occasion.[1]

I. **Gold *quinarii*.** In this series, which apparently only began in the *Signa Recepta* period of Augustus (p. 165)—but had its roots in the third century B.C.[2]—the following issues seem to be due to anniversary occasions:

(1) Augustus, Gaul, 11–10 B.C.[3]—inaugurating, as far as we can tell, consecutive series of at least five years: *vicennium* of Actium and of *Aegyptus capta*, much favoured occasions for anniversary commemoration (pp. 164 f.).

(2) Augustus, Gaul, A.D. 1–2[4]—seemingly inaugurating a nearly consecutive series for at least five years, after a gap of apparently five years: *tricennium* of *Aegyptus capta*.

(3) Nero, A.D. 55–65[5]—an isolated issue, believed to have been the first for thirteen years, followed by a gap of at least nine years: centenary year of Julius Caesar's death (began in A.D. 56), a great occasion of which the sesquicentenary seems likewise to have been commemorated (pp. 100, 162).

---

1 It needs to be stressed, however, that these *quinarii* are nearly always exceedingly rare, so that—as I have emphasised in the Introduction—the possibility must be borne in mind that hitherto unknown specimens will from time to time come to light and help to fill the apparent gaps. Perhaps some further pieces have appeared since the publication of the various volumes of *BMC. Imp.* and M. & S.; but I have not searched the museums of continental Europe or of America for *quinarii*, so it is these works that form the basis of the present Appendix. The material collected in them is remarkably extensive; but for rare series with many variants, such as these *quinarii*, it is naturally not complete— that is to say, hitherto unknown specimens are likely to turn up from time to time. The consequent element of uncertainty, in the present state of our knowledge—though it would need a lot of unexpected new pieces to upset the validity of my general thesis—is one reason why the *quinarii* are dealt with here rather than in the main part of the book (which contains, however, references to this Appendix). Another reason for segregation is the exceptionally homogeneous character of the series.

2 Mattingly, *Roman Coins*, p. 15.

3 *BMC. Imp.* I, p. 80. 467. For the mint see *CSNM*.

4 *Periodico di Numismatica e Sfragistica*, 1868, p. 14 (Florence), cf. *BMC. Imp.* I, p. 86 n.

5 *BMC. Imp.* I, p. 202. 11.

(4) Domitian, A.D. 88[1]—apparently the first since a single piece of A.D. 75–9,[2] and followed by a gap of eight years: in connection with the secular celebrations later in the year, which may have been timed to coincide with the centenary of the imperial high-priesthood (pp. 5, 95).

(5) Septimius Severus, A.D. 208[3]—the first with his head since his and Albinus' on their accession in c. 193–4 (the only intervening ones are isolated issues for Julia Domna—but empresses' types are apart from the customs governing other coinages, p. 109 n. 5—and Geta): the quarter-millenary of 43 B.C., a celebrated year until much later than this (p. 152) owing to the conferment on Octavian of his first consulship, his first salutation as *imperator*, and (especially) the *imperium* (pp. 84 and n. 8, 164).

(6) The only recorded gold *quinarii* of Valerian's reign, issued for Salonina[4] and Saloninus[5] (the latter perhaps a *triens*),[6] are of c. A.D. 256–7 —the tercentenary year of the great events of 44 and 43 B.C. (cf. p. 133 and n. 12).

(7) The only two gold *quinarii* of Postumus to bear dates, according to Webb,[7] are of A.D. 261—the tercentenary of 40 B.C. The latter year was one of several long-remembered landmarks at the beginning of the Principate,[8] for the somewhat unexpected reason of Octavian's first *ovatio* (p. 29), following the Treaty of Brundusium (pp. 29 f., n. 7. See also Appendix II). Two of Postumus' three undated gold *quinarii*[9] are likewise of an anniversary character, being issued for his *quinquennalia*.

(8) The only dated gold *quinarius* of Victorinus (who, like Postumus, seems to have been interested in anniversaries [p. 137]) is of A.D. 270[10]— the tercentenary of Actium and *Aegyptus capta*.

II. Silver (later billon) *quinarii*:

(1) Vespasian revived this denomination in A.D. 71–3,[11] unless this had just been done by Galba.[12] This revival is noteworthy in view of the previous total absence of silver *quinarii* from *BMC.* since the early days of Augustus.[13] The revived *quinarii* very probably formed part of the

1 *BMC. Imp.* II, p. 325. 126.
2 Ibid. p. 50. 283. It is conceivable that this too (apparently the first since Nero's [3]) was of an anniversary character, and celebrated the centenary of the great administrative reform of 23 B.C., though its provisions were in practice largely obsolete by the time of Vespasian (see above, p. 90).
3 M. & S. IV, 1, p. 120. 223.
4 Ibid. V, 1, p. 40. 25, p. 109. 15.
5 Ibid. p. 125.
6 Mattingly, *Roman Coins*, p. 127.
7 M. & S. V, 2, p. 340. 47, p. 341. 48.

8 Gagé, *RGDA*. p. 184.
9 M. & S. V, 2, p. 341. 50 f.
10 Ibid. p. 390. 34.
11 *BMC. Imp.* II, p. 17. 91, p. 18. 92 (Titus), p. 23 (Domitian), are of A.D. 73.
12 Ibid. p. xxvii n. 2; ibid. I, p. 353. 244: VICTORIA GALBAE AVG.; but cf. above, pp. 87 n. 3, 143–4 n. 10.
13 But not since as early as 29–27 B.C., as *BMC. Imp.* II, p. xxvii n. 2 (no doubt thinking of Rome only), since P. Carisius (ibid. I, p. 54. 293) is a little later—probably c. 23 B.C., *FITA.* p. 120.

numismatic celebrations—detected by Laffranchi and Mattingly—for the centenary of the *respublica restituta* of 27 B.C. (p. 91) or of Actium— *Aegyptus capta* (p. 88), or of both (see Appendix III).

(2) Domitian's *quinarius* of A.D. 83,[1] which quite exceptionally deviates from the usual 'Victory' type and shows the *caduceus* which figured at the half-centenary of the Augustan *saeculum* (p. 45), was issued for the centenary of the same event (pp. 96 f.).

(3) Marcus Aurelius issued silver *quinarii* with several types in A.D. 163–4[2] and subsequent years, after a long period in which Antoninus Pius, unlike his predecessors, had struck very few indeed, and those undated.[3] The revival under Aurelius significantly coincided with the sesquicentenary of that long remembered occasion—the death of Augustus (cf. p. 163).

(4) The only 'silver' *quinarius* of Elagabalus known to bear a date[4] was issued in 221—the quarter-millenary of *Aegyptus capta*.

(5) The only billon *quinarius* of Postumus known to bear a date[5] was struck in 260—the tercentenary of 40 B.C., and the year before his only dated gold *quinarius* (see above, no. [8]), which was probably issued in connection with the same anniversary.

(6) The only dated billon *quinarius* ('half-*sestertius*') of Probus (A.D. 281)[6] coincided with the tercentenary of Tiberius' Parthian success under Augustus (*signa recepta*, 20 B.C.; p. 65).

(7) The only pre-reform billon *quinarius* ('half-*sestertius*') of Diocletian is attributed by Webb[7] to 295, the tenth year of the new collegiate monarchy.

The supposition that all or most of these coincidences, as regards gold and silver alike, were deliberate is supported by other evidence suggesting very strongly that this denomination, in both metals, was largely devoted to commemorative purposes. This view was put forward—without consideration of anniversaries—by that keen distinguisher between main and special issues (p. 60), Karl Pink;[8] and Pearce makes the same point about the even rarer half-*siliquae* which continue the series.[9] This interpretation is corroborated by many unmistakable coincidences of gold[10] and silver (or

---

1 *BMC. Imp.* II, p. 305. 38.

2 Ibid. IV, p. 419. 254, pp. 420, 423.

3 Ibid. p. 24. 144 (Faustina sen.; accession?), p. 80 (Hercules).

4 M. & S. IV, 2, p. 31. 47.

5 Ibid. V, 2, p. 346. 104.

6 Ibid. p. 44. 260.

7 Ibid. p. 231. 114.

8 *NZ.* 1936, p. 13; cf. *NZ.* 1933, p. 20 and n. 7, and 1934, p. 5.

9 *NC.* 1943, pp. 98 f.

10 (a) Tiberius, A.D. 15 (*BMC. Imp.* I, p. 121. 12)—the first known specimen since c. A.D. 7–8, and the inaugurator of a long series: part of a great output of accession issues, cf. *APT.* ch. I, sect. ii, subsection B, and ch. III, sect. iv, subsection B; (b) Claudius, A.D. 41–2 (*BMC. Imp.* I, p. 167 n.), two known varieties, apparently the only gold *quinarii* of the reign, again forming part of a large accession series, see above, pp. 70–5; (c) Nerva, Sept.–Dec. A.D. 96 (*BMC. Imp.*

billon) *quinarii*[1] and half-*siliquae*[2] alike with imperial accessions. This emphasis on commemorative occasions is entirely in harmony with the present identification of a marked anniversary element. It would not be true to describe the *quinarii* as *wholly* commemorative or medallic, since for considerable periods both the gold[3] and the silver[4] denominations were, if not common, at least regular and often annual, and so played their part as currency. But we are left with an altogether abnormally large residue of great rarities, far more than would occur in the main stream of imperial coinage. Surviving examples are the relics of small commemorative issues, timed to coincide with special occasions such as accessions and anniversaries.

This emphasis on anniversaries by the gold and silver *quinarii* may well be connected with their traditional character and traditional type of Victory, inherited from the silver *quinarii* of the Republic.[5] In particular, the preference for Augustan anniversaries is relevant to the long persistent link of the concept *Victoria Augusti* with the memory of the first *princeps*.[6]

III, p. 3 n.)—two varieties, apparently the first since 88, and demonstrably issued immediately after Nerva's accession; (*d*) Trajan (ibid. p. 34. 20); (*e*) Hadrian (ibid. pp. 245 n., 246 n.); (*f*) Lucius Verus (ibid. IV, p. 392. 39); (*g*) Commodus (ibid. p. 690. 5); (*h*) Septimius Severus (M. & S. IV, I, p. 93. 20, cf. p. 44. 3 [Clodius Albinus]). (*a*), (*b*), (*c*) and (*h*) are all preceded or followed by long chronological gaps in our lists of known gold *quinarii*, and so particularly stress concentration of this denomination on special occasions such as imperial accessions.

1 (*a*) Titus (*BMC. Imp.* II, p. 241); (*b*) Trajan (ibid. III, p. 34. 19 and 24); (*c*) Hadrian (ibid. p. 246. 52); (*d*) Antoninus Pius (ibid. IV, p. 24. 144, of Faustina sen.)—only one other silver *quinarius* of this reign seems to be known, and that is in its latter half (ibid. p. 80); (*e*) Septimius Severus (M. & S. IV, I, p. 93. 20); (*f*) Caracalla (ibid. p. 238. 186); (*g*) Severus Alexander (ibid. IV, 2, p. 72. 12); (*h*) Maximinus (ibid. p. 138. 1); (*j*) Balbinus (ibid. p. 170. 8); (*k*) Florian (ibid. V, 1, p. 354.

50)—apparently the first billon *quinarius* ('half-*sestertius*') since Gallienus; (*l*) Maximian (ibid. V, 2, p. 279. 519, p. 280. 520 and 531). The chronological incidence of (*f*), (*h*), (*j*) and (*k*) is particularly noteworthy (see end of last note).

2 (*a*) Gratian, *c.* A.D. 367 (Pearce, *NC.* 1943, pp. 97 ff.)—the first known issue in the series (only one specimen recorded); (*b*) Theodosius I, *c.* A.D. 379 (ibid. p. 98)—the second known issue of this extremely scarce denomination.

3 E.g. in the latter part of the reign of Augustus, and in the reigns of Tiberius, Trajan-Caracalla and Gallienus.

4 E.g. under the Flavians, Trajan and Hadrian, Aurelius-Caracalla, Valerian and Gallienus.

5 Cf. Mattingly, *Roman Coins*, pp. 9 f., 13, 17.

6 Gagé, *Revue archéologique*, XXXII, 1930, *Revue historique*, 1933; cf. Nock, *JRS.* 1947, p. 114, *APT.* ch. II, sect. 3.

THE ANNIVERSARY CHARACTER OF ALEXANDRIAN ISSUES WITH NAMES OF 'NOMES'

It has been recognised that the Alexandrian pieces with names of Nomes (administrative regions of Egypt) were primarily commemorative.[1] It should be added that many of them possess an anniversary character. This conclusion is based not on types,[2] for the types convey no suggestion of anniversaries, but on a series of chronological coincidences.

As far as is known, these issues occur under four emperors:[3]

(1) Domitian, year 11 (A.D. 91–2)—seven Nomes.

(2) Trajan, from year 12 (A.D. 109–10) to 15—thirty-three Nomes; also year 20 (A.D. 117)—one Nome.

(3) Hadrian, from year 6 (A.D. 121–2) to 8, and chiefly year 11 (A.D. 127–8)—fifty Nomes.

(4) Antoninus Pius, year 8 (A.D. 145–6)—eighteen Nomes.

The dates at which these four emperors seem to have started their issues with the names of Nomes are in every case those of important imperial anniversaries (in two cases these have a special importance to Egypt). These anniversaries are the following: (i) Domitian: centenary of death of Nero Drusus (p. 96); (ii) Trajan: sesquicentenary of first *ovatio* of Octavian (p. 29 and Appendix I), who was regarded in Egypt as 'the founder of the Roman dynasty';[4] (iii) Hadrian: sesquicentenary of Octavian's capture of Egypt (pp. 164 f.), that is to say of 'the foundation of the Roman dynasty'; (iv) Antoninus Pius: half-centenary of the death of Nerva, founder of the adoptive Antonine dynasty (p. 99 n. 2). Moreover, the dates at which, after pauses of a few years, Trajan and Hadrian revived and repeated their 'Nome' coinages—A.D. 117 and 127–8—were, respectively, those of the *vicennium* of Trajan's rule (viz. the *vicennium* of Nerva's death, cf. above, p. 31 and n. 4), and (posthumously) the *tricennium* of the same events.

The anniversaries of these events are familiar to the Roman mint also. In the case of Nero Drusus' death the same anniversary as occasioned the

1 Head, *Historia Numorum*[2], p. 864.

2 For the problems raised by these, see Poole, *BMC. Alexandria*, pp. xcviii ff.

3 Milne, *Catalogue of Alexandrian Coins in the Ashmolean Museum*, p. xxxi. Each

emperor used a fresh denomination until Antoninus repeated Domitian's, Poole, loc. cit. p. xcviii.

4 *FITA.* pp. 132 f. (references p. 132 nn. 18, 19, p. 133 n. 1).

'Nome' coinage under Domitian inspired Roman coinages too (p. 96). The situation with regard to Hadrian's first 'Nome' issues is not far different: for medallions of his (p. 100) seem to celebrate the sesqui-centenary, if not of *Aegyptus capta*, at least of the battle of Actium which was often associated with it in retrospect (pp. 164 f.). Both of these events received celebration on other anniversaries also. So did the remaining occasions to which 'Nome' issues seem to look back. Augustus himself (pp. 29 f.), and perhaps Postumus (Appendix I), seem to have commemorated anniversaries of the former's first *ovatio*; Septimius Severus signalised centenaries of the reign (if not the death) of Nerva (p. 116); and the accession of Trajan was particularly long remembered,[1] like other events connected with that emperor (pp. 150, 158).

It should be said at once that there is nothing surprising in the fact that Alexandrian coinage should celebrate imperial occasions. The Alexandrian series was imperial and official; traditional types predominate on it,[2] and among them are many referring to Roman events and coinages[3] (e.g. p. 107 and n. 4). Furthermore, this mint provides many instances, from all periods, of the apparently deliberate coincidence of issues with anniversary occasions. For example, the last two large bronze pieces ever struck there, those of Gallienus (p. 136) and Claudius Gothicus (p. 139), both seem to possess this character; and Domitian's introduction of the 'Nome' coinage on an anniversary occasion is paralleled by the coincidence with such occasions, under at least five emperors, of Alexandrian monetary innovations (p. 41 n. 5; cf. pp. 61, 73, 83, 124 and 136).

It is true that the 'Nome' coinages are not quite in the same 'official' category as the main Alexandrian series. The exact *nuance* of their official-dom is, as so often[4] (but never more so than here), obscure; that is to say we cannot assess the character and extent of the collaboration—if any— between the authorities of Alexandria who issued them and those of the Nomes which are recorded on them. It might seem at first sight that the appearance of such local designations entitled these pieces to be regarded as the Egyptian counterpart of local peregrine coinages.[5] But such a conclusion must be radically modified by the centralisation of their mintage[6] (as befits the bureaucratic structure of Egypt itself), by the not truly local character and appearance of the types,[7] and by the local designations in adjectival form,[8] i.e. not in the Genitive Plural ethnics characteristic of

1 Cf. the *Feriale Duranum*: Fink, *YCS*. 1940, p. 79.
2 Cf. Hoey, *YCS*. 1940, p. 30 n. 50.
3 Cf. Head, loc. cit. pp. 862 f.
4 On this general question see *SMACA*.
5 This peculiarity, and the extreme rarity of the whole series (Poole, loc. cit. p. xcvii;

cf. Appendix I), are features which make it preferable to segregate the present discussion in an Appendix.
6 Poole, loc. cit.   7 Ibid. p. c.
8 E.g. ΕΡΜΟΠΟΛΙΤΗΣ, ΣΕΘΡΟΥΕΙΤΗΣ: sometimes with ΝΟΜΟΣ added, e.g. ΣΑΕΙΤΗΣ ΝΟΜΟΣ.

peregrine coinage. So the difference in administrative origin from the official series of Alexandria may not be great.

Whatever difference may remain does not make these 'Nome' issues any the less likely to celebrate anniversaries. On the contrary, it may even increase the likelihood of this. For the Nomes were essentially religious in character:[1] and Egyptian religious ceremonies during the empire, however native and Ptolemaic their procedure,[2] were—as we should expect—largely concerned with official Roman occasions. This is illustrated by papyri such as the *Feriale* of Tebtunis (*c.* A.D. 169–76),[3] which is largely preoccupied with the imperial cult.[4]

It is an aspect of this cult, the commemoration of the death of Nero Drusus, which I believe to have caused the initiation of these pieces, or at least to have inspired its timing.[5] This is not the only evidence that we have of attention to the memory of Nero Drusus by Domitian. Silver and *aes* medallions of A.D. 92 seem to bear witness to the celebration of the very same anniversary occasion. Domitian's interest in Nero Drusus (and his son Germanicus) is due to his characteristically Roman linking of his own German victories with theirs: he adopted the name Germanicus (which Nero Drusus too had borne), and it appears in emphatic unabbreviated form (cf. p. 5) on Roman *aurei* of this very centenary year A.D. 91 (p. 96).

These themes were of particular significance in Egypt, since Nero Drusus was the father of its great 'benefactor' Germanicus (p. 61 and n. 6). Indeed, there is independent evidence of the interest of the Alexandrian mint under Domitian: for it is in his reign that Nike is specified for the first time, and the specifying phrase is ΚΑΤΑ ΓΕΡΜΑΝѠΝ.[6] Our carefully timed Nome coinages provide further evidence of this interest; whereas later 'Nome' issues, as has been suggested, likewise seem intended to celebrate imperial anniversaries,[7] those of Hadrian again stressing an occasion of special importance to Egypt.

1 Cf. A. H. M. Jones, *Cities of the Eastern Roman Provinces*, p. 297. On the 'Nomes', ibid. pp. 297 ff., 313 ff., 468 ff., 474, and H. Gauthier, *Les Nomes d'Égypte depuis Hérodote jusqu'à la Conquête Arabe* (1935).

2 Hoey, loc. cit. pp. 36, 190 n. 915.

3 Eitrem, *Papyri Osloenses*, III, p. 47, cf. Hoey, loc. cit. Compare, for example, a papyrus showing imperial celebrations at Syene, Wilcken, *Chrestomathie*, 41, col. III; cf. Hoey, loc. cit. p. 37 n. 100.

4 Cf. Fink, *YCS.* 1940, p. 75.

5 The seven 'Nomes' mentioned on these issues of Domitian are the Heracleopolite, Memphite, Mendesian, Oxyrhynchite, Saite, Sebennyte and Sethroite. In the present state of our knowledge it does not seem possible to say why these were selected, or why other such selections were made for subsequent 'Nome' issues.

6 Head, *Historia Numorum*², p. 864.

7 The dates are otherwise inexplicable; cf. Poole, *BMC. Alexandria*, p. xcvii.

VESPASIAN'S CENTENARY ISSUES OF
c. A.D. 69–71 AND 73–74

━━━━◆━━━━

The following are some of the types which led Laffranchi and Mattingly to detect references to the centenary of Actium, and Mattingly to indicate also allusions to the centenary of 27 B.C.:[1]

c. A.D. 69–70

adlocutio type: cf. similar type shortly after Actium.[2]
DIVVS AVGVSTVS.[3]

A.D. 71

S.P.Q.R. ADSERTORI LIBERTATIS PVBLICAE:[4] cf. LIBERTATIS P. R. VINDEX shortly after Actium.[5]
VICTORIA NAVALIS:[6] especially suggesting Actium.[7]
SIGNIS RECEPTIS:[8] cf. coins of Augustus.[9]
PROVIDENT., altar:[10] cf. coins of DIVVS AVGVSTVS PATER.[11]
Eagle on globe:[12] ditto.[13]
TVTELA AVGVSTI.[14]

A.D. 73

VESTA, temple: closely associated with Divus Augustus.[15]

A.D. 74

Oak-wreath:[16] cf. conferment[17] and coin of 27 B.C.[18]
Two laurel-branches:[19] cf. conferment of 27 B.C.[20] and coins of Augustus.[21]
IVSTITIA AVG.: cardinal virtue on *clipeus virtutis* conferred in 27 B.C.[22]

---

1 See above, pp. 9, 88 and n. 3.
2 See above, p. 88 and nn. 7, 8.
3 See above, p. 88 and n. 9.
4 *BMC. Imp.* II, p. 189. 781, etc.
5 *BMC. Imp.* I, p. 112. 691 (28 B.C.).
6 *BMC. Imp.* II, p. 129. 597, etc.
7 Laffranchi, *R. it.* 1911, p. 430 n. 2.
BMC. Imp. II, p. xlvii, suggests associations with Vespasian.
8 *BMC. Imp.* II, p. 190. I am grateful to Mr C. M. Kraay for calling my attention to this coin and to its Augustan reminiscence.
9 *BMC. Imp.* I, p. 110. 679 ff.
10 *BMC. Imp.* II, p. 132. 611.
11 See above, p. 62.

12 *BMC. Imp.* II, p. 132. 612.
13 See above, p. 44.
14 See above, pp. 88 ff., and p. 89 n. 1, where it is pointed out that Mr C. M. Kraay (as he has kindly informed me) questions the attribution of the same type to A.D. 70 (*BMC. Imp.* II, p. 112. 527).
15 See above, p. 91.
16 Ibid.
17 *Res Gestae*, ch. 34.
18 *BMC. Imp.* I, p. 106. 656.
19 *BMC. Imp.* II, p. 25. 133.
20 *Res Gestae*, ch. 34.
21 *BMC. Imp.* I, p. 63. 351.
22 See above, p. 91.

Rudder on globe:[23] cf. coins of Augustus, and others issued on the 60th anniversary of 27 B.C. (i.e. half-centenary of the Augustan *saeculum*).[24]

Winged *caduceus*:[25] ditto.[26]

Heifer or cow:[27] cf. coins of Augustus.[28]

---

23 *BMC. Imp.* ii, p. 162. 706, cf. p. li.

24 See above, p. 45.

25 *BMC. Imp.* ii, p. 25. 137.

26 See above, p. 45.

27 *BMC. Imp.* ii, p. 25. 132, cf. p. xxxviii.

28 *BMC. Imp.* i, p. 107. 659; *CSNM.*

CONJECTURAL ATTRIBUTIONS TO ANNIVERSARY OCCASIONS

The attributions of coins and medallions to anniversary occasions in this book include a small proportion for which the grounds of such an attribution are largely or purely conjectural. These are mintages of which the occasions are, and remain, uncertain; ascription to an anniversary is merely one of a number of unproven possibilities.

This may not, in itself, seem sufficient reason for the inclusion of these pieces in the present study. If it does not, I would excuse this further by urging the inadequate attention which they have hitherto received. Some of them—despite their official character—are little known and have been very rarely cited or described; others are well enough known, but the occasions of their issue have been insufficiently considered or, in any case, have remained doubtful. That is to say, these conjectural cases have been admitted here, partly indeed because they seem to deserve at least marginal mention in an attempted assessment of anniversary issues, but partly also in pursuit of a second, subordinate—and, strictly speaking, irrelevant— aim. This aim is the stimulation of interest in these problematical pieces, in the hope that further research may be directed towards the occasions of their issue. Such research may well be able to show, in some or many cases, that my present tentative attributions to anniversary occasions are wrong. Meanwhile, pending more probable suggestions, these attributions have been included here.

But the indulgence of this secondary aim, leading as it does to the introduction of material of only doubtful relevance to my main theme, may have risked obscuring that theme itself. That is to say, the dubious instances may have tended to distract the reader from the many far more plausible examples of anniversary issues, with which—owing to the chronological arrangement of this book—they have necessarily been placed in juxtaposition. If this be so, I can only urge that the latter, *divisim et seriatim*, be considered on their merits.

It may be of assistance, in counteracting the confusing effects of this juxtaposition, if the partly or wholly conjectural instances are recapitulated and segregated here, so that they may duly receive both the suspicion and the further consideration that they deserve. Among the pieces, then, whose attributions to anniversary occasions are based on guesswork rather than on convincing evidence, are the following:[1]

Augustus: quadrantes (p. 28 and n. 2, pp. 29 f. n. 7).

Tiberius: PONTIF. MAX. in wreath (p. 42); Divus Augustus (pp. 42 f., 62 f.); CIVITATIBVS ASIAE RESTITVTIS (pp. 65 ff.); *asses* of Drusus jun. (pp. 67 f.); T. Helvius Basila (p. 69).

Caligula: silver of Caesarea and Antioch (p. 70).

Claudius: Germanicus (pp. 75 f.), Agrippina senior (p. 76) and junior (p. 77).

Nero: AVGVSTVS AVGVSTA (pp. 82 f.).

Domitian: S.C. as reverse type (pp. 97 f.).

Hadrian: AVG. P.P. REN. (pp. 102 f.).

Pescennius Niger: ROMA AETERNA (p. 114).

Maximinus II: RESTITVTOR ROMAE (p. 151).

Valentinian I: certain contorniates (pp. 158 f.).

Also some of the gold and silver *quinarii* mentioned in Appendix I.

---

1 This list does not include coins and medallions discussed only in footnotes.

ADDENDA

pp. 3 f., 15. The dedication by Tiberius of the restored temple of Castor and Pollux, as usually dated to A.D. 6 (Gagé, *RGDA.* p. 166), fell within the 501st year after one of the traditional dates for the vowing of their temple, 496 B.C. (for round numbers + 1, see p. 11 and n. 6).

pp. 4, etc. The term *respublica restituta* is here employed loosely to describe either or both of the two stages of the change in 27 B.C.—the 'transference of power', and the assumption of the name 'Augustus' etc. As Professor R. Syme and *BMC. Imp.* II, p. xxxvii (in regard to the centenary issues of Vespasian) point out, celebration could as well be accorded to the latter stage as to the former.

pp. 5 n. 7, 96, 178. For another aspect of the significance of unabbreviated names, see Syme, *JRS.* 1948, p. 125.

p. 10 n. 4. For the *Ara Pacis* see also now Moretti, *Ara Pacis Augustae* (1948), Ryberg, *Mem. Amer. Acad. Rome,* 1949, and—if, as I hope, it is published— a lecture by Dr J. M. C. Toynbee.

pp. 20 and n. 2, 25, 43. The importance attached by Augustus to vicennial intervals, and particularly to the *vicennia* celebrated successively in 7 B.C. and A.D. 14, was stressed by Mommsen, *Die röm. Chronologie bis auf Cäsar²,* p. 167.

p. 24. When Moretti, loc. cit., p. 221, labelled the medallion with IMP. XV. SICIL. 'Tiberius', was he too thinking of the latter's arrival in Gaul in A.D. 4, or did he regard the piece as post-Augustan?

pp. 33 and n. 6, 65 f. Most of the onus for the theory of delayed tribunician dating under Tiberius falls on the issue inscribed S.P.Q.R. IVLIAE AV-GVST.; but this in my opinion can scarcely be prior to Livia's death (cf. *APT.* Ch. III, sect. IV b).

p. 35 and n. 1. E.g. *BMC. Imp.* I, p. 61. 342 (Augustus). In a dedication to Augustus from Potentia (*ILS.* 82), a similar Victory is accompanied by an inscription apparently attributing her shield (again defined as *clipeus virtutis*) to the same four 'Virtues' as had figured on the Roman *clipeus.*

pp. 41 f. n. 5, 169. There are analogies elsewhere for this sort of commemoration of the dead by reforms in fields not obviously connected with their memory: e.g. the Magliano (Heba) Tablet explicitly links posthumous celebration, first of Gaius and Lucius and then of Germanicus, with electoral reforms (Ehrenberg and Jones, *Documents Illustrating the Reigns of Augustus and Tiberius,* pp. 154 ff., no. 365).

p. 56. The arguments postulating numismatic celebration of an electoral change in *c.* A.D. 14–16 are by no means strengthened, and are perhaps diminished, by the Magliano (Heba) Tablet (Ehrenberg and Jones, loc. cit.), on which (*a*) attention is rather diverted to other dates in electoral history, (*b*) *destinatio*, at least, is shown not to have become, after all, the exclusive prerogative of the senate; cf. de Visscher, *Bull. de la Classe des Lettres et des Sciences Morales et Politiques de l'Académie Royale de Belgique*, 5 sér., XXXV, 1949, pp. 190 f., 199.

pp. 99 nn. 1 and 2, 127, Appendix II. Hadrian's *vicennalia* were still commemorated in the *Feriale* of Tebtunis (c. A.D. 169–76), Eitrem, *Papyri Osloenses*, III, no. 77, pp. 52 f.

p. 116, Appendix II. Nerva's birthday still figured in the *Feriale* of Tebtunis, Eitrem, loc. cit., pp. 47, 53.

p. 129. Censorinus, X, writing in A.D. 238, notes its centenary character—as the 100th year of a new *magnus annus* dating from A.D. 139. The latter may have something to do with the popularity of the early coinages of Antoninus Pius as objects of anniversary commemoration (pp. 167 f.).

p. 131 n. 3. For the imperial issues add Saria, cf. Radnóti, *Numizmatikai Közlöny*, XLIV/XLV, 1945/6 (Trajanus Decius), against Ambrosoli (Trebonianus Gallus).

pp. 141 f. In the third century the '*Anni Augustorum*' were said to have begun in 27 B.C. (Censorinus, X f.).

p. 144 n. 2. Or is this mint (R.S.R.), after all, neither Rotomagus nor Gesoriacum, but Rutupiae? See now *Ashmolean Museum, Heberden Coin Room, Guide*, etc., cf. Carson, *JRS*. 1949, p. 188.

p. 150 nn. 10, 11. See now Jones, *Constantine and the Conversion of Europe*, Alföldi, *The Conversion of Constantine and Pagan Rome*, Moss, *JRS*. 1949, pp. 167 ff., Powicke, ibid., pp. 169 f.

p. 152 n. 7 (cf. pp. 84, 162, 164). But these medallions could also bear witness to the other early Christian tradition, which reckoned the reign of Augustus from 44 B.C., cf. Henderson, *JRS*. 1949, p. 123.

p. 157 n. 8. Add Schuurmans, *L'Antiquité Classique*, 1949, pp. 25 ff.

pp. 162 ff. The commemoration accorded by *Fasti* to these Augustan occasions is now conveniently tabulated by Ehrenberg and Jones, loc. cit., pp. 44–54.

p. 15 n. 4. As Vessberg sees, features and title (*cos.*) invalidate the attribution of Cesano, *Studi di Num.* I, 2, 1942, p. 143, to the legendary A. Postumius Regillensis.

ABBREVIATIONS

AC.	M. Grant, *The Augustan 'Constitution'. Greece and Rome*, London, 1949, pp. 97 ff.
APT.	Id., *Aspects of the Principate of Tiberius. Numismatic Notes and Monographs*, New York, No. 117, 1950.
Augustus	*Studi in occasione del Bimillenario Augusteo.* R. Accademia dei Lincei, Rome, 1938.
BMC. Imp.[1]	H. Mattingly, *Coins of the Roman Empire in the British Museum.* London, from 1923.
BMC. Rep.[1]	H. A. Grueber, *Coins of the Roman Republic in the British Museum.* London, 1910.
CAH.	*Cambridge Ancient History.* Cambridge.
CIL.	*Corpus Inscriptionum Latinarum.* Berlin.
CMG.	M. Grant, *The Colonial Mints of Gaius. Numismatic Chronicle*, 1948, pp. 113 ff.
Cohen[1]	H. Cohen, *Description Historique des Monnaies frappées sous l'Empire Romain*, 2nd ed. Paris, 1880–92.
CSNM.	M. Grant, *Complex Symbolism and New Mints. Numismatic Chronicle*, 1949.
de Laet, *Samenstelling.*	H. J. de Laet, *De Samenstelling van den Romeinschen Senaat gedurende de eerste eeuw van het Principaat. Werken uitgegeven door de Faculteit van de Wijsbegeerte en Letteren*, 92ᵉ *Aflevering*, Gent Univ., 1941.
Dura	*The Excavations at Dura-Europos*, Yale (especially *Final Report*, VI: A. R. Bellinger, *The Coins*, 1949).
FITA.	M. Grant, *From Imperium to Auctoritas.* Cambridge, 1946.
Gagé, *RGDA.*	J. Gagé, *Res Gestae Divi Augusti. Publications de la Faculté de Lettres, Textes d'Études*, v, Strasbourg Univ., 1935.
Ginzel	F. K. Ginzel, *Handbuch der mathematischen und technischen Chronologie.* Leipzig, 1906.
Gnecchi	F. Gnecchi, *I Medaglioni Romani.* Milan, 1912.
IGRR.	*Inscriptiones Graecae ad Res Romanas Pertinentes.* Paris, 1911–27.
ILS.	H. Dessau, *Inscriptiones Latinae Selectae.* Berlin, 1892–1916.
JHS.	*Journal of Hellenic Studies.* London.
JRS.	*Journal of Roman Studies.* London.

1 Where references have two Arabic numerals, in the form *BMC. Imp.* 1, p. 236. 86, the second of the two numerals refers to the number not of the page but of the coin.

M. & S.[1]	H. Mattingly, E. A. Sydenham, C. H. V. Sutherland, and P. H. Webb, *The Roman Imperial Coinage*. London, 1923–1949.
NC.	*Numismatic Chronicle*. London.
NZ.	*Numismatische Zeitschrift*. Vienna.
OCD.	*Oxford Classical Dictionary*. Oxford, 1949.
PIR.	*Prosopographia Imperii Romani* (Klebs-Dessau), Berlin, from 1897; 2nd ed. (Groag-Stein), Berlin-Leipzig, from 1933.
PR.	M. Grant, *Pax Romana. University of Edinburgh Journal*, Edinburgh, 1949, pp. 229 ff.
PW.	*Real-Encyclopädie der Classischen Altertumswissenschaft* (Pauly-Wissowa-Kroll-Ziegler). Stuttgart, from 1894.
RGDA.	See Gagé, *RGDA*.
R. it.	*Rivista Italiana di Numismatica*. Rome.
Rn.	*Revue Numismatique*. Paris.
Röm. Mitt.	*Mitteilungen des Deutschen Archäologischen Instituts, Römische Abteilung*. Berlin.
RS.	*Revue Suisse de Numismatique* (*Schweizerische Numismatische Rundschau*). Geneva.
SHA.	*Scriptores Historiae Augustae*.
SMACA.	M. Grant, *The Six Main Aes Coinages of Augustus*. Edinburgh (in press).
Strack	P. Strack, *Untersuchungen zur römischen Reichsprägung des zweiten Jahrhunderts*. Berlin, 1931–7.
SWC.	M. Grant, *A Step towards World Coinage*: 19 B.C. Princeton, 1950.
Toynbee	J. M. C. Toynbee, *Roman Medallions. Numismatic Studies No. 5*, New York, 1944.
YCS.	*Yale Classical Studies*. Newhaven, Conn.
YCS. 1940	R. O. Fink, A. S. Hoey and W. F. Snyder, *The Feriale Duranum*, and W. F. Snyder, *Public Anniversaries in the Roman Empire*. *YCS*. VII, 1940.
ZfN.	*Zeitschrift für Numismatik*. Berlin.

1 Where references have two Arabic numerals, in the form M. & S. I, p. 236. 86, the second of the two numerals refers to the number not of the page but of the coin.

INDICES

[These Indices do not include references to the Introduction or to the Appendices; but anniversary occasions identified in the Appendices are mentioned in footnotes to the text, and references to these footnotes are included in the Indices.]

INDEX I
PERSONS[1]

1 This Index is drawn up according to *gentilicia*, except that imperial personages (including 'usurpers') and writers are entered according to their most familiar names. Principal references to emperors are given in bold type.

INDEX II
PLACES

TYPES AND LEGENDS[1]

INDEX IV
GENERAL

For EU product safety concerns, contact us at Calle de José Abascal, 56–1°,
28003 Madrid, Spain or eugpsr@cambridge.org.

www.ingramcontent.com/pod-product-compliance
Ingram Content Group UK Ltd.
Pitfield, Milton Keynes, MK11 3LW, UK
UKHW010337140625
459647UK00010B/648